Books are to be
the las

MANAGERS
AND
THE SOCIAL WORK SERVICES

John Triseliotis
Moira Borland
Malcolm Hill
Lydia Lambert

LONDON: HMSO

Moira Borland worked for several years as a social worker and in recent years has participated in a number of research projects on services for children, including fostering, adoption and residential care. She currently works in the Department of Social Policy and Social Work at the University of Glasgow, where she combines research with teaching on the Master of Social Work Course.

Malcolm Hill worked in London as a social worker, then moved to Edinburgh to carry out a study on early parenthood. Subsequent research has concerned adoption, foster care and social services. He has taught on social work, child care, comparative social policy and family issues. He is currently Baring Fellow in the Centre for the Study of the Child and Society, University of Glasgow.

Lydia Lambert trained and worked as a diocesan social worker before becoming a researcher. She was co-author with Jane Rowe of 'Children Who Wait' and then joined the team for the follow-up at 16 of the National Child Development Study. She continued to work at the National Children's Bureau on other studies related to child care, adoption and family issues. She moved to Edinburgh University as a Research Fellow in 1988.

John Triseliotis is Emeritus Professor and Senior Research Fellow at the International Social Sciences Institute, the University of Edinburgh. He has practised as a social worker and has carried out extensive research in child care. His most recent book, with others, is on the Theory and Practice of Foster Care published by Batsford.

Contents

Acknowledgements

List of Tables

Foreword

Acknowledgements

A great many people have helped us with this study. Firstly, we would like to thank the Department of Health for sponsoring the project and especially members of the Advisory Group for their support and constructive comments. Dr Carolyn Davies chaired the group and Peter Marsh of the University of Sheffield acted as external adviser. Next, we are extremely grateful to the Directors and staff of the local authorities in which the study was conducted. Taking on board any research is an additional burden at the best of times and this period coincided with the introduction of much new legislation and internal changes.

The perspectives provided directly by the teenagers and their families undoubtedly form the core of this study and we acknowledge our particular debt to them for talking to us at often difficult stages in their lives. We depended on the efforts of many social workers to gain the agreement of these young people and their parents. The social workers also generously gave interviews about their work with them. Keyworkers and foster carers were very helpful as well in arranging access and in recording their views on the initial placements. We would also like to thank the young people who participated in additional group discussions.

The research team was ably assisted by our secretaries Anne Walsingham in Edinburgh and Irene Ramsey in Glasgow. Jean Ollerton, Kate Stewart and Larry Anderson undertook some of the more distant interviews. Tony Dickinson helped with some computing and vital advice and support was provided by members of the Social Science Support Team of Edinburgh University Computing Service. We are grateful to Roger Bullock at the Dartington Social Research Unit for his helpful comments on the draft of this final report.

List of tables

Foreword

This report covers a three year research project carried out jointly by the Universities of Edinburgh and Glasgow which set out to study local authority social services' responses to the needs of teenagers who are placed on formal or informal supervision or who are looked after in care. The impetus for the study came from the relative absence of studies focusing on the type and effectiveness of services provided for this particular age group. With child abuse capturing the headlines as a result of a number of tragedies involving younger children, less attention has been paid to the type, process and outcomes of programmes designed to respond to the needs, circumstances and requirements of this age group. Yet soon after the project started, as a result of a number of incidents involving young people and sometimes their carers in residential establishments, this age group suddenly came under intense scrutiny. There have been calls for tougher measures to control young people who get into trouble, including imprisonment for children.

Concern about the behaviour of young people is not new and documentary evidence goes back at least to classical Greece. Each successive generation seems surprised and astonished at what is seen to be unacceptable behaviour by young people. The antics and disturbances caused in the fifties by the so called 'mods' and 'rockers', especially at sea-side resorts, have been replaced by 'joy-riding', drugs and teenage law-breaking on council estates. There is a significant difference in the family and social circumstances of a high proportion of young people to-day compared to those of earlier generations. The present generation of young people has experienced a rapid change in family structures through the extension of single parenthood, reconstitution and step-parenthood. Almost four out of every five young people featuring in our study came from such a background. This is not a condemnation but simply to draw attention to a new social phenomenon that cannot be simply attributed to individual or family pathology. Nevertheless, and as a result of these changes, a number of young people to-day have to cope with changing family and social relationships, which on occasions become sour, conflictual and acrimonious leading to instability and sometimes rootlessness. Added to this, as we have found, is the despair that long term unemployment and continued marginality generate. In spite of these often depressing circumstances, only a few of the young people featuring in the study were totally alienated from their families and society. Neither was there evidence of an 'alternative' youth culture. The ordinariness of most of the young people featuring in the study was their main characteristic.

In Chapter 1 the report introduces the study and outlines its aims and methods. The child care policies of the participant agencies as well as the wider legal context are described with specific reference to teenagers. This chapter also summarises major themes from the literature relevant to young people requiring social work intervention. Chapter 2 describes the characteristics of the young people at the start of the study, including their age, previous care or social work involvement, legal status, health, adjustment, self-esteem and education. The young people's family situations and networks are also outlined as well as the quality of these relationships and the support they provided. Issues relating to identity and the provision of background information are also addressed.

Chapter 3 identifies firstly, the dominant issues and circumstances that led to measures of supervision or care being taken. It presents the views of the three main actors, that is young people, their parents and the social workers. The chapter then moves on to examine the setting of expectations and the extent of congruence and coherence among the three parties. In Chapter 4 we describe the services available and consider ways in which they had been combined to form 'care packages' during the year. We outline the teenagers' movements during the year and identify some of the factors which prompted change and influenced access to services. Gaps in resources are identified.

Chapter 5 describes how the direct work of the social workers was regarded by each of the three parties. It examines their views of social work activities and explores the nature of the relationships between social workers and the families they were trying to help. Comparisons are also made with perceptions of other professionals, including residential staff. Chapter 6 begins with evaluations of home-based supervision, a curiously neglected topic. The helpfulness and impact of supervision are considered both in general terms and with respect to specific problems. Feedback is given on group work, befriending, outreach activities and psychological/psychiatric services. Chapter 7 concentrates on arrangements for young people living away from their parental home. This covers residential schools, foster care and 'independent' living. The positive and negative aspects of each kind of placement are described. The limitations of preparation and support for young people leaving care are reaffirmed.

In view of the emphasis placed by the Children Act, 1989 on partnership in planning, questions of participation and decision-making are examined in Chapter 8. The chapter presents the perspectives of young people, parents and social workers covering consultation, participation and choice, and how these influenced decisions and outcomes. The report moves on to provide, in Chapter 9, an account of the overall progress of the sample during the year. This uses the participants' reflections and comparisons of standard data gathered in both interviews on items such as behaviour, adjustment and self-esteem. The chapter also investigates how far expectations were met. Chapter 10 describes a summary measure which identified the most 'successful' cases in the sample and those where progress was extensive. Connections between outcomes and initial circumstances are examined as well as the relationship between overall success and the intervention. Factors which contributed to successful packages of services are discussed and notable differences between agencies reported. Finally Chapter 11 summarises the main findings of the study and discusses the implications for policy, practice and training.

1 Introduction to the Study

This report describes a three-year research project concerned with social work intervention with teenagers. A high proportion of the children dealt with by social workers come into this age-group but their particular needs have not been studied closely in recent child care research, except in relation to specific issues like offending or leaving care. There have been extensive discussions amongst policy makers and practitioners about the relative merits of different forms of care, particularly in the community (through foster care or supervision at home) and residential care, but little has been done to examine the services actually provided to teenagers or to identify the best combinations of care for them. As a result local authorities have developed a range of services which vary considerably in the content, balance and degree of co-ordination achieved. The shift away from institutions towards community care has been more marked in some authorities than others, notably Warwickshire and Fife which introduced well publicised policies to reduce the use of residential care to a minimum. An evaluation of the Warwickshire experiment, published after our project had begun, concluded that 'we still know very little about the experiences of older adolescents in care and which interventions are the most fruitful' (Cliffe with Berridge, 1991).

In the present study we investigated the arrangements made over the course of a year once it had been decided to admit teenagers into care (or to 'accommodation' since the Children Act 1989), or else to provide formal or informal supervision at home as an alternative. The research was based primarily on interviews with 116 young people aged 13–17, their social workers and parents in five local authorities in England and Scotland. Our overall approach was to examine the relationship between needs, as stated in the expectations held by the participants, the services deployed and outcomes. Important objectives of the research were to understand:

- how one or more services would be made available over a period of time in response to the initial problems;
- how these services were evaluated by the key participants;
- what impact they had on the teenagers and their families.

When carrying out these programmes, social work with teenagers has to take account of the many changes already going on in these young people's lives as they grow to maturity and come to school-leaving age or after. This is a period when a great deal of experience is visibly crammed into a short space of time and responses to external influences are correspondingly heightened. The year during which they were followed up may not seem long in which to monitor the effects, but by the end of the year it could have been too late for the social workers to go back and make another attempt to put things right.

We followed the lead given by the Working Party on assessing outcomes (Parker *et al*, 1991) who provided a thoughtful analysis of the nature of outcomes in child care. They cited two main approaches: the production of welfare and the developmental. The first approach has a systemic, economic focus and analyses inputs (of services and clients) in relation to the quantity and quality of outputs. The second perspective derives from developmental psychology and is concerned with the nurturing of competence. Drawing on both of these approaches, the authors noted that the 'outcomes' or dimensions of progress need not be located in the child or family, but can also include wider professional, public, and service outcomes. Parker *et al* also stressed that timing is crucial and in many respects there are sequences or chains of outcomes, a notion also explored by Quinton and Rutter (1988). The progress of children and families with difficulties is usually complex, with improvements and reverses, different patterns on different dimensions.

Most child care studies have concentrated on indicators related to the child as an individual or to placement sequences. Typically, the child's development, behaviour and health are examined. A few have also examined family relationships. Often this has been done using the single quantifiable variable of contact with birth parents and occasionally other relatives (Millham *et al*, 1986; Fanshel *et al*, 1990). Measures of the quality of family relationships are much harder to operationalise, although a number have been developed in the United States (Yuan and Revest, 1990).

Placement factors have been used as indicators of outcome too, although strictly these describe a living arrangement and do not necessarily correlate with particular consequences for the child or family. Typically, the breakdown or unplanned ending of a placement has been a prime measure used in studies of residential care, foster placements and adoption (Berridge and Cleaver, 1987; Kadushin and Martin, 1988). The analysis of placement patterns by Rowe *et al* (1989) sought to differentiate the nature of endings by whether placements lasted as long as needed and as long as planned and also whether the aims had been met. In addition Thoburn (1990) showed how different criteria can result in quite diverse pictures of the apparent success of permanent placements.

Besides the nature of the ending of particular placements, it is also possible to consider the culmination of a care career. Return home is one outcome of care in this sense although it cannot be assumed this is always a satisfactory conclusion (Farmer and Parker, 1991; Bullock *et al*, 1993b). An alternative outcome describes a living arrangement which has come to be known, somewhat misleadingly, as 'independence', ie living alone or with peers, supported or unsupported. In North America many evaluations have judged outcomes according to the 'restrictiveness' of the post-placement living environment with respect to space, movement and involvement in 'normal' community activities (Hawkins *et al*, 1992).

The present study breaks new ground by examining the use of supervision as an alternative to care and how this was viewed by the participants. Supervision at home has been a key provision under the children's hearings system in Scotland and was also available in England and Wales under the Children & Young Persons Act 1969. Yet little is known about the nature of this type of supervision or its effectiveness.

When the project began in January 1991, social services agencies throughout England & Wales were preparing for the implementation in the autumn of the Children Act 1989. This Act marked a drawing together for the first time of civil and state responsibilities for children into one piece of legislation. The 1989 Act not only simplified the means of committing children to local authority care and the orders that could be made, but also replaced the so-called 'voluntary' care process with 'accommodation' by the local authority. In addition, it formally introduced the principle that no order should be made 'unless it can be shown to be beneficial to the child' (DOH, 1989). In making these changes, the Government took note of a long consultation process which was itself informed by new developments in practice, major research studies and the findings of inquiries and inspections which had highlighted instances where social work practice had failed to live up to expectations (House of Commons, 1984; DHSS, 1985a; 1985b; Levy and Kahan, 1991; DOH, 1991a; 1991b; DOH, 1992).

With regard to teenagers in care, the 1989 Act made it easier for young people over the age of 16 to make their own requests for accommodation. The Act also strengthened the requirement for social workers to consult young people about plans being made and when these are reviewed or changed. In addition, the rights of young people to complain if they felt aggrieved were addressed through a new 'representations' procedure which is now available in all local authorities. The previously contradictory and unsatisfactory clauses covering arrangements for providing 'advice, guidance and assistance' to care leavers were also overhauled. Some of these changes were given an additional focus through the worldwide impetus for member nations to ratify the UN Convention on Children's Rights.

Scotland was affected by part of the 1989 Act relating to services for children aged under 8, but at the time of writing (December, 1994) a new Children (Scotland) Bill is yet to be enacted. This is based on a White Paper which emphasised the continuing and extended role of the children's hearings system in Scotland and made some recommendations, such as ending the power of local authorities to assume Parental Rights, which have similarities with the provisions of the Children Act 1989 (Scottish Office, 1993). It also noted the desirability of extending support to young people from 16 onwards and committed support to Who Cares? Scotland.

Although some of these improvements were targeted at the difficulties facing older adolescents and care-leavers, teenagers as a whole were not singled out for special attention towards their particular needs and problems. In part this was due to a pre-occupation with other pressing issues, especially the ever increasing referrals for alleged child sexual abuse. It is possible, too, that practitioners and policy makers relied on the information gained from 'Who Cares?' groups and NAYPIC and thought they knew enough about these young people's situations and worries. These groups have, indeed, persisted in keeping certain facts and issues in front of those responsible for dealing with them (Fletcher, 1993).

During the study period there was great public concern about juvenile crime and especially the apparent increase in persistent offending. Events which came to a head in Tyneside during the autumn of 1991 provoked much discussion of the underlying causes of the rioting and 'joy-riding' that took place. It was clear that poor social conditions, the effects of the recession and unemployment played a part, but questions were also asked about the responsibilities of parents, teachers and others in authority as well as the degree to which the young people should accept blame personally for their actions. More recently these debates reached an even higher level of 'moral panic' over the killing of James Bulger by two 10 year olds. The extreme youth of these boys disturbed everyone and led to demands for clearer boundaries between right and wrong to be enforced. These are difficult tasks for parents, teachers and others. They become more so when increasing numbers of families are split and problems such as bullying and truancy are rife.

Considerable changes to the care and treatment of young offenders have resulted from the Criminal Justice Act, 1991 which came into force in England & Wales a year after the implementation of the Children Act. This led to greater Social Services involvement with 17 year olds through Youth Justice schemes and a consequent need for closer collaboration with the Probation Service and also the Police. Although influenced by populist concerns to deal with serious offenders more severely, the 1991 Act also supported the increased use of community sentences (Worthington, 1993). Changes in Scotland which had followed arrangements for 100% funding and the introduction of National Standards for adult offenders led in a rather different direction as offenders over the age of 16 became the responsibility of specialist teams within generic social work departments (who combine, as they have done since the Social Work (Scotland) Act 1968, the functions of probation officers with those of social workers). These arrangements may, however, be affected by proposed alterations to Local Government boundaries and functions.

While the study was in progress, it was too early to note many direct links between the services provided to the teenagers in our sample and new developments in assisting other client groups through 'Care in the Community'. Nevertheless, the social workers and possibly some families were likely to have been affected by preparations for these changes within their departments and by the switch in the training of social workers from the CQSW to the DipSW. The movement towards more specialist child care teams has accelerated and already a whole new approach to the task of service delivery is evident through the split between purchaser and provider and the contracting out of services. In this new environment the language of 'quality assurance' does not exclude children. The study therefore spans a period in which very rapid developments were taking place within social work in response to the radical redefinition of the needs of many groups in society.

Method of Investigation

We aimed to base the study on a target of 120 teenagers as this number seemed likely to provide sufficient data for analysis. In fact 116 young people were eventually recruited, each of whom agreed to participate. The criteria for selection, besides being aged between 13 and 17 at referral, were a decision to admit the young person to care or accommodation, or to undertake formal or informal measures of supervision, or else to make a major change to an existing care or supervision arrangement. Further information about the sample is provided in Chapter 2.

The core study material was collected through interviews conducted with the young people, parents and social workers firstly when each case was referred to the research team and again one year later. In the first round, the social worker responsible for each of the 116 teenagers was interviewed. We were, however, unable to see 11 of the young people who had originally agreed to participate in the study, so that 105 initial interviews were carried out with young people. Some parents were dead or no longer in contact with their children and others declined to take part but we were able to conduct initial interviews with 78 parents (or other significant carers) in respect of 82 young people.

The semi-structured interview schedules contained a mixture of pre-coded and open-ended questions. Some self-completion charts and lists were also used with the young people. Provided that they and their parents were in agreement, we usually tape recorded all or part of these interviews but not those with social workers. Many of the interviews with all parties took place in fairly noisy surroundings but the ones with social workers were especially liable to be interrupted by telephone calls, tannoy messages and the general bustle of an office.

The schedules used in the first round of interviews obtained some descriptive details about the participants and the background to the referral. They then focussed on the decisions made, the programmes set up to carry out the plans, the participants' views about the actions being taken and their expectations about the likely outcomes of these interventions. If the young person was in a residential or foster care placement we asked for details of these arrangements. Otherwise we explored the plans for supervision in the community. In order to compile baseline information with which to compare subsequent progress a year later, we also enquired about some of the many aspects of a teenager's life such as health, education or work, relationships with family and peers, ability to cope with practicalities and aspirations for the future. Each party was asked to complete a modified version of the Rutter behaviour scale and the young people also completed the Coopersmith Self-Esteem Inventory (these instruments are described in Chapter 2). Finally we asked people to look ahead and anticipate how the young people's situation might be working out in 6 months to a year.

If the young person was in a care placement we asked their foster carer or key worker to complete a short questionnaire about general aspects of their work and about the needs and plans of the particular teenager. The researchers also completed a 'records form' of basic information on each young person from their files. This included details about the legal basis (if any) of the intervention, household composition at referral, schooling, any placements or moves and particulars about previous contacts with social workers or admissions to care.

After the first round of interviews had been completed a series of meetings were arranged in two of the study agencies with groups of teenagers who were not included in the sample. The purpose of these group meetings was to check how typical the views expressed by the sample were of other young people in various care or supervision situations. They also enabled us to test reactions to some 'word choice' charts and, as these were well received, we used them in the second round of interviews with the young people who were in the sample.

At follow-up, one year later, we again sought to interview as many as possible of the 3 parties. We succeeded in interviewing 97 young people, including 7 of the 11 whom we had not managed to see first time. Similarly, we obtained interviews with 73 parents, 9 of whom had not taken part in the first round. We conducted follow-up interviews with social workers for 109 young people, in 3 cases over the phone rather than in person. In some instances where cases had been closed or not re-allocated we contacted the worker who had been interviewed first time.

Overall, the two rounds yielded a total of 582 interviews. In 56 cases (48%) all 3 parties were seen both times. At the other extreme, there were 3 cases where only the social worker was interviewed. In between came a variety of permutations for 57 cases. Table 1:1 records the number of interviews conducted with the 3 parties in these 116 cases.

Table 1:1 Interviews conducted

	Social Worker	Young Person	Parent
Both times	109	90	64
1st interview only	7	15	18
2nd interview only	0	7	9
Neither time	0	4	25

Before being interviewed for the follow-up, social workers were asked to complete a short additional questionnaire, mainly about their methods of working with the young person. We also obtained a list of each teenager's known moves during the year. Otherwise the interviews with the 3 participants employed the same basic framework as the first round, with some modifications to cover a variety of situations. If the young person had been in a care placement at referral, we asked for an update on this placement and we then concentrated on the current or most recent placement for those who had moved or come into care during the year. With regard to formal or informal supervision, we just asked one set of questions but made some differentiations according to the timing of the intervention. Since many of the teenagers were aged 15 or older at follow-up, the preparation given to young people for becoming independent was an important facet, as was the experiences of those who were already living independently. Participants were asked to assess their level of satisfaction with the services provided and to say how they viewed the young person's prospects for the future and ability to cope as an adult. The Carers' questionnaire was not repeated, and we did not update information from the casefiles.

Interviews were undertaken by all the researchers and we recruited three free-lance interviewers to assist with some of the more distant interviews with young people and their parents. Some interviews took place in quite difficult circumstances and it was not always possible to cover every question, so responses are sometimes missing. Base numbers also vary sometimes due to interviews with participants taking place at different times. We tried to conduct these close together, but this did not always work out in practice.

All the answers to pre-coded questions from both rounds of interviews and many of the open-ended questions, especially from the first round, were analysed using the Datadesk statistical package. The package included Chi-square tests for statistical significance and these were carried out routinely unless the numbers in particular groupings were too small. Variables were usually examined for differences according to the age, gender and living situation of the young people as well as the agency and type of intervention. Some 3-way tables were run but numbers were mostly not large enough for meaningful conclusions. We have only made reference to these when significant differences were present. Most of the tape-recorded interviews from both rounds of interviews were transcribed, as were many of the answers to the open-ended questions, and this material was re-grouped under topics for qualitative use during analysis.

The Study Agencies and their Child Care Policies

The 5 local authorities were all very different and included both urban and rural communities. The involvement of agencies from both England and Scotland was partly pragmatic, due to the locations of the sponsors and the researchers. The study was designed principally to consider the impact of services for teenagers rather than to contrast policy and practice between the two countries, or between different agencies within them. However, we were able to examine some naturally occurring differences which resulted from variations in the legislation of the two countries. The inclusion of several agencies was deliberate as it increases confidence in the generalisability of the findings compared with a focus on a single agency. We had planned to work with 4 agencies but it became necessary to recruit an extra English agency because of unexpected problems in one authority, which were not connected with the research. The fifth agency was chosen partly on the grounds of its significant ethnic minority population. Depending on the number of referrals, either 2 or 3 Areas or Districts were selected from each authority.

During the initial fieldwork period we conducted interviews about the child care policies of each of the study agencies with senior personnel who held responsibility for child care services. Further interviews were carried out towards the end of the study to ascertain whether there had been any changes or new developments.

When the research began none of the 5 agencies had a specific or comprehensive policy for work with teenagers. Sometimes adolescents were considered but not singled out within a global age-range of children from 0 to 18. Policies which did target teenagers were confined to particular dimensions such as offending, truancy, leaving care or types of placement and were often presented in separate documents. Many initiatives were designed to keep certain groups like truants or offenders away from formal measures of care and had led to the construction of broadly based collaborative strategies in conjunction with a range of other statutory and voluntary agencies. For example, both of the Scottish agencies had developed very close links with the Education Department and all 5 agencies were involved in diversion schemes for young offenders.

Each authority had been reviewing its residential provision and fostering services but these reviews had usually been conducted separately from each other so that the placement needs of teenagers had not been considered as a whole. Policy about placements was also interrelated with the resources available or allocated. Falling numbers of children in care had contributed to massive reductions in the use of residential care during the 1980s. Various 'gatekeeping' procedures were operated and choices sometimes appeared wider than they were in reality. While none of the policies stated that residential care should be the first or only type of placement to be offered to adolescents, there often seemed little chance of foster care being offered as an alternative. Even though most agencies ran specialist Community Placement schemes for teenagers, the numbers were limited and very careful assessments had to be carried out first. Each of the agencies had some residential units designated for assessment and reception purposes, and community based methods of assessment were also being developed. Policy statements expected that many young people would return quickly to their families and where restoration was unlikely the emphasis was on preparation for independence rather than on continued support into early adulthood. With this aim in mind, community placements were often time-limited and/or designated as task related.

Two of the 5 agencies did not provide any secure accommodation and the policy in all of them was to use such placements as little as possible. As a result, residential units and also some foster carers were expected to care for some very difficult teenagers and the threat of violence and other disturbance was frequently acknowledged. Agencies were under pressure to increase staffing ratios and institute new training schemes in response to these problems. All the agencies found it necessary to make some placements outwith their boundaries and one had only recently embarked on a concerted withdrawal from this practice. Another strategy was to 'stagger' entry to care resources, especially residential schools, by forcing young people to stay at home until a placement became free. In Scotland, this process could cause particular difficulties in respect of making decisions at a Children's Hearing as these must include specific requirements about residence if it is thought best for the young person to be placed away from home. If no suitable placement is available, the Hearing must either adjourn or else make temporary arrangements which have to be reviewed whenever a change is contemplated.

The follow-up interviews with senior agency staff revealed that the intervening period had been a tumultuous one for all of the agencies with the introduction of much new legislation as well as major restructuring in three departments. However, there were several indications of more attention being focussed on teenagers though this still tended to concentrate on older adolescents and arrangements for leaving care. For example, one agency has set up a specialist team to work with all those aged 16 or over.

Two agencies had developed policies for 'through care' programmes which include more specific preparation for adulthood while the young people are in care, as well as support and after-care once they have left care. Another aspect of this 'through care' policy is increased attention to prevention through the provision of family support services, including more flexible contact points, community groups and short periods of accommodation during crises. One of the agencies had already set aside funding for 'through care' work and had begun to make operational changes for new posts which would be attached to teams throughout the agency. The other had successfully initiated some preventive measures but plans for a more comprehensive response were less advanced and there was uncertainty about whether the money would be forthcoming. It was evident that financial and political constraints were affecting the extent to which agencies were able to put some of their proposed policies into practice, especially those with longer-term implications. In the absence of coherant preventive services to families and young people, most choices were reduced to the traditional ones of formal supervision or residential care.

All the study agencies had continued to review their policies for residential services in response to the considerable concerns expressed by Central Government and because of changing needs. Interestingly, the thrust has been mainly to redefine the purpose of residential provision or to improve conditions in existing units for both residents and staff rather than to close them. Where there had been closures, new smaller and more localised homes had usually been opened in their place. Two agencies referred to the closure of specialist units providing preparation for independence; in one preparation was now a generic task in all residential units, while the other had no system at the time. A third agency had been developing satellite flats attached to residential schools as there were growing numbers of teenagers aged 16+ attending them. Some reductions in numbers had occurred within establishments through providing individual bedrooms and generally creating more space in recognition of the older age-group of residents and their expressed wishes for greater privacy. Much attention had been given to improving pay and service conditions as well as providing better training for staff. In addition, new procedures and standards had been set and there was evidence of more consultation with young people.

There had been few policy changes in these agencies with regard to fostering teenagers since the study began and foster care continued to be a restricted service for this age-group. One agency was experimenting with the use of foster care as an alternative to secure accommodation. Another planned to provide more choice for teenagers by recruiting specialist foster carers at the same time as reducing the number of beds in residential care. A third agency decided to improve the allowances for 'ordinary' foster parents, only a few of whom take teenagers, instead of expanding its specialist provision which caters for adolescents and those with 'special needs.' The restructuring of child care teams in two agencies had led to the development of area based responsibility for providing both foster care and residential services. In one, this had resulted in an increase in the number of foster carers but mainly for younger children so that teenagers still had to wait several weeks or even months for places. Contracts between carers, young people and their families and the agency appeared to be more widely used than in the past but there were problems in monitoring or enforcing them. Agencies varied in their more general approach to the issue of young people's participation in decision-making and acknowledgement of their rights but here, again, there was evidence of greater attention. Some agencies now had, or were developing, a Charter of Rights, with officers appointed to promote them, while others had consulted with groups of young people in care.

There had been changes in policy with regard to the supervision of offenders in the English agencies since the Criminal Justice Act 1991 as Social Services Departments were now responsible for 17 year old offenders. This had greatly increased the work of the renamed Youth Justice teams. Joint services had been developed with Probation and great effort had been put into reducing the high numbers of young people remanded into custody. On both sides of the border existing schemes which provided diversion or alternatives to custody had been strengthened. Some of these were run by voluntary bodies. There had also been policy initiatives to develop closer links with these organisations and with other statutory departments such as Education, Housing and the Health Service.

These links provided better support and after-care for teenagers moving to independent living. Some of the study agencies had many young people who were homeless, while in others tenancies could be obtained quite easily but there was no follow-up or support. Generally speaking, only one agency seemed to have moved towards putting a concerted policy for teenagers into operation. In the others, despite the various policy changes referred to, a strategy for teenagers as a distinct group still seemed to be missing. Many of the efforts were piecemeal and were acknowledged to be short-term reactions to individual situations.

The Legal Context

As the study covered authorities in both England and Scotland we now provide a brief account of the different legal contexts within which the social workers were operating. The study took place at a time when the Children Act 1989 and Criminal Justice Act 1991 were being implemented in England though many of the young people featuring in the study were already known to the social services for some time and had been, at least initially, processed under earlier legislation. Previously the English Social Services operated largely within the context of the Child Care Act 1980 and Children & Young Persons

Act 1969. Since 1970 most of the services offered by Social Work Departments in Scotland come under the Social Work (Scotland) Act 1968.

There are some commonalities in the child care legislation of the two countries but also major differences. In both countries local authorities have powers to support families and children on a voluntary basis, including making available residential provision, where necessary in order to help hold the family together. The legislation in both countries also aims to prevent children appearing before Courts or Hearings by encouraging the use of alternative measures in the community. Both systems, albeit differently, are meant to focus on children's needs rather than deeds.

When it comes to compulsory measures, whether in the form of home supervision or residential provision, then the process and emphasis differ. A major difference is the continued retention in England of the Juvenile Court system (now renamed Youth Courts) which in Scotland was replaced in 1970 by the Children's Hearings which are composed of Panels of lay people (Martin and Murray, 1982). The English Children & Young Persons Act 1969 was viewed as incorporating justice principles similar to those of the Scottish legislation which moved decidedly towards a more welfare orientation, especially in its treatment of troublesome children and young people up to the age of 16 (Pitts, 1988). Referring to the ambivalence of the 1969 Act, Harris (1991) commented on some of its contradictory ideologies such as the view that crime by youngsters was a transient part of growing up (therefore leave alone) and that it was indicative of personal or social distress (requiring 'treatment').

The Children Act 1989 emphasises the 'non' criminal side of child care and distinguishes children who offend from those in need of protection. Many of the teenagers who come into the first category will now be treated within the 1991 Act. However, the 1989 Act introduced the concept of a criminal supervision order with a residence requirement for some serious offenders. The maximum period which may be specified is six months.

In contrast to the English system, the Scottish system gave wide discretionary powers to the Reporter to the Children's Hearings over whether to bring a child before a Panel or not, though these powers are somewhat curtailed in the case of 14–16 year olds involved in serious crime. These young people are referred to the Courts, although the Hearing may still be involved in some of the disposals.

Unlike the Juvenile or Youth Court, the Hearing is not a judicial process. If the grounds of referral are accepted by the child/parents or have been established by a Court, then the main role of the three lay Panel members is to decide what should be done. This can range from no action, to the making of a supervision requirement or a residential requirement. A 'condition of residence' can apply to any named address, including that of one parent and not the other. Unlike in England, it is the Panel's responsibility to name the residential establishment or foster home or other address where the child/young person will live. Another difference from the English system is the regular review carried out by Panels for any child or young person subject to a statutory order. Furthermore, in such cases, any change of placement has to be approved by the Panel.

Review of the Literature relating to Teenagers

In order to set the work undertaken with teenagers by the study agencies in a wider context we reviewed some of the enormous literature relating to adolescent and child development, family and social circumstances and the care of children and young people in need of social work assistance. The review is divided into seven sections which correspond with some of the main concerns of the study. Where reviews have been conducted by other researchers (eg on residential care) we refer to them rather than going over the same ground again.

A Adolescent Development

We tend to take for granted that the teenage years represent a distinct and significant life stage. Yet often in the past the transition from childhood to adulthood activities happened much earlier than nowadays and was sometimes quite abrupt. The creation of an extended 'intermediate' phase is closely linked to the extension of compulsory schooling, together with the more recent comparative affluence of many though not all young people and the commercialisation of adolescence (Hurrelmann and Engel, 1989). Those processes have deferred certain rights and responsibilities for this age group, but also expanded their material aspirations which can lead to frustrations when these are not met.

General Features

The teenage years bring rapid changes in all dimensions of development. There are near-universal alterations in physique, sexuality and cognitive capacities which are normally linked with improved abilities to be responsible for oneself and for others. Physical growth and the changes associated with puberty alter the interests and self-perceptions of young people, as well as the responses of adults. In most cases, the capacity for abstract and hypothetical thinking develops considerably. There are usually improvements in the ability to anticipate future events and the consequences of current actions, to consider the views of others and to question information and assumptions (Smith and Cowie, 1991; Steinberg, 1993). The variations in the nature, pace and contexts of these transformations are wide, between individuals and across social circumstances.

The process of differentiation from parents, other carers and household members tends to accelerate in the teen years, although the extent and nature of this is much affected by cultural norms. In most Western societies, there are expectations of greater autonomy and of the formation of a definite separate identity, but also risks of confusion and diffusion in self-perceptions (Erikson, 1965). This period is often characterised as one of growing independence, although it can also be seen as developing new forms of interdependence in which the balance of reciprocity in relationships alters but mutual responsibilities remain (Youniss and Smollar, 1985). Relatively little is known about the quality and meaning of sibling relationships in adolescence, although this is clearly affected by such factors as gender, birth order, age-spacing and prior relationships to each other and to parents (Sutton-Smith and Rosenberg, 1970; Dunn, 1984; Wedge and Mantle, 1991).

Typically, the peer group, the media and youth cultures assume greater importance in a child's life during adolescence. Generally, more time is spent outside the home, often with peers, and conversations with friends increase in intimacy (Berndt, 1982; LeFrancois, 1990). Friends are sometimes seen as negative influences (a deficiency or pathology view of peer relations), but often perform important positive functions (Hartup, 1992). Mostly peer relationships do not subvert respect for and closeness with parents (Youniss and Smollar, 1985). Nevertheless, those adolescent behaviours regarded as problematic by adults are often initiated by and with peers (Colten and Gore, 1984). Group relationships are most important in early and mid-adolescence. At this stage, associations are often mainly with several members of the same sex, but sooner or later this usually cedes priority to heterosexual or in some cases homosexual pairing.

Progress through the teen years leads to the transition from school to the adult world of work, further education, training or unemployment, although for increasing proportions the transition to the world of work has been deferred or even indefinitely postponed compared with two decades ago. Limited prospects for work and training have an impact on the orientations of younger adolescents who may feel alienated and marginalised, especially when they have difficulties in conforming to standard expectations at school (Coffield et al, 1986; Jones and Wallace, 1992).

All these alterations can challenge both the individual young person and members of the immediate household and social network. The manner of response to such challenges is affected by the degree of success in negotiating earlier developmental stages and has implications for later relationships and life-satisfaction (Erikson, 1965). Adults may not adjust helpfully to the transition, perhaps affected by their own life-stage concerns and by influences from their own experiences as teenagers. On top of the perennial disjuncture of outlook between generations may be a failure to adjust to the rapid changes in technology, activities and *mores* of present day society which mean that being a teenager now is very different from 20–30 years ago. There is also a need to respond differently to the stages within adolescence (Petersen, 1988).

In spite of the common image of stress, conflict and 'storminess', most families negotiate this period without major tensions and upheavals. The majority of teenagers get on well with parents and value their advice (Fogelman, 1975; Coleman and Hendry, 1990). Most parents successfully give progressively greater latitude to their offspring, whilst maintaining definite limits and expectations. Teenagers usually want and respect parental authority, although they resent some particular rules (Youniss and Smollar, 1985). These positive findings in the literature suggest a model for the successful negotiation of this life-stage by adolescents and their families.

Our study, though, is concerned with the minority of families who have such significant difficulties that intervention from social services is sought or imposed. Research such as the well known Isle of Wight study indicates that between 10 and 20% of teenagers experience serious inner or outer turmoil, although not all will receive professional attention (Rutter *et al*, 1970).

Problems within the family and outside often go together, as our study was to bear out. There is a strong association between poor relationships with parents, strong peer influences and 'anti-social behaviour' – such as law-breaking, drug and alcohol abuse, running away, suicide attempts and early pregnancies (Petersen, 1988; Noller and Callan, 1991). Likewise, internal characteristics (like self-esteem) are closely linked to external performance, as at school (Coopersmith, 1990). Adolescents are more likely to succumb to environmental pressures to engage in activities disapproved of by adults when their parents are very strict or very weak and when there is a low level of monitoring of the teenagers' activities. Difficulties are often exacerbated because both parents and teenager interpret each other's behaviour more problematically than is necessary (Dickerson and Zimmerman, 1992). Intervention is important, since problems which start in adolescence often persist into adulthood (Petersen, 1988). Although many teenagers do 'grow out' of delinquency, especially as they settle into stable partnerships, there is considerable continuity between juvenile and adult offending (Farrington, 1992).

Individual and Social Variations

Social class affects adolescence directly through variations in access to resources and environments, but also through the cumulative implications of earlier childhood experiences and present parenting patterns. The close relationships between class, income and educational attainments has been well documented (eg Davie *et al*, 1972). There are differences in parenting aims and styles in relation to young children, which are partly related to social class and may well have longer term consequences (Newson and Newson, 1968; 1970; Hill, 1987).

At least since early anthropological studies, it has been well known that the meaning, status and duration of the intermediate period between childhood and adulthood varies greatly from one culture to another (Mead, 1961). Adolescents with parents from overseas may experiences value tensions, but their exposure to multiple frameworks can also be seen as a strength rather than a disadvantage (Ahmad, 1990; Gambe et al, 1992). Similarly adolescents of mixed parentage often identify positively with both strands of their heritage (Tizard and Phoenix, 1993).

Many differences have been noted between boys and girls. The focus for identity of females tends to be more oriented towards intimacy and personal relationships, whilst for boys it involves autonomy and activities (Bernard, 1981; Gavin and Furman, 1989). More girls respond to stresses by internalising their feelings of anxiety or depression, whereas more boys act out (Colten and Gore, 1984; Lerner, 1985). Partly as a result, more boys are engaged in offending and activities like substance abuse (Kerfoot and Butler, 1988; Farrington, 1992). There is some evidence that girls who develop physically earlier are more likely than others to be unpopular and engage in activities like smoking (Brooks-Gunn and Paikoff, 1992; Jackson and Bosma, 1992). Both boys and girls tend to confide in mothers rather than fathers (Monck, 1991; Youniss and Smollar, 1985). Adults tend to judge differently the actual, potential or suspected sexual behaviour of boys and girls. Partly in consequence, girls are more likely to be subject to social control and have less freedom (Salmon, 1992).

B Family and Social Circumstances

The association between admission to care and disadvantaged socio-economic and family circumstances has been known for many years (Packman, 1968; Wedge and Prosser, 1973) and still continues (Bebbington and Miles, 1989). The factors examined have usually included living in single parent or large families, overcrowding or other indicators of poor housing and the receipt of benefits as a measure of low income. Intensive studies of children from some of the groups most at risk (eg Ferri, 1976) highlighted further the difficulties of coping with these conditions and the effects on developmental progress. Pilling (1990) teased out some of the factors which enabled young people from disadvantaged situations to succeed against the odds. However, economic conditions generally have worsened in the last 10 years or so for many sections of society with the recession and continued unemployment. Government policies with regard to benefits and housing have exacerbated the difficulties and there has continued to be a high rate of marriage breakdown and reconstitution. Stewart and Stewart (1993) argued that these factors accounted for the difficulties found by supervising social workers in persuading many older teenage offenders to give up crime.

Two studies have set the context in which young people were growing towards adulthood in the late 1980s. One (Banks et al, 1992) was based directly on the ESRC's 16–19 Initiative; the other (Jones and Wallace, 1992) used some material from the same Initiative, as well as from the Scottish Young People's Survey and also other sources, including the National Child Development Study. Between them, these two reports collated some of the mass of material relevant to teenagers' family and background circumstances. Although those who come into contact with social services may suffer particular disadvantages, they obviously share in the impact of influences affecting their generation as a whole. While both studies concentrated especially on economic and labour-market forces, they also examined their effects within the family and on the young people's social life and showed how these interacted to shape future directions.

Many influences went much further back into childhood and Banks et al (1992) demonstrated how career routes had their origins deeper in the structures of society, so that by puberty family and peer group pressures were reinforcing each other and shaping the path to adulthood. The paths still differed, as they had in the past, according to gender and class as well as family backgound and these interacted with education and training. Family circumstances also influenced progress at 16 in material ways through the extent to which families were able to offer financial support. For example, most young people on Youth Training schemes lived in situations where their allowance was critical to the family budget, while those pursuing further education could only do so if they were supported financially by their families. Banks et al (1992) described how the young people struggled to achieve their identities in a 'landscape of inequality' and disliked or resisted much of what was happening to them.

Jones and Wallace (1992) showed that many other aspects of the relationships between parents and children have an economic basis and affect issues of dependence and independence. They described adolescence as a phase of considerable ambiguity, involving delicate negotiations between children and their parents, especially in reconstituted families. Throughout this period there is a tension between the parents' desire to keep children dependent and allowing them to grow into independent adults. In recent years some of the normal attempts at emancipation have been discouraged by state policies, which have placed additional strains on these relationships. For example, one of the ways in which teenagers begin to exercise their independence while living at home is through 'leisure' spending. Making provision for this may have a privileged position in the family economy or it may be impossible due to poverty. The media emphasis on youth culture and consumption, together with peer group pressure, mean that denial of funds can lead to a sense of exclusion or to problems such as debt.

For most young people leaving home is a symbolic step towards independence but this has become more extended, spaced and complex in recent years. Jones and Wallace (1992) support their thesis with data on social class and gender variations in the timing and spacing of these transitions. One consequence of the changes has been that leaving home, or living away from home, is not necessarily synonymous with independence or with the attainment of adult status. Many young people move into intermediate households, including staying with relatives, hostels or live-in jobs and may risk homelessness or the need to return home. This latter recourse is less likely to be available for young people from poorer, one-parent or reconstituted families and is therefore another source of inequality. However, the authors refute the notion that young women may get pregnant to jump housing queues and obtain welfare benefits. Both studies found that few teenagers had attained independence through marriage as the age for this event has continued to rise into the twenties, although more couples are living together first (Banks *et al*, 1992; Jones and Wallace, 1992). Both studies concluded that the state's expectation that parents should continue to offer shelter and support to their children after they have reached adulthood required a more integrated approach to the needs of young people and their families.

It is well known that higher proportions of children are now growing up in households which have experienced separation, divorce and reconstitution (Kiernan and Wicks, 1990). Besides poverty, unstable adult relationships constitute the main factor associated with reception into care (Packman *et al*, 1986). It has been suggested that adolescents are more able to cope with the consequences of family conflict and disruption, particularly when they have a good relationship with the custodial parent, but many do face serious social and emotional difficulties (Parkinson, 1987; Buchanan *et al*, 1991; Hill, 1993). Evidently, many teenagers are content in lone parent and reconsituted households, but strained and more distant relationships with parents do appear to be more common when there is a step-parent, whether permanently or irregularly (Ferri, 1984; Steinberg, 1990).

C Social Work with Teenagers in the Community (excluding Independence)

As the boundaries of this topic could become extremely blurred, we have divided it into sub-sections which concentrate separately on prevention & diversion, supervision and rehabilitation. However, it should be emphasised that many of the teenagers who come to the attention of social services experience all these types of activity, albeit varying in intensity and quality, so that we are not looking at discrete groups. The aim is to highlight some recent research findings which are relevant to these particular services.

1 Prevention and Diversion

The concept of prevention has been broadened in recent years. The idea that the aim of prevention is to keep children out of care has given way to the notion that there is a spectrum of levels and strategies seeking to prevent family stress, crises and breakdown and to minimise the negative consequences of any of these events (Hardiker *et al*, 1991; Marsh and Triseliotis, 1993). By this view, a placement away from home may have preventive functions in forestalling long-term family disruption.

Gibbons (1990) in her examination of the idea of prevention refers to the DHSS review of Child Care Law (1985b) which suggested that local authority community based provision for families with children had two main aims: i) to provide 'family support' to help parents bring up their children and ii) to seek to prevent admission to care or Court proceedings except where this is in the best interests of the child. Her study concentrated on the first aim and was restricted to families containing children under the age of 14. Although this age-range is mostly younger than in our study, it provides detailed information about families who seek help from social services at this earlier stage. The concluding hypothesis that 'parents under stress more easily overcome family problems . . . when there are many sources of family support available in local communities' (p.162) is one that seems likely to apply also to parents of teenagers.

However, one difference in preventive work with adolescents, compared with younger children, is that their individual needs tend to be focussed on more directly and there may be a tension between dealing with these and attending to problems in the family as a whole. Consequently, the second aim of preventing admission to care becomes more of an issue. Swanson (1988) described a new initiative in Strathclyde which aimed not only to prevent the breakdown of families and reception into care of older children but also to extend and develop appropriate supports for all young people with social problems. The study related to the first year's service provided by a short-stay refuge and counselling service for older children. Nearly half the referrals were for clients aged under 16 and almost two-thirds had experienced some kind of social work involvement prior to referral. All were said to have relationship difficulties with their parents or carers varying from fairly typical problems of adolescence to ones which were more deep-rooted and there were often other presenting problems as well. In some cases the refuge was unable to prevent family breakdown and the young people went into residential care. Some of those with educational needs were especially at risk of admission. The refuge also became caught up in the issue of homelessness, but was often able to achieve a reconciliation with the young people's families. The work of the refuge emphasised the need to perceive prevention in a broader sense but also showed the desirability of clarity about aims and objectives.

Even if these can be specified with some clarity at the outset, the original objectives may undergo revision as Fuller's evaluation of the MARS project (1988) showed. The project worked intensively with adolescents on the brink of removal from home but the passage of time could result in other events or crises bringing to the fore a different set of problems and needs which entailed changes in the help given. Some of the Unit's cases did enter care, so that taking admission to care as the only outcome measure would have misrepresented the Unit's work. The study attempted to use a typology of preventive objectives to assess the project's effectiveness. These were derived from Holman's overview of prevention and child care (1988) and were rated over a six-month period. Approximately three-quarters of the objectives were achieved with complete or partial success but there was some tendency for objectives directed at parenting behaviour to be less successful than work concerned with preventing admission to care.

A recent study of juvenile justice issues for local government in England (AMA, 1993) draws attention to the interrelationship between responsibilities for prevention through family support and the promotion of community safety which are contained in the Children Act 1989 and those for work with offenders which are laid down in the Criminal Justice Act 1991. The study refers to strategies outlined in other reports (eg NACRO, 1991) for Outreach, Community Support and involvement and work related to the problems of drugs and alcohol which would put the needs of young people on the agenda. Another important point is that preventive work with young people who have left school requires a very different style from working with those still at school. The study urges that the needs of 10–16 year olds should not be overlooked when seeking to respond to issues such as homelessness, unemployment and lack of benefits which affect older teenagers. Similar issues are examined by Utting et al (1993).

In North America, many programmes have been established to target with intensive services families where removal of a child from home is thought to be imminent (Yuan and Revest, 1990; Pecora et al, 1989; Rossi, 1992). Social workers in these 'family preservation' schemes typically have a very small caseload (2–4) and spend several hours per week assisting a family with a combination of counselling, practical assistance and advocacy. Contracts are used and work is time-limited (up to 6 months). Evaluation suggests that this approach has resulted in most of the children staying at home, though in some cases this was probably because of slackness in determining that removal really was otherwise inevitable.

The term diversion has been used mostly in relation to offenders and serves to indicate efforts to limit a young person's involvement with the judicial or care systems on the grounds that labelling and net-widening processes often lead to further anti-social behaviour or more drastic measures when otherwise the problems would have diminished (Parsloe, 1976; Bilson and Thorpe, 1987; Thoburn, 1993). At times this has meant doing as little as possible other than severe warnings or cautioning, but some people have also included as diversionary schemes which act as alternatives to care or custody, where the distinction between diversion and prevention becomes more blurred. Pratt (1985), for example, views the avoidance of further trouble, provision for the constructive use of enforced leisure, understanding of the social damage caused by crime and other similar situations as reasonable social work and probation objectives.

Intermediate Treatment schemes can range from targetted projects providing alternatives to custody through to programmes available to youngsters who may have had no formal involvement with the police. Intermediate Treatment has been used both as a condition of a statutory order and on a voluntary basis (Jones and Gallagher, 1985; Pitts, 1988; Bottoms *et al*, 1990). Police in England and Wales and Reporters in the Scottish system also exercise considerable discretion in diverting young people away from formal involvement with the courts and hearings. The use of such discretion varies greatly from one area to another (Asquith, 1992; Thoburn, 1993).

2   Supervision

Unlike the supervision of adults within the probation service, which has received extensive attention over the years, that involving children and teenagers, whether on compulsory or voluntary measures, has been largely ignored by the theoretical and research literature. Even less attention has been paid to the purpose, content and outcomes of work with children supervised by local authority social workers. In the latter case, debates have mostly focused on an examination of the legislative provision and of administrative procedures. In addition, the split within the English system which existed until recently between the social services and the probation service for the supervision of young people aged 14–17 did not help to provide a clear picture of how this affected practice locally or nationally.

When the purpose of supervision for teenagers is examined in the social work literature, it is almost always in relation to compulsory measures for those supervised by probation officers. The debate has centred mostly on issues of 'care and control'. The positions taken by those championing either of these models reflect ideological or else empirically based arguments. For example, Harris (1980) argued for a separation of 'caring' and 'controlling' functions on the grounds that supervision makes no difference to re-offending and yet the controlling aspect limits the assistance made available to those who are supervised. Critics of this view have singled out the impracticality of separating these two functions and often the difficulty of distinguishing between them (Raynor, 1985).

In contrast, Singer (1989) substitutes 'support and surveillance' for 'care and control'. From an analysis of responses made by teenagers, supervisors and probation officers, he could find no evidence for the existence of incompatibility between notions of 'support and surveillance'. He went on to add that 'no support-surveillance conflict was indicated between either counselling and directing, assisting and monitoring or any other configuration of mixed aims' (p.38). In fact he found that both probationers and supervisors had difficulty in distinguishing when an action was 'care' and when it was 'control'.

Singer's conclusions find theoretical support from Spicker (1990) who argues that social workers should reconcile themselves to the use of authority on the grounds that, as they are acting to change the client's situation, at least in part they are there to affect the behaviours and responses of their client and therefore are exercing some control. He comments that 'the social work relationship is often formed in a context of authority and approaches which seem to be non-directive are realised within this context' (p.227).

In one of very few articles on the supervision of children by local authority social workers, Spalton (1976) had no doubt that there could be advantages from a compulsory social work relationship with children. A compulsory relationship, she contends, is based upon the external reality of the decision 'which was preceded by certain specific admitted or proved events. These events may signify little or much, but they do provide *a focus on external reality*' (her italics, p.136). She equally asserted that, to be meaningful to a child or adult, any attempt to exercise control must be rooted in a demonstrated concern for the basic essentials for life.

In the 1960s and 70s many practitioners and commentators saw the primary purpose of supervision as being the treatment of perceived underlying problems in the interests of the young people's welfare. It was contended that this would indirectly help the young people become more willing to conform. Bottoms and McWilliams (1979) shifted the discussion to an attack on the 'welfare' model because of what they describe as the 'treatment' objectives. In their influential article they accepted that supervision should maximise client choice within limits set by the court or any other statutory body but supervisors should concentrate on providing help for client-defined problems rather than treatment for professionally-defined difficulties. Their emphasis was on 'help', shared assessment and joint definition of tasks as the basis for social work action. On this basis, the idea of addressing intangible 'needs' without the knowledge and agreement of the supervisee would have no place. The raising of issues by the social worker, far from limiting the client, increases his/her power to choose from a range of alternative actions and behaviours. Senior (1984) captured the essence of this by making the suggestion that supervisors should undertake work that is directly of benefit to the individual concerned and work on those issues agreed with him or her as problematic and in ways acceptable to them.

The two sides of the argument at this time were mainly about different approaches to assessing need. This led to criticicism of both approaches by Giller and Morris (1979). They found that supervisors in their wish to demonstrate that their primary concern was 'the child and the family' tried to relegate 'the significance of the child's offence and the court order to a mere formality' (p.154). Willis (1983) also asserted that research in the 1970's had found that 'criminality' was seen as 'rather unimportant and inconsequential' as a subject for discussion within supervision, while work concentrated on a problem-solving approach aimed at the relief of presenting needs. This led to approaches which concentrated more specifically on targetting offending behaviour, often using group work. Public attitudes towards those who commit crimes have hardened since and concern has been expressed within social work that supervision is being tilted towards greater control and surveillance within the community (Walker and Beaumont, 1985).

3 Rehabilitation

The return home of young people from placements in care is another aspect of social work with children in the community which ranges from the regulated supervision of children 'Home on Trial' to after-care arrangements made with varying degrees of planning and execution. Farmer and Parker (1991) discuss the tensions inherent in this work when the day-to-day care of the children is in the hands of parents or others whose capacity to provide adequate care or control has previously been put in question.

They divided the children in their study of children on Care Orders or Parental Rights resolutions who returned home on trial into two groups: the 'protected' who were mainly pre-teen and the 'disaffected' who were mostly teenagers. The second group contained all the children subject to orders for offending, for not attending school or for being beyond their parents' control. Two-fifths returned to the same household that they had left but two years later half the placements for the disaffected group had broken down. The extended family appeared to be an important resource for some of the adolescents but the researchers noted the remarkable mobility of some young people and suggested that moving may be regarded as a solution to a variety of problems. In other respects the dominant impression left by the disaffected group was of little change. It proved impossible in most cases to obtain from the records a detailed picture of what the social work activity with these placements actually comprised. Their findings led the authors to question the priority attached to work with difficult adolescents at home. However, the study noted a significant association between special education and successful placements. It also seemed that good preparatory work assisted more successful rehabilitation.

Bullock *et al* (1993b) observed that return home was often an extended process rather than a specific event. Three quarters of the children went home to relatives directly and some of the rest eventually did so after one or more stopping off points. Most reunions appeared to be reasonably successful but there was a significant minority who oscillated in and out of care or joined the homeless. Factors which hindered successful reunification included previous discontinuities of family relationships; disappearance or displacement of the child's role or territory at home; new family crises; unrealistic expectations. Social work preparation and support could be crucial, especially in terms of advice, finance, schooling or work. Help from a 'particularly sensitive' foster or residential carer could also be decisive. They concluded that 'return is as fraught and stressful an experience as separation, that the management of reunion is far from simple and that, while the majority of conciliations are successful, those that fail can carry with them serious long-term implications for the rejected child' (p.229).

D Entry to Care

Several recent studies have underlined the complexities involved in looking at admissions to care and have demonstrated that patterns of entry differ from the population in care at any one time. National statistics for children in care on 31 March during the 1980s appeared to indicate that teenagers were increasingly the main group in care but Rowe et al (1989) showed that during a year more than half of all admissions were children under 11 years old. Nevertheless, they confirmed the finding of Bebbington and Miles (1989) that 14–15 year olds were especially vulnerable to admission. In Scotland, about 85% of those in residential care are aged 12–17 (Scottish Office, 1992). Rowe et al noted that girls seemed particularly prone to coming into care at this age. Above that age, admissions of girls dropped more sharply than for boys, 10% of whom were admitted aged 16+.

The considerable turnover of children in care and the fact that the majority are already known to social services (Millham et al, 1986) mean that entries may be re-admissions rather than first-time experiences of care. Rowe et al (1989) found that 38% of the adolescents in their sample had experienced at least one previous admission beforehand and nearly one quarter of adolescents were re-admitted during the 2 years of the project. Millham et al attributed the re-admission of adolescents to a resumption of difficult behaviour at home or school.

Packman et al (1986) classified entrants to care into 3 groups: victims, volunteers and villains. The majority of those needing protection or voluntary support were younger children, so that teenage entrants were most likely to be 'villains'. However, the researchers emphasised that there were many areas of overlap between the 3 groups and they could represent different life-stages, so that some 'villains' were 'victims' or 'volunteers' grown older. They had all been admitted to care because of their behaviour. Besides often being described as 'unmanageable' at home, many were offenders, truants and run-aways. Poor parental control was a factor in three quarters of the admissions and poor emotional care in nearly two fifths.

Millham *et al* (1986) state that admitting a child to care is very much a social work decision and this process has been detailed by Vernon and Fruin (1986) and others. An important factor in this process is the choice of legal route into care, which may be pre-determined by the reason for admission or may be subject to negotiation between the professionals and perhaps also the parents and the young person. Although the Children Act 1989 has altered classifications of 'voluntary' care in England & Wales, the 'compulsory' route remains broadly the same. Some studies (eg Bebbington and Miles, 1989) distinguish admissions for offences from other children admitted on a compulsory basis for their welfare. However, the definition of 'offender' seems to vary between studies and Fisher *et al* (1986) discuss the inconsistency of this intervention as a route into care. Rowe *et al* (1989) found that the proportion of voluntary admissions quickly declined among the older teenagers and 42% of 16 year olds were admitted on remand.

While most studies describe the background circumstances of the children included in their samples, Bebbington and Miles (1989) provide the most recent overview of children who enter local authority care compared with those not in care (using data from the 1985 General Household Survey). This demonstrated that deprivation was a common factor among all types of children entering care, but was less significant for offenders than for the others. They concluded that though the majority of delinquent children come from deprived backgrounds, deprivation was not an invariable explanation why children offend. The researchers noted the particularly high correlation between single-parent families and entry to care and they discuss some of the alternative explanations and implications of this association. They also found that variations between areas reflected local social conditions which, in turn, were related to variations in social work practice.

E Placements for Teenagers Away from Home

Foster Care

1 *In General*

We need to distinguish children who grow up in foster care and become teenagers within that setting (often in the same family) from those who enter foster care as teenagers. The former have always been common, the latter less so (Berridge, 1994). However the trends have been in opposite directions. The permanency planning movement aided by legal and practical changes such as adoption allowances has meant that many young children in stable foster homes are nowadays adopted (Hill *et al*, 1989). Conversely, the development of specialist or professional foster care schemes has enabled more children needing placement in their teens to be fostered, although this development has not been uniform. Moreover, some agencies have moved to a position where nearly all children are accommodated in foster care without special arrangements (Cliffe with Berridge, 1991).

Most reports of fostering up to the 1970s tended to assume that most children placed in foster care would be fairly young (Dinnage and Pringle, 1967; Prosser, 1978). Shaw (1988) observes that 'the fostering of older children originated with Nancy Hazel and her colleagues in Kent' in the mid-1970s (p. 56). Yet it is clear that teenage children were being placed in the 1950s and 1960s, although with a much higher risk of placement breakdown than younger children (Trasler, 1960; Parker, 1966). The association between age and placement discontinuity has persisted, but possibly with a reduced difference which may be related to improvements in assessment, support and training for foster carers (Berridge and Cleaver, 1987; Triseliotis, 1989).

The high rate of placement turnover in foster care even with respect to younger children (Triseliotis, 1989) means that many younger children will have moved elsewhere by the time they reach their teens. When placements do survive (and many do), they can be very successful in terms of current progress and providing a family base for adulthood (Rowe et al, 1984; Triseliotis and Russell, 1984). A helpful guide to the practice issues and theoretical concepts relevant to fostering adolescents is provided by Aldgate et al (1989).

The large scale survey by Rowe et al (1989) showed that the proportion of children fostered who were aged 11+ ranged from 16% to 37% in the authorities taking part. Nearly all of these placements were defined as 'task-centred'. They found that twice as many placements for teenagers as for younger children did not last as long as planned. The peak age for placements in this category was 14–15 (59%). In general, the aims of placement were also less likely to be fulfilled in relation to older children.

2   Specialist Schemes

The earliest specialist scheme set up in Britain was the well-known Kent Family Placement Project established in the 1970s. It was intended to demonstrate that youngsters in their mid-teens with substantial difficulties could be placed in family settings, provided that a model of fostering was used which differed from traditonal conceptions. Carers were explicitly recruited to carry out negotiated tasks and to act as fellow professionals; intensive preparation and support was provided; carers received pay for work done in addition to maintenance costs; there were specific time-limited plans specified in written agreements (Hazel, 1981). This project was developed in conjunction with a University department and was evaluated both independently and by project staff at different points in time (Hazel, 1990). Results showed that teenagers aged 14+ with major difficulties could be held and helped in foster family placements. An initial external evaluation found that 64% of placements were completed as planned and 76% benefitted the young person (Yelloly, 1979). Later results produced by the Project itself showed that similar levels of success were being maintained (Smith, 1986; Kent SSD, 1986). Although success was generally good, the combination of truancy and behaviour problems was a particularly high risk factor for breakdown whilst experienced foster carers had a lower probability of breakdown (Fenyo *et al*, 1989). In the United States, matched comparisons of similar children have shown specialist foster placements to be more successful than the usual alternative arrangments in terms of personal development and subsequent avoidance of institutional care (Bogart, 1988; Almeida *et al*, 1989; Chamberlain, 1990).

Internal reports from both statutory and voluntary agencies indicating low breakdown rates have confirmed the positive findings from Kent and North America (O'Brien, 1990; King, 1991). However the survey of all child care placements made in 6 local authorities by Rowe *et al* (1989) indicated that the apparent success rates of the specialist placements was mixed. Just over half had ended sooner than planned, whilst slightly under half lasted as long as needed (according to social work judgements). However, one third were thought to have been 'very helpful' and a further 40% 'fairly helpful'. The teenagers placed in these specialist schemes tended to have more behaviour difficulties than teenagers in other kinds of foster homes.

Besides the outcome data, some information is available about how young people experience specialist foster care. For example, Downes (1982; 1992) noted the importance of viewing foster care within the context of other significant attachments past and present. Colton (1988) conducted comparative observations of specialist foster homes and residential units. His findings showed that the family setting was more 'child oriented' on all of four major dimensions – the child's choice and flexibility in daily living; participation in ordinary 'community' activities; the physical environment (eg privacy, individuality); and the nature of discipline.

Two important descriptive surveys of specialist fostering schemes were carried out in the early and late 1980's by Shaw and Hipgrave (1983, 1989a). The first study showed that specialist schemes had become widespread and mostly concentrated on difficult or delinquent adolescents. The second revealed that the number of schemes had continued to expand. They had also diversified to embrace a wider variety of children. Some of the newest developments cater for young people on the threshold of adultood, so that the clients have more autonomy than is usual for adolescents, although there is still an emphasis on tight planning (Graham *et al*, 1992). Some act as alternatives to custody for offenders or help prepare for independent living (Field, 1992; Kosonen 1993). Only some of these newer developments have achieved the levels of success of the original Kent scheme (Triseliotis, 1989).

By the late 1980s, misgvings had surfaced about the possible unfairness of a two-tier system of 'traditional' and specialist fostering (Shaw and Hipgrave, 1989b). Some agencies responded by paying fees and increasing support to all or most of their foster families (Maclean, 1989; Lowe, 1990; Hill *et al*, 1993). When authorities have sought to place nearly all their teenagers in foster care it has been hard to find sufficient suitable families (Cliffe with Berridge, 1991).

Residential Care

Major reviews of the research and literature on residential child care have been undertaken recently by Bullock *et al* (1993a) and Kendrick and Fraser (1992) and earlier by Parker (1988). The latter two were commissioned as part of an overall review of current provision, first in England by the Wagner Committee (1988) and later in Scotland by Skinner (Scottish Office, 1992). In both countries there have been large reductions in the numbers of children in residential care since the 1970s. Although some of the changes are due to demographic factors, there has been a particular shift away from using residential care for children under the age of 12. A survey by Knapp & Smith (1984) found only 11% children aged under 10 in residential care and Skinner (Scottish Office, 1992) reported that in 1990 only 11% of children in residential care in Scotland were aged 5–11. Thus the service is now almost entirely geared towards adolescents and the issues and concerns examined in these reviews overlap very strongly with those of our research with respect to this particular dimension of care.

All these writers emphasise the enormous variety of provision within the umbrella term of 'residential child care' which makes accurate definition and differentiation a difficult task. By sub-dividing the diagrams in their 'Directory of Publications' into 13 separate categories Bullock *et al* (1993a) enable readers to see at once which types of institutions have received most or least attention from researchers. They note that research undertaken since 1975 'reflects a changing view of child-care services' and has been patchy. There have been few studies of residential services in their own right and the gaps cannot be filled by earlier knowledge because the establishments and their residents have changed so much. In particular, older adolescents present different problems from younger children and 'should not be viewed as the latter writ large'. They are increasingly young people with serious difficulties and these pose new control problems for staff. Although many children are said to prefer residential care to fostering because it is less restrictive and minimises conflict with family loyalties, there is a risk of a poor outcome. Young people's views and wishes are important but their long-term interests also need to be understood. For example, admission to residential care creates secondary problems associated with stigma, separation and strained relationships within the institution. Dealing with these can lead to neglect of the primary problems which necessitated removal from home. However, research suggests that residential care confers educational benefits and offers stability and an environment in which to grow up and acquire social skills.

The chief areas identified by Bullock *et al* (1993a) as having been neglected in research since 1975 are short-stay residential care and the quality of the care offered to children. In addition the outcomes of different combinations of intervention should be studied. Although there has been improved under-standing of the functions of residential care for the wider child-care system, it has lacked careful analysis of children's background characteristics and needs. Among the many other aspects which the Dartington researchers highlight for investigation are: health, the special needs of girls, concepts such as identity, personal growth and development, sexual behaviour and the risks of already abused children facing further abuse while in residential care.

Parker (1988) divided his examination of residential care into various groupings and attempted, wherever possible, to make comparisons with data about alternative provisions, especially foster care. However, he too concluded that few studies systematically address the alternatives although there were some good small-scale studies (eg Triseliotis and Russell, 1984). Parker's call for an integrated approach to child care planning is taken up strongly by Kendrick and Fraser (1992).

Their review makes a sharper contrast between what they term 'enclosed' communities such as residential schools, secure units and therapeutic com-munities and 'community-based' resources in the shape of Children's Homes and other types of centre sited on local estates near the residents' families. In making this contrast the reviewers acknowledge that using the word 'commu-nity' raises questions not only about a child's home environment but also about the use of foster care. For example, they note that the term 'community carer' is commonly used instead of 'foster parent' in Scotland. Like the Wagner Committee they argue that residential child care cannot occur in isolation from other community services and must be part of a 'continuum of care'. Instead of being seen as a last resort and an admission of failure, it should be a positive choice in the goal of preventing family breakdown. This, they say, should include providing young people who need care with opportunities to define their needs and make choices between real and valid alternative placements.

Within this broad consensus these reviews examine many individual issues relevant to the functions and running of residential establishments. While some concern the basic nurturing and attention to the developmental needs of children and young people, Parker (1988) noted how these can get over-looked or be difficult to maintain in an institutional setting. The changes in the age-range have meant that some aspects, such as the need for privacy or relationships between the sexes, have become more important. Appropriate control and discipline continue to be major factors in all group settings and have been the subject of specific guidance following enquiries into abuses.

There has also been much attention given to the issue of contact between young people and their families and to the need for preparation for returning home or else for moving to independence.

The conduct and success of all these activities depend to a large extent on the selection, training and deployment of the staff for these Homes and these aspects are also covered by these reviews. Although there are still gaps, a considerable amount of information and knowledge about residential child care has been accumulated. Nevertheless, Kendrick and Fraser (1992) point out that many of the issues which still require further attention are not new.

The future role of residential child care is discussed by Cliffe with Berridge (1991) in their study of the Warwickshire experiment of closing down its Children's Homes. The topic is also central to Sheriff Kearney's report of the inquiry into child care policies in Fife which discouraged residential place-ments (Kearney and Mapstone, 1992). While Warwickshire explicitly retained a positive commitment to residential placement through other agencies for children who required this, the Fife Inquiry found a universally negative attitude pervaded the council's policy towards the use of residential child care. Despite these apparently divergent attitudes the end result in both authorities appeared to be similar as the residential placements which were made usually followed a series of foster home breakdowns. A special study of 42 children who were placed residentially by Warwickshire revealed that only 4 went straight into a residential placement on admission to care. In their conclusions, both reports reiterate the importance of taking into account the individual needs of children and they warn of the dangers of over-simplifying or confusing messages about the most appropriate methods of achieving these aims. In doing so, these reports provide a salutory reminder of the complex and difficult tasks involved in residential work with children, especially now that these are mostly older adolescents.

Harris and Timms (1993) have reviewed the situation of children in secure accommodation following legislative changes in 1983. The study grew out of research but is primarily a piece of social analysis on the relations of state, family (especially the deviant family) and child. The theme is one of ambiguity, both in respect of the disposal and of the behaviour and experiences of the child under consideration. Secure accommodation is described as a range of disparate institutions having in common only the possession of a licence and the turning of a key. Where a youngster is sent is often chance and a confluence of body, bed and criteria. The stories of 5 children are recorded in detail and the authors conclude that in the absence of secure accommodation it is difficult to see where they would go. The study urges caution about extending the provision, especially as it could be used to fill the more general gap between poorly staffed and under-resourced alternatives. A detailed study of a Scottish secure unit showed how it highlighted the gap between the justifying rhetoric of treatment in a supposedly welfare-based system and the reality of containment by well-meaning but inadequately trained staff (Kelly, 1992). This research echoed the findings of a German investigation which argued that the main function of 'closed' institutions is to handle those whom the rest of the system cannot cope with and thus enable other establishments to function in their accustomed way without needing to adapt to 'misfits' (Wolffersdorff *et al*, 1989).

F Leaving Care/Moving to Independence

Many of the research studies about young people in care have focused on the transition out of care. Garnett (1992) included an appendix giving a brief description of 14 studies dating from 1983. Her own study is based on social workers' responses to a questionnaire relating to 135 young people from three of the authorities which participated in the 'Child Care Now' study (Rowe *et al*, 1989). There was a gap of 2–3 years between the two stages of the study which resulted in some loss of information. Garnett divided the group according to their pattern of care into:

1   Long-term stable placements   (21%)
2   Long-term unsettled placements   (19%)
3   Teenage entrants   (59%)

She provided interesting data about their care situations and the contrasting educational qualifications and employment status of these groups at discharge. A striking finding was the amount of movement in the run-up to discharge from care and also in the first 12 months post care. Much of this movement was experienced by the older, more difficult to place teenage entrants and concern is expressed at the lack of provision, as well as the lack of choice, for this group, especially for young women with small children. Nearly one in seven of the female care-leavers in the study were reported to be pregnant or already had children by the time they left care. The survey raised the issue of the lack of formal planning at the time of discharge from care but urged that leaving care should not be treated in isolation from the care experience as a whole.

The study examined the nature of support and assistance received from social services once the young people had left care and found that none of the three authorities made specific provision for after care. One-third of the sample had plans to continue contact with their social worker and many of them still had some involvement 2–3 years later. For the other two-thirds the most common arrangement was for the young people to come back at their own initiative if and when they needed help. More than one-third of them did seek help later, often on a one-off basis, and were not necessarily dealt with by their original social worker. This raised further questions about the duty to 'advise' young people, who should do it and the need for co-ordination with other local authority and voluntary services. In addition the study suggested that there should be more concentration on 'sustained relationships' with people other than social workers who can act as support systems during the transition to independence.

Many of Garnett's findings are supported and amplified by the Leeds University Leaving Care project (Biehal *et al*, 1992). This survey too was based originally on social workers' responses but the researchers have now carried out follow-up interviews which include the young people as well. The authors discuss the concept of 'independence' and define it for their purposes as:

> 'neither living under the direct supervision
> of social services nor within the family home'.

Consequently, 'the only young people we consider not to be independent are those who returned to or remained within the family home when legally discharged from care'. The study noted the very early age at which young people who have been in care move to independence compared with the population as a whole. The questionnaires were completed within 3–9 months of discharge or moving to independence. As Garnett found, there was a considerable amount of movement during this early period. There was a small but noticeable shift towards permanent tenancies and a reduction in the numbers living in more temporary forms of accommodation. However, the numbers in custody increased as did the numbers where social workers had lost touch. Some 15% of young people were considered to be homeless and 16 or 17 year olds appeared to be at greater risk than older teenagers, also young people with special needs were over-represented. The survey found similar findings to Garnett's with regard to the lack of educational and employment prospects, and the number of young parents.

Each of the three authorities in the Leeds study had developed leaving care schemes and the survey also examined the on-going support offered to all the young people, plans for further contact and what financial assistance the young people had received. Within a few months of leaving care one-quarter of the sample were reported to be receiving no professional support at all, but nearly half were still in contact with their social workers and some young people received help from several sources. Nevertheless, there was a worryingly low level of contact with former foster or residential carers. Just under one-quarter of the young people were involved in leaving-care schemes. The study showed that high levels of unemployment and changes in eligibility for benefits meant that local authorities increasingly had to provide assistance with weekly incomes in addition to making leaving care grants of varying amounts. Some two-thirds of the sample had already received financial help from social services and the transition from care may be impossible without such help for those who have no family support.

The study paid particular attention to the experiences of 'Black' young people and those with special needs. There were no substantial differences in the pattern of on-going support received by 'Black' and 'White' young people.

However, there was a surprising lack of current support or expected future social work contact with young people who were likely to have special needs because of disabilities, mental health problems or past emotional or behavioural disturbance.

G   Rights and Decision-Making

Until recently debates about child care principles have tended to focus on children's needs and interests together with parents' rights and responsibilities, but over the last decade approaches which use the concept of children's rights have become increasingly prominent. Some individual agencies began to create children's rights officer posts. The UN Convention (ratified by the UK with some reservations in 1991) gave further impetus to this development.

Although attention to children's rights in philosophy and law has a long history, children's rights issues came to prominence in the 1960's as a result of the children's liberation movement. This mainly had adolescents in mind and argued for the extension to children of the same rights as adults, for example as regards not going to school, being able to work, sexual relations (Franklin, 1986). This challenged the prevailing protectionist view of children's rights, that they needed special exemptions from adult rights because of their vulnerability (Adler, 1985). Lindley (1991) accepts that younger children should be treated separately because of their capacities and emotional labililty, but argues that teenagers should have the same rights of agency and consent as adults. The question of giving due recognition to the ability and understanding of adolescents to decide matters for themselves has been much discussed in relation to agreement and refusal for medical treatment (Buchanan and Brock, 1989; Freeman, 1993).

The UN Convention includes rights to express an opinion and to have that taken into account (Article 12); to information and freedom of expression (13); to periodic review of placement (25). It also embraces a different set of social rights – to protection and services, which are pertinent to our present study. It is vital that children subject to public intervention should continue to have the same basic entitlements as those brought up by their families, including the right to love, good quality care, appropriate education and continuity of experiences and relationships. Triseliotis (1983) also highlighted the importance of having an understanding of your past and of a sense of belonging. Dennington and Pitts (1991) outlined a set of additional rights. These include:

- a personalised response to their needs and difficulties;
- access to friends and trusted family members;
- having their views listened to and taken account of;
- being involved in key decisions about their lives.

There are at least 4 necessary elements for exercising rights in relation to key decisions (Barford and Wattam 1991; Batty and Robson, 1992):

1　procedures for consulting young people;
2　access to information, skills and processes which enable young people to express themselves well;
3　decision-making which genuinely takes account of their expressed views;
4　opportunities for complaint or appeal.

In the UK the prime legal duty under both the Children Act 1989 and the Social Work (Scotland) Act, 1968 is for social work agencies and professionals to act in the best interests of children and young people (as the professionals perceive it), which may conflict with a young person's own view of what is best.

The implications of rights in decision-making gradually alter as a child becomes an adolescent (Triseliotis *et al*, 1993). Firstly, most teenagers have more developed cognitive abilities compared with younger children. As we saw earlier they are more comfortable with abstract concepts, more able to take a longer term perspective and to consider the viewpoints of others. This means that they generally have a greater capacity to articulate their own needs and wishes, although their communicative skills will vary considerably according to their personal confidence and ability. Just as significantly, this will depend on the ways in which adults shape the contexts for communication.

Secondly, teenagers normally have much greater physical and emotional autonomy that younger children. They are much more able to initiate events and to modify what happens to them. Compared with young children, teenagers are more likely to run away from a situation they are unhappy about or to undermine plans they do not agree with. Positively, they are also more capable of maintaining links with significant people and usually do not need to be visited or transported in order to secure access to relatives or friends, as is often the case with younger children (Millham *et al*, 1986).

The exercise of participatory rights by teenagers is affected not only by their usually improved intellectual capacities compared with younger children, but also by their greater ability to take practical steps to alter their own circumstances (eg by running away; by visiting parents or friends unaided).

With increasing age, the issue of the young person's responsibilities become more prominent. They can do more for themselves. Their need for receiving care gradually diminishes, although advice and support remain vital. Indeed it can be argued that teenagers have the right to be assisted in taking increased responsibilities for their self-care and life plans. This has been the basis of most recent thinking about teenagers leaving care and moving to independent living, although there are dangers that young people from care are thrust into a situation of self-reliance much sooner than most of their peers and without comparable social and practical resources or emotional supports (Aldgate *et al*, 1989; Jones and Wallace, 1992).

Implications for the Study

When dealing with people at any age, it is important to consider the implications of their developmental life-stage, their interactions with social networks and social institutions and the wider societal and policy contexts. Adolescence in present day Britain is generally a period of competing pressures and issues which need to be resolved successfully to ensure a reasonably satisfactory transition to adulthood, as happens in most households. Teenagers are moving from the relative dependence and restrictions of childhood to the autonomy of full adult citizenship, often within rapidly changing family structures. Most remain responsive to adults but are increasingly subject to peer influences, youth cultures and subcultures, whose nature and impact vary according to gender, class, ethnic and cultural background and geographical location. In recent times, educational developments, the media and commercial forces have raised aspirations at the same time as high unemployment and financial restrictions have constrained opportunities. Deferment of adult status and responsibilities can be liberating, but can also be frustrating, especially when the accompanying material rewards are also absent (Chisholm, 1990; 1993).

As a result of all these and other factors, teenagers, parents and professionals concerned with them are often engaged in delicate balancing acts. The need and right to protection which persists from childhood has to be balanced against the right for gradually increased self-determination and participation of adulthood. Likewise the need for care and control or freedom with responsibility have to be balanced against the availability of educational and material resources. It becomes easy for disequilibrium to occur, if the desires and expectations of teenagers and their parents, teachers or the law diverge and conflict. This may be a temporary phenomenon, a period of readjustment in attitudes or expectations on either or both sides. It can also be superimposed on deep-seated problems (such as abuse or long-term educational failure) to produce circumstances or behaviour which are much harder to deal with.

When social services become involved, there is a need to restore the balance (within the family, at school or in the community) or in more extreme cases to create a new context for the care or control of the teenager. Over the years, social work has been subject to a number of guiding nostrums. These too should be carefully weighed for their relevance to particular situations, because they are incompatible as absolutes but each contains truths which apply in some cases. For example:

a   children should be kept out care at all costs,
b   care can be a positive choice;

a   institutions can provide controls when parents cannot,
b   institutional care is harmful;

a   every child should live with a family,
b   fostering is not appropriate for teenagers.

Each of these has acted as a lodestone for the direction of policies and services, but there has been a tendency to adopt just one of them as a generalisation at any one time, rather than recognise that prevention, diversion, fostering and residential care may all have a part to play depending on the circumstances.

When the problem is one of temporary imbalance, minimal or brief intervention will often suffice. Indeed excessive intrusion can be counter-productive because of the well-known secondary consequences of judicial action and substitute care. Some behaviour like sexual intercourse or school non-attendance is unacceptable at 13 or 14 but becomes normal by 18. Many, though not all, young offenders grow out of crime. Some families rapidly adapt to conflicts and crises. On the other hand, illegal behaviour is sometimes more deep-rooted, including self-destructive activities such as drug-abuse. There are families where the lack of basic attachments and mutual respect makes transitional tensions into major ruptures. In these instances more substantial input is necessary, but the role of the state in protecting its younger members and in protecting others from the depredations of some adolescents still has to be tempered with respect for the rights and duties of teenagers and their parents. Social workers have to reconcile all these dilemmas when they are called upon to help families with teenagers in serious difficulties.

Summary

The study examined the services provided to teenagers referred for social work intervention by means of a longitudinal survey of 116 young people aged 13–17, their social workers and parents in 5 local authorities in England and Scotland. None of the agencies had specific policies for this age-group although some were developing programmes of 'through care'. Policy directives usually concentrated on situations such as offending behaviour or leaving care and on placement requirements. These topics and others relating to adolescents and their families have been extensively researched and a review of the literature sets the work of these agencies in a wider context. Over the last decade the concept of children's rights has become increasingly prominent and the involvement of teenagers in decision-making has been recognised to be particularly relevant to the satisfactory provision of services. This is just one of many interrelated themes which will be covered in more detail in later chapters.

2 Characteristics of the Sample

The main part of the research was an intensive study of a sample of 116 young people aged 13–17 (73 males, 43 females). They were followed for a period of approximately 12 months from the point at which decisions were made about the need for care or supervision or when major changes to existing arrangements became necessary. Starting in the summer 1991, the young people were identified through their social workers and their agreement was sought for participation in the study. Although 11 teenagers changed their minds about being interviewed during the usually brief interval after their social workers had given an initial interview, we decided not to exclude these cases from the study as we hoped that some of them would reconsider their position at the follow-up stage and agree to participate then, as in fact happened.

Fifty six other young people were known to have declined to take part for a variety of reasons. Where information about their age and gender was provided this indicated that the distribution was broadly similar to the sample included in the study. Social workers were often reluctant to divulge further details once participation had been refused. Many of the young people were in such crisis at the time of their social work contact that they (or their social workers) could not cope with the research request, while others were still at loggerheads with their parents and/or the department and wanted nothing to do with anyone connected with this involvement. In spite of trying to obtain a higher representation from ethnic minorities, we only succeeded in interviewing 3 young people who were black or of mixed ethnic origin.

The study was successful in obtaining the consent of 78 parents for interviews. These parents had 82 children in care or on supervision as there were some pairs of siblings in the study. Whilst there were some refusals from parents, other factors also contributed to not being able to see more parents. Some parents were dead, in prison or ill and some had dropped out of the life of the young person or the teenager did not want any further contact. About half of the parents who were interviewed were in paid employment. Two out of five of these had non-manual occupations and some other parents were studying at Universities.

It will become more apparent in later chapters that the circumstances of intervention were often complex and subject to change. Some of the young people who were in the sample because they were newly admitted to care or placed on supervision in the community had, by the time we came to interview them only a few weeks later, already been discharged from care or had their supervision arrangements radically altered. Indeed, it was this fluidity of activity that convinced us that we would obtain a truer picture of the reality of social work practice with this age-group if the selection criteria included unexpected moves and changes of plan.

Agency Distribution

We had planned to include 30 young people each from four agencies but it was often uncertain until the last minute whether their agreement would be obtained. In three agencies more than this number were approached and the figures were just over 30. This helped to compensate for the low number of cases in the fourth agency resulting from problems unconnected with the research. We also obtained additional cases from a fifth agency. The eventual distribution for the 116 cases included in the study was:

Agency A	33 cases
Agency B	8 cases
Agency C	34 cases
Agency D	10 cases
Agency E	31 cases

Age at Referral to the Study

Provided that the young people were aged between 13 and 17, no deliberate attempts were made to control for any specific age or gender among those referred to the study. The eventual distribution turned out to be fairly typical of 'care' populations as it contained more 15 year olds than any other single age and also boys outnumbered girls by two to one (cf Rowe *et al*, 1989). The 13–14 year-olds formed 44% of the total compared with 31% 15 year-olds and 25% in the 16–18 age range (one young person had turned 18 as she just managed to be admitted to care before her birthday). There were considerably more younger boys (13–14) and somewhat more older girls (16+) in our sample, but the differences were not statistically significant.

Table 2:1 Age of young people at referral by agency

	Agency						
	A	**B**	**C**	**D**	**E**	**Total**	
Age	%	%	%	%	%	N	(%)
13–14	33	25	50	30	58	51	(44)
15	46	12	29	20	26	36	(31)
16–18	21	63	21	50	16	29	(25)
Total	100	100	100	100	100	116	(100)

There was, however, a significant difference between the 5 agencies in the ages of the young people included in the study (Table 2:1). A higher proportion of younger teenagers (13–14) came from Agency E while the sample for Agency A contained more 15 year-olds than the other agencies. The two agencies with fewer cases (B and D) both provided more older teenagers (16+). The age distribution in Agency C was closest to the overall composition of the sample.

Previous Care or Social Work Involvement

More than half of the young people who were currently being supervised in the community said they had been in care during the last year and provided details of this experience. We also used information from the case records to build up a more extensive picture of previous care episodes and social work involvement with the young people in the community or with members of their family, particularly during the last 5 years. This revealed that only a handful of teenagers or their families had been previously unknown to the agencies concerned. Table 2:2 shows that 73% of our sample were either in care at the start of the study or had been admitted to care on previous occasions.

Table 2:2 Past and present care experience at referral to study

Care experience	N	%	
In care now and previously	24	21	
In care now, not previously	32	27	73%
Not now, in care previously	29	25	
Never in care	24	21	
Information missing	7	6	
Total	116	100	

Social workers had previously been involved in work with 13 of the 24 young people who had never been in care and in a further 4 cases they had been involved with their families in some other capacity. Full information was missing in 3 cases, which left just 4 young people who appeared to have had no social work contact before the current episode. Three of these 4 came from Agency E, which puts considerable emphasis on diversion from social work involvement.

Two-thirds of those with previous experience of care had only been admitted once before. The highest recorded number of previous admissions was 7 (2 cases). The length of these earlier admissions varied from a few days to several years but even a brief episode, or memories of other children's experiences, could colour the attitude of the young people and/or their families towards care in general or towards particular placements.

Legal Status of the Current Intervention

Referrals to the study were comprised of care episodes or supervisions which had been made on either a statutory or a voluntary basis. We included within the 'statutory care' category young people in Scotland who were placed under Supervision Requirements with a 'condition of residence' away from home. The 'voluntary care' group included teenagers who were 'accommodated' after the Children Act 1989 was implemented. Information on the legal status of the current intervention came from case records and varied in the precision with which the relevant Acts and sections were recorded so that some informed guesses were necessary. In addition, quite a few young people were subject to more than one type of legislation at the time of referral to the study (eg on remand while under a care order, or in voluntary care awaiting the outcome of a Children's Hearing).

Young people referred from Agency A were much more likely to be in voluntary care or in receipt of voluntary supervision than those referred from Agency E, where more statutory work was included, while referrals from Agency C came in between (Table 2:3). The two agencies with smaller numbers complemented each other as more statutory referrals came from B and more voluntary referrals from D. Despite the difference in proportions of statutory referrals between Agencies A and E, both provided more supervision than care cases while the reverse was true for Agencies B, C and D.

Table 2:3 Legal status by agency

	Agency						
	A	B	C	D	E	Total	
Legal status	%	%	%	%	%	N	%
statutory care	9	50	41	30	39	36	31
stat supervision	27	12	18	0	45	30	26
voluntary care	36	12	23	60	0	27	23
vol supervision	27	25	18	10	16	23	20
Total	100	100	100	100	100	116	100

Girls were somewhat more likely than boys to be in both statutory and voluntary care, whereas more boys were on statutory supervision – often as a result of offending. Overall, statutory measures were in force for 63% boys compared with 46% girls. We noted earlier that more of the younger teenagers were boys and 90% of those on statutory supervision were aged 13–15. Approximately half of the young people in voluntary care or voluntary supervision were aged 13–14, but the inclusion of teenagers who had moved in care probably accounted for there being a similar proportion of 16–18 year-olds in statutory care as in the two younger age-bands.

Contextualisation of the Study Sample

In order to set the study cases in context information was obtained in two agencies one English and one Scottish about their overall work with teenagers. The purpose of this exercise was two-fold: firstly to establish what proportion of cases which met the study criteria had in fact been included in the sample and secondly to determine how representative the sample was of work in these agencies.

We were only partially successful in meeting these aims. To minimise the demands on agency staff we did not ask for information to be collated specifically for this purpose but primarily used data which were already available. Consequently we obtained somewhat different information from each agency and sub-groupings by age were not always directly comparable with those of the study sample.

The criteria for inclusion in the study could not be applied readily to existing statistics as the study contained young people who experienced a significant change in the type of intervention as well as new admissions. In both authorities we were able to assess the proportion of admissions to care which had been included, and in the Scottish authority separate information from the Reporter to the Children's Panel enabled us to gauge how many cases of new or changed supervision status were in the sample.

The overall response rate in these agencies was between a third and half the potential sample. This is perhaps as high as might be expected in a study which involves interviewing teenagers in trouble from a number of geographically dispersed offices. The effect on the sample of social worker bias and some young people's reluctance to take part can only be inferred.

On the basis of this information it was possible to identify two particular groups which were under-represented in the sample: young people admitted to care on a voluntary basis and teenagers aged 15 and over. Social workers had not informed us of most of the voluntary admissions, perhaps because many were of very short duration. We had been aware that several older teenagers, particularly those involved in offending, had refused to take part in the study.

The second purpose of the contextualisation exercise was to ascertain the extent to which the composition of the sample reflected the overall current pattern of work with teenagers of these agencies as opposed to new interventions. Information on age, gender and legal basis was provided by two districts in the English agency and one in the Scottish.

The gender distribution of the sample from the Scottish agency reflected the total workload in this district in that approximately one third of all cases were female. The age breakdowns of the sample and the total workload were also broadly similar though the sample had a slightly higher proportion of the younger age group. A higher proportion of statutory cases appeared to have been included in the sample than were in the overall workload. This difference is partly accounted for by the fact that the figures for the total workload included young people who were not cases in their own right but whose families were receiving social work support on a voluntary basis. Teenagers in that position would not have met the study criteria.

In terms of age and gender the composition of the study sample from the English agency was very similar to the overall workload in one district. A completely accurate picture could not be made with the second district since the figures included young people with physical or learning difficulties, none of whom were in our sample from this agency. Totals from both districts indicated that young people accommodated or in voluntary care were over-represented in the sample but those in statutory care were under-represented. The study sample contained a higher percentage of cases subject to statutory supervision in the community than in the overall workload. While these proportions appropriately reflected the study's focus on new interventions this appeared to differ from the overall workload in these districts

Because the two agencies worked within different legal contexts it was in most respects not possible to make comparisons between their work from the information outlined above. It did seem, however, that a higher proportion of receptions into care were voluntary in the English than in the Scottish agency. Less than a third of the English agency's admissions were on a statutory basis, and these were virtually all remands, while two thirds of the young people admitted to care in the Scottish agency were on an order. This difference will be explored more fully in Chapter 4 which examines the care placements in the light of the progress of the young people in the study. Further research would ascertain whether the Hearing system, by being a non-judicial process, brings more children under 'surveillance' compared to the English system.

Baseline Data about the Young People in the Sample at Referral

The particular circumstances which led to the current social work intervention and inclusion of these young people in the study will be discussed in Chapter 3. Inevitably, these circumstances were intertwined with the teenagers' developmental progress and it was therefore important to establish at the outset some baseline data about their health, education, behaviour, self-esteem and other features. These would serve as a basis for comparing outcomes at the follow-up stage. Here we present information about the position of the young people at the start of the study. Details of changes and levels one year later are given in Chapter 9 after considering what happened to the teenagers in the intervening period.

The information was supplied by the participants and supplemented by details held in case records. We were unable to be as systematic as we had hoped in extracting recorded information, sometimes for lack of time but often because it was not there. If the young people were placed in residential or foster care, current medical and school records were quite often lodged with the key worker or carers and copies took longer to reach social work files. If they were living at home, background data were sometimes limited, depending on the reason for the referral. The issue of what information should be available was addressed in guidance on the Children Act 1989 and has also been considered by an Independent Working Party on assessing outcomes (Parker *et al*, 1991).

Health

When asked to describe their present health, 75% of the young people said it was good or very good, 19% said it was average and 6% said it was poor or very poor. Social Workers also assessed 70% as having good health but there were some differences of opinion over these assessments. In part these may have related to differences in the number of categories and wording of the questions. Perceptions of health are, however, commonly accepted as based on many different factors (Blaxter, 1981).

Parents as well as the young people and social workers were asked whether there were any current health problems. One or more of these respondents said there were problems for 54% of young people but often they were not in agreement with each other. For example, in the 71 cases where replies were available from all 3 participants, 7 (10%) all said 'yes', 29 (41%) all said 'no' and the remaining 35 (49%) gave different answers. The 'majority' view (ie 2 out of 3 responses) in these 35 cases was 'yes' for 9 young people and 'no' for 26. Interestingly, there were almost equal numbers of young people, parents and social workers taking the dissenting view in these cases.

None of the problems was described by parents as life-threatening at the time, though some could be. The most prevalent of these conditions was asthma (5) followed by pre-epileptic or epileptic attacks. Two young people were on medication for depression whilst another three had attempted suicide in the previous twelve months. Significantly more illnesses were reported on behalf of young people supervised or looked after by one of the agencies featuring in the study compared to the rest. With one exception, medical advice had already been sought.

Where information was available from records it usually confirmed the concerns shared by more than one respondent about a young person's health and provided details about the chronic conditions such as epilepsy and asthma, serious physical illness and psychiatric disorders. At least 40% of the young people had at some point been referred to a psychologist or psychiatrist. By comparison, there were very few references to problems with weight, teeth, ears or eyes. Just two were reported to have been involved in accidents.

We asked the young people whether they smoked, drank, took drugs or abused solvents and, if so, whether they did this frequently or occasionally. Their answers depended to some extent on the teenagers' willingness to answer questions about their personal behaviour. Table 2:4 shows that smoking was by far the most frequently admitted of these activities, especially by girls. Half the young people said they drank alcohol occasionally and a quarter admitted taking drugs occasionally. There were no significant gender or age differences among those who drank, took drugs or abused solvents although the latter activity occurred mainly among younger participants. Nearly all the young people said they were aware of the dangers of these activities and at least three-quarters had received health education about them. More (86%) said they had learnt about drugs than about the other topics with glue sniffing covered the least well (76%).

Table 2:4 Extent of smoking and other activities reported by young people

	Frequently	Occasionally	Not at all	Total
	%	%	%	(N)
Smoke	58	13	29	(95)
Drink	14	51	35	(90)
Take drugs	10	26	64	(93)
Abuse solvents	2	11	87	(93)

One in four of these teenagers claimed not to have had health education about unsafe sex in relation to the risks of pregnancy or AIDS and 10% said they were not aware of the dangers involved. We did not ask directly about their sexual activity but some young people indicated that they were indeed at risk of becoming pregnant or of contracting AIDS. Social workers thought there were issues with regard to the sexuality of about 25%, especially among females. They also thought girls were more in need of help than boys to prepare for close personal relationships. Altogether, social workers thought two-thirds of the young people needed help in this respect and they were uncertain about another 15%. When asked from where such help might be available, workers most often mentioned themselves, with parents and other settings such as IT groups next. Social education classes at school were mentioned least, possibly because workers were aware that many of the young people were no longer attending school. However, social workers themselves did not know whether two-fifths of the young people had had advice about contraception or avoiding sexually transmitted diseases. Those who did know almost all answered in the affirmative.

Behaviour and Adjustment

Problems with behaviour were frequently precipitating factors in the referral to Social Services/Work Departments which will be examined in Chapter 3. It was important therefore to be able to measure the perceptions of parents and others in these cases against a more 'objective' assessment of behaviour for the sample as a whole.

For this purpose we used the Rutter scale, which has been widely used in other studies and so makes for easy comparisons. The scale consists of brief statements concerning the child's behaviour such as:

> often worried, worries about many things
> often appears miserable, unhappy, tearful or distressed
> is often disobedient
> fussy or over-particular
> often tells lies

We took a version of the scale which had been approved for an education study of 16 year-olds. This converted the questions into direct first person statements and simplified some items, or made them more relevant to an older age-group (eg 'I frequently chew the end of my pen or pencil' was substituted for 'frequently sucks thumb or fingers'). The scales administered to parents and social workers followed the same sequence of questions as for the young people but were mostly worded according to the more familiar Rutter 'B' scale. There were, however, 25 questions instead of the usual 26 items. Each scale invited the respondent to say whether a question 'doesn't apply', 'applies to some extent', or 'certainly applies' to the young person.

The ratings for the three scales were each based on a maximum score of 50 points (the higher the score, the more problematic the behaviour). A score of 9 points or more on the 'B' scale is considered to indicate the possible existence of problems requiring further investigation (Rutter et al, 1970). Other studies have sometimes also made internal sub-divisions of scores in their analyses (eg Fogelman, 1983). We used a 3-way sub-division into 'low' group (score 1–8 points), 'medium' (score 9–19 points) and 'high' (score 20+ points).

Only a few young people or parents failed to answer one or more items and a check showed that even if these had applied 'certainly' they would not have altered the position with regard to the cut-off point for a 'low' score. There was rather more of a problem with the social workers' responses as about a quarter did not know whether the young person bit their nails or chewed their pencils and in 4 cases this could have changed the scores to above the cut-off point. Further investigation showed that when these two items were answered there was little congruence between young people and social workers. The social worker ratings may therefore be somewhat less reliable than the other two scales. For this reason we decided to repeat the exercise just with parents in the follow-up interviews.

Table 2:5 Rutter scores

Scores	Social Worker %	Young Person %	Parent %
Low	16	6	4
Medium	36	40	33
High	48	54	63
Total %	100	100	100
N	111	103	78
Missing	5	13	38

The main finding was the very high proportion of young people who were rated by themselves, their parents and their social workers above the usual cut-off point (Table 2:5). Indeed, over half the young people were given 'high' ratings by themselves or their parents and just under half by social workers. This confirmed that our study had a population with above average levels of difficulties. When the scores from each of the 3 respondents in a case were compared there were no significant differences between parents' and social workers' ratings. There was some disagreement between social workers and young people, with young people more likely to give themselves 'high' ratings when the social workers' ratings were 'low'. By contrast, parents and young people disagreed more often over 'low' and 'medium' ratings.

There were no significant differences when the scores for each scale were compared by age and gender. Parents in Agency C were, however, rather more likely than parents in the other agencies to give a high rating. Neither the young people's nor the parents' ratings varied according to where the young people were living at the start of the study. Social workers' ratings did, however, show a significant difference as more young people in foster homes than in other types of residence were given low scores. None of the young people in residential schools and only a few of those in residential care were given a low rating by social workers, while those living with parents did not fare much better.

In addition to completing the Rutter scale, social workers and parents were asked whether the young people had 'any other emotional or behavioural problems not already mentioned'. Just over half the social workers said there were other problems, but parents had often already spoken at length on this issue and only one-third mentioned further difficulties. The young people were questioned more directly about the current problems they were 'most keen to sort out over the next year'. Two-thirds shared their worries with the interviewer, while one-third said they did not have any particular problems at the time. There were no significant differences in their Rutter scores, so that the young people who did admit to having problems were not more likely to have 'high' scores than those who disclaimed any problems.

Self-Esteem

Another characteristic which is an important element in teenage development is the level of self-esteem. This aspect is notoriously volatile during this period but adults who know a young person well are usually able to guage his/her overall mood. Allowances are frequently made for 'bad patches' or untypical reactions and comments may indicate behaviour that covers up true feelings of self-worth, such as 'he seems very sure of himself but underneath he's not'. In order to reach closer to these feelings we used the Coopersmith Self-Esteem Inventory with the young people.

The Inventory is designed to measure attitudes to self and provide a personal judgement of worthiness (Coopersmith, 1990). High scores indicate high self-esteem and a good feeling of self-worth. In the first round of interviews we used the full-length 'school' version of the Inventory devised for students aged from 8–15 years. On this, a total score (max = 100) is made up of 4 sub-scales which allow for variations in perceptions in different areas of experience. These relate to: general self; self and peers; home and parents; school and academic. However, some of the questions are inappropriate for school-leavers or school-refusers and the form can also be scored as a 'short' version which is comparable to the form used with adults. At the follow-up we used the 'adult' form for all who were not attending school and, in order to be able to compare the first and follow-up scores, all the forms were marked to obtain a 'short' score. As with the Rutter scale, we used a 3-way division into sub-groups of 'high' (80+), 'medium' (76–60) and 'low' (56 and below). The 2 scales do, of course, go in opposite directions as a 'high' Coopersmith score is the most positive rating whereas a 'high' Rutter score is the most negative.

Just under a quarter of the 88 young people who completed the Coopersmith inventory at the start of the study had a 'high' self-esteem score and the remainder were evenly divided between 'medium' and 'low' scores (39% each). Boys were significantly more likely than girls to have 'high' scores and nearly 60% of girls had 'low' scores compared with 28% of boys. Younger rather than older teenagers tended also to have 'high' scores, but the age difference was not significant. There were no agency differences. The relationship between self-esteem and type of placement is explored in Chapter 4.

We asked the young people's social workers to assess their overall level of self-esteem and they rated this as low for 56%, medium for 34% and high for 8% of the sample (2 did not answer). When these ratings were compared with the Coopersmith scores there was agreement over only one case with a 'high' score. There was a tendency for either the social worker's or the young person's to go up or down to the 'medium' range rather than stay within the same bracket but the differences were not significant. Parents' ratings of the teenagers' levels of self-confidence also varied when compared with their Coopersmith scores and these differences were significant. Parents were more likely to rate young people as 'very self-confident' who had 'medium' rather than 'high' Coopersmith scores. It is possible, though, that parents were assessing a quality that was not quite the same as self-esteem. Overall, parents described 36% as 'very self-confident', 32% as 'fairly self-confident' and the remaining 32% as 'not self-confident'. One-third of the young people were said to be less self-confident than usual in certain situations.

Table 2:6 Young people's ratings on Coopersmith and Rutter compared (N=87)

	Coopersmith		
	Low	Medium	High
Rutter	N	N	N
Low	0	4	2
Medium	11	17	7
High	23	12	11

When we compared the young people's self-rating on the Coopersmith inventory with the ratings by each of the 3 participants on the Rutter scale there were no significant differences. This may have been due in part to the small numbers with 'low' Rutter scores. However, the results indicated that perceptions of behaviour and self-esteem were broadly in agreement, although a considerable amount of variation was still evident. One in four of the young people whose own ratings on the Rutter scale were high (indicating problematic behaviour) also had low scores on the Coopersmith inventory (indicating low self-esteem) but only 2 teenagers rated themselves in the opposite direction with a 'low' Rutter score and a 'high' Coopersmith score (Table 2:6). Parents also only gave 'low' Rutter scores to 2 young people with 'high' self-esteem whereas they rated one in five of those with 'low' self-esteem as having 'high' Rutter scores. Thus both the young people and their parents tended to link together the ratings that were negative rather than more positive.

Education

Schooling was obviously a major element in the lives of the majority of our sample as three-quarters were aged below the official leaving age at the start of the study. Much will be said in later chapters about the difficulties over schooling experienced by many of the young people and the extent to which these related to their contact with Social Services/Social Work Departments. In order to set these problems in context we obtained as much data on their educational circumstances as we could from the records held in the social workers' files. Nineteen young people had officially left school (all of those aged 17 or over and half of the 16 year-olds) and they will be looked at separately from those who were still within the education system.

a *Young People Formally Within the System* (N=97). Table 2:7 shows that just over half the teenagers were enrolled at mainstream comprehensive schools and most of the rest were in receipt of special measures or else had exhausted the available resources. Eight or possibly nine pupils were subject to a Statement or Record of Need. One other pupil who had been subject to a Record in the past was now back in mainstream schooling. Three of those attending residential schools were currently there on a day basis as part of their preparation for returning to the community and one 16 year-old was attending College as well as school. Another younger boy was receiving part-time tuition at a special school as well as in his comprehensive, while several others were being given extra help by support or remedial teachers within their schools. Two of those excluded from school were being allowed back just to take exams. There were no plans for the rest to return, though some were awaiting placement in another school or unit. A few simply left early after a fragmented school career.

Records of attendance held in social work files varied. Some included copies of the school's sheets (which were usually submitted along with other reports for teenagers referred to the Reporter to the Children's Hearing), others comprised written notes and some had no details. About one in four pupils either had a high percentage attendance or this was recorded as 'good' or 'no problem'. At least 40 others were noted as truants – sometimes the truancy was only suspected but more commonly it was 'regular' or 'chronic'. Among the young people who were registered at school but not attending were teenagers who were suspended because of their disruptive behaviour and others who refused to attend. Some of those who were now placed in residential schools were still running away or avoiding lessons.

Table 2:7 Type of school attended (currently or most recently at the start of the study)

	N
Day comprehensive	54
Residential school/secure unit	21
Special school	5
Private school	1
Home tutor	2
Excluded or none	11
No information	3
Total	**97**

The behaviour of at least 40% of those still formally within the education system was reported as troublesome at school and 17 were recorded as having had a compulsory move from one school to another because of behaviour problems. Three of these teenagers were now excluded from school, ten were in residential schools, 1 had a home tutor, another was in a special school and just 2 were still in a mainstream comprehensive.

Although it was unusual to find a record of an IQ test, we were able to ascertain some measure of three out of four of the young people's general ability. Nineteen were reported to be 'above average', 34 'average' and 18 'below average' in ability. However, we failed to find specific estimates of reading, writing or maths ability for the great majority of our sample. Even when school reports were available, these items were not always completed. It was also rare to find any mention of the young person's interests in school. However teachers' reports quite often acknowledged the efforts made by the teenagers in an often uphill struggle and these were deemed to have been 'good' or 'reasonable' efforts by 41 and 'poor' by 23 of the 97 pupils.

Only two of the young people still at school were recorded as successfully having passed formal exams but 29 were preparing for them. Half of the 16 year-olds who had stayed on were taking exams and the others making preparations were 15 or 14 year-olds.

b *Young People who had Left School* (N= 19). The information available in the social work files about the educational performance of the school leavers was patchy and depended on the circumstances of the current referral and whether the young person had been in care before or for some time. Three were known to be of low intelligence and one at least of them had probably been the subject of a Statement in the past. Several were former truants or had exhibited troublesome behaviour in school.

Two of the leavers had passed exams and one of them was now attending a College of Further Education. Several others were hoping to get onto courses which might improve their chance of a job. Only 3 young people were recorded as working and 4 were on YTS programmes. One young woman had recently had a baby and a young man was now in a Young Offenders Institution.

Young People's Household Situation and Networks

At the initial stage we obtained information about the young people's current family and social networks in order to identify to whom these teenagers would turn for support. This also enabled us to find out whether the teenagers' social contacts and support networks changed during the year as a result of being admitted to care or being supervised by a social worker.

The vast majority of the teenagers were living with at least one parent figure at the time of the first interview or before the recent reception into care (Table 2:8). However, only one in five were in families with both their own parents still living together. This is a lower proportion than in the general population. Two-fifths were in single-parent households. One-quarter were in reconstituted families, compared to a national average of about 21%. One in ten of the teenagers were being cared for by relatives or were living independently with friends or boyfriends. Two young women were caring for their own child.

Table 2:8 Main carers

Both parents	26	(22%)
Parent & step parent or partner	30	(26%)
Single parent	48	(42%)
Other	12	(10%)
Total	**116**	**(100%)**

The size of households ranged from one person living alone to a home shared with seven other people. Nearly two thirds of the young people lived with three or fewer other people. Siblings were part of almost two-thirds of the families. The number of siblings ranged from one to five with only seventeen young people (15%) sharing the household with more than 2 siblings.

The teenagers named between one and 15 relatives as key people in their immediate or extended family. Half named five people or less and half named six people or more. After members of their current household, young people (55%) most frequently named grandparents as important, 40% mentioned aunts and almost a quarter named uncles. A quarter cited peer relatives such as cousins, nieces and brother/sisters in law as key people. The teenagers indicated that some of these relatives would offer practical help, such as accommodation or money, but they also valued people who could be relied on simply to be available. Having a large family was in itself no guarantee that young people could rely on family support. Some teenagers were estranged from their relatives and few had more than weekly contact with adult relatives outwith the immediate family.

Networks of Friends

Almost a third of the young people included an adult friend in their social network. These included friends' parents and friends of their own parents as well as neighbours and other people whose company they enjoyed.

However most friends were themselves teenagers. Approximately half the young people said that their friends were around the same age as themselves but 37% spent much of their time with older teenagers and 13% had mostly younger friends. At the time of the first interview a third of the young people had a boyfriend or girlfriend.

The range of information young people gave about friendships with their peers was often lacking in detail. Some were reluctant to name friends and only volunteered that they were part of a group. Some groups were clearly defined but others consisted of a loose collection of individuals who changed from week to week. A few young people were very isolated and said that they had no friends while one had taken the trouble to count his fairly constant group and said that it totalled 32.

One means of assessing the relative importance of family and friends or of peers and adults was to note the frequency of contact with each network member. Data on this was incomplete but in the cases where it was complete it clearly indicated the importance of the peer culture for these young people. While contact with adult relatives outwith the main family was usually less than weekly, most young people spent each day, whether at school or outwith school in the company of their peers. Most said they spent each night with one or more friends. The typical pattern was for young people to spend more time with peers than with the other people they lived with.

Family Support

At the first interview young people were asked to name family members in whom they would confide or would ask for help in a difficult situation. Their responses indicated that over half the sample (54%) felt they could rely on someone. The people they named were:

parents	31
other relative	15
sibling	8

Of those who named a parent over 80% identified their mother as the person who would help. Almost 60% of boys but just over 40% of girls said they would confide in a family member. Among teenagers aged 16 and older the difference between boys and girls was marked. Sixty per cent of girls compared with a quarter of boys said they would *not* confide in any member of their family.

In general the older age group seemed somewhat less able or willing to turn to family members for help. Over half (54%) of those aged over 16 compared with 43% of 13–14 year olds said that they would not confide in any family member. In each age group approximately half of those who would confide in someone said they would choose to speak to a parent. Despite the family difficulties many young people had experienced, twice as many parents as other relatives were identified as likely to help. Some older teenagers may have been less willing or able to approach their parents for help but it did not seem that other family members had taken over from parents as major sources of support in these cases.

Over half the young people from reconstituted families said that there was no member of the family in whom they could confide and this compared with 35% of those living with both or a single birth parent. A somewhat lower proportion of young people who had been admitted to care compared with those living at home named a relative they would confide in (half compared with two-thirds) but the difference is not substantial. Overall a quarter of those in care said they would confide in a parent or ask a parent for help compared with 40% of those not in care.

Peer Support

At the beginning of the year 63% of the young people said that they would confide in a friend or ask a friend for help. Almost three quarters of the girls said they would confide in a friend compared with just over half of the boys. Similarly two thirds of those aged 15 and older were able to turn to friends for help compared with just over half of 13–14 year olds.

A quarter of the young people gave reasons why they would not discuss problems with friends. Some said that confiding or discussing problems was not in their nature. All but two of the young people who gave this reason were young men. Other reasons included that they did not have any close friends, that they did not trust their friends or that they had other sources of help and support.

Social Workers' Perceptions of Social Networks

At the initial interview social workers said that they believed that 67 (58%) of the young people had a close relationship with an adult friend or relative but their responses corresponded with those of the young people who were interviewed in only about a third of the cases. Only 19 (29%) of the 67 said either that they were friendly with a non-related adult or that they got on well with or would confide in a member of their wider family. A total of 13 young people identified no adult friend and no family member at all with whom they got on well or in whom they could confide yet social workers considered that 8 (61%) of these young people did have a close relationship with an adult relative or friend. Social workers therefore did not seem to know which young people felt devoid of adult support.

There was closer agreement about whether or not young people had a peer confidant. Social workers and young people's responses were consistent in 55 (52%) of cases. In 38 instances social workers and young people agreed that there *was* a friend in whom the young person could confide and in 17 cases they agreed that there was not.

Young people's responses about whether or not they would confide in a family member or friend were compared with the Coopersmith scores to explore whether the availability of this type of relationship had a bearing on the level of self-esteem. A higher proportion of young people who said they would be able to turn to friends for help obtained the highest scores (7 or 8 out of a possible 8) in the section which measured self-esteem in social situations: 64% of those who identified a peer confidant, compared with 44% those who did not, had the high scores. There was a similar relationship between being able to confide in a family member and the sub-scores which rated self-esteem within the home: 36% of those who identified a confidant in the family had a high score compared with only 11% of those who did not. Two thirds of those who had no family confidant scored 2 or less in this section. There was no relationship, however, between the existence of a peer or family confidant and the overall level of self-esteem.

Close Support Networks

In order to obtain an additional perspective on what the people who made up their support network meant to the young people they were asked:

  1   who they felt closest to;

2   who were best at helping;
3   who were most fun or whose company they most enjoyed.

Up to three people could be named in response to each question. Any category of response was only counted once for each young person so that, for example, if someone named two brothers or two residential workers this was included only once in that category (Table 2:9).

Table 2:9 Support networks (N = 101)

	Closest	Best Helpers	Most Fun
Mothers	46%	34%	8%
Fathers	20%	10%	6%
Siblings	30%	8%	16%
Grandparents	15%	5%	2%
Other adult relatives	6%	6%	4%
Friends	42%	27%	65%
Peer or child relatives	6%	4%	4%

These responses confirmed that the people most important to the teenagers were the immediate family and friends. Despite the fact that there had often been family difficulties, parents, particularly mothers were cited as emotionally important and helpful. Brothers and sisters were also significant relatives.

The importance of friends in each category is also clear. Friends were mentioned as close companions by twice as many people as mentioned their fathers and by almost as many as named their mother. More friends than social workers were described as good at helping and almost two thirds said they found their friends' company most enjoyable. It is not surprising that parents who tried to change their son or daughter's choice of friends had little success.

By comparison with immediate family and friends, professionals did not usually figure as significant members of young people's support networks except that half the sample named at least one professional as a best helper. Approximately 20% of social workers were identified as good at helping so that they were in third place to mothers and friends. Of the 44 young people in residential care 15 (34%) named their key worker as a good helper and 44% of foster children identified their carer. Thirty three young people had said that they were in contact with a project worker, befriender or other type of worker and 27% of them were identified as good at helping. All 5 young people who felt close to their social worker were in Agency A. They were a mixture of boys and girls and some were in care and some not.

Relationships with Parents

Assessments of the quality of the relationships with their parents were also provided by young people, 95 of whom rated how well they got on with their mother and 72 gave a rating for their father (Table 2:10). Although the teenagers were rather more positive about how well they got on with their mothers than their fathers, many were cautious about either relationship saying they got on 'quite well'.

Table 2:10 Young people's ratings of relationships with their parents

	With Mother		With Father	
Get on very well	25	(26%)	14	(19%)
Quite well	39	(41%)	32	(44%)
Not well	18	(19%)	18	(25%)
Varies	13	(14%)	8	(11%)
Total	**95**	**(100%)**	**72**	**(100%)**

If the young people had step-parents or their parents had a new partner, they were also asked how well they got on even though the young people were not necessarily part of the same household. The numbers who gave a rating were small, especially for step-mothers (11), but they indicated that relationships were generally less positive with step-parents than with birth parents. However there were a few examples of them being important sources of help and advice.

Overall young people currently in care did not rate their relationships with their parents substantially differently from those supervised at home nor did social workers' ratings show any significant difference between these two groups. At the initial stage there was a close association between the young people's level of self-esteem and their perception of the quality of the relationship with their mothers. One third of the teenagers who said they got on very well with their mother had a high Coopersmith rating compared with none of those who thought the relationship was poor. Conversely, nearly half those who said they did not get on well with their mother had a low Coopersmith score. The association between self-esteem and young people's relationships with their fathers was less marked.

Social Workers' Initial Perceptions of Family Relationships

Social workers were asked at the first interview to rate the relationships between young people and their parents on a scale which was worded slightly differently to the young people's and did not differentiate between step or birth parents.

Table 2:11 Social workers' assessment of relationships
(N = 116)

	Mother/stepmother	Father/stepfather
Get on well	28 (24%)	15 (13%)
Quite well	26 (22%)	25 (22%)
Not well	31 (27%)	41 (35%)
Varies	23 (20%)	10 (8%)
NA/DK	8 (7%)	25 (22%)

The social workers and young people rated similar proportions of relationships with both parents as good but young people more often gave a middle rating when the social worker's assessment indicated that the relationship was poor. This difference may have been due to the young people being reluctant to be too negative about their parents or to the fact that the social workers' responses included step and birth parents.

In 49 of the 95 cases (52%) where both responses were available there was complete agreement between young people and social workers on the quality of the relationship with the mother. There was full agreement about fathers between young people and social workers in 26 (40%) of the 64 cases in which both gave a rating. A clear divergence of views emerged in only 5 cases.

Fewer younger teenagers rated how they got on with their mothers negatively than older teenagers. Only 10% of 13–14 year olds thought this was poor compared with 42% of those aged 16–18. Correspondingly 80% of 13–14 year olds said that they got on well or quite well with their mothers compared with 38% of those aged 16+. However this may reflect the fact that most older teenagers in the sample were living away from home. The social workers' responses showed a similar trend.

It seemed that more boys enjoyed a good quality of relationship with their mothers than the girls. While almost a third of boys (32%) rated this as very good and 12% as poor, only 17% of girls said that they got on very well with their mothers and almost a third (31%) gave a negative rating. In all age groups almost twice as many girls as boys rated the relationship with their mother as poor. Social workers believed that only a third of the girls compared with 61% of the boys got on well or quite well with their mothers or step-mothers.

Overall most young people saw their relationship with their father in a less positive light than with their mother. A higher proportion rated it as poor and a lower percentage considered it was good. The more negative ratings of girls and of the oldest age group noted in relationships with mothers were, however, not replicated in relation to fathers. The fact that teenage girls' relationships with their mothers were particularly conflictual and that teenagers of both sexes had a less intense relationship with their father than their mother were consistent with findings of other studies (Youniss and Smollar 1985).

Parents' Initial Perceptions of Relationships

In spite of the frustrations and tensions described elsewhere by the majority of parents, when it came to rating the quality of their relationship with the young person, two thirds rated them as 'very good' or 'quite good' (Table 2:12). One explanation for this is that once parents had ventilated to the researcher a lot of angry or frustrated feelings about the young person, they felt more benevolent when it came to rating this aspect. Another explanation is that a poor relationship would not reflect well on them as parents. In half the cases there was full agreement between young people and their parents and there were no examples of one party believing the relationship was very good and the other rating it as poor.

Table 2:12 Parent/carer's assessment of the quality of the relationship between themselves and young person

	N	%
Very good	25	35
Quite good	22	31
Not good	16	22
Variable	9	12
	72	**100**

Parents reported that approximately six out of every ten young people got on quite well or well with their siblings and in the rest of the cases the relationship was either not good or variable. Relationships between individual siblings are not static and can vary from time to time. Rivalry is, of course, not unusual among siblings and it is only one aspect in what is usually a multi-dimensional set of interactions. Though a young person's dealings with some siblings would be described as 'bad', 'competitive', or 'hostile', there was usually at least one sibling with whom the young person would get on well.

Parents gave examples of particularly good relationships involving young people and an adult sister or brother, some of whom were now married and had their own children. The teenager would spend a fair amount of time at the older sibling's home and sometimes babysit. Sibling relationships of this kind could be of crucial importance to young people who were planning to move on to independence.

Identity

When asked at the first interview whether there were aspects of the family history on which the young person should have more information or understanding social workers were much more likely than the other parties to identify issues in response to this question. Their training tends to place particular emphasis on the importance of a good understanding of personal and family history. In 63 cases (57%) social workers believed that there was an aspect of the family background of which young people were ignorant or which they did not understand. In contrast only 18 parents (22%) and 19 young people (19%) mentioned a relevent topic. Similar proportions of social workers in the three largest agencies identified gaps in the young people's understanding but there were considerable variations in the responses from parents and young people (Table 2:13). They were most likely to feel the need for more information in Agency A, and least likely to do so in Agency C.

Table 2:13 Percentage identifying a gap in the young
person's understanding of family
background

	Social Workers	Parents	Young People
Agency A	51%	46%	31%
Agency C	58%	9%	7%
Agency E	58%	18%	13%

A higher proportion of girls than boys said themselves that they wanted more information though neither parents' nor social workers' responses reflected any gender difference. Similarly social workers and parents identified an equal proportion of children currently in or outwith care as requiring information about an aspect of the family background but a higher proprtion of young people in care identified an issue themselves. Three quarters of the young people who were concerned about a background issue were currently in care though young people in care accounted for only half the sample.

There was little consensus among social workers, young people and their parents about who required information. Social workers mentioned only half the cases which parents cited and they identified only half the young people who spoke of gaps in their own knowledge. This low level of agreement between social workers and young people was the same in all agencies, including Agency A where a higher percentage of parents and young people had identified issues. The level of agreement was lower still between parents and young people as only five of them agreed that further information was required, four of them from Agency A. From the total sample there was agreement by all three parties in only two instances.

Three-quarters of the social workers who identified a gap in background information spoke about past events in the family which had not been fully explained to the young person. The break-up of the parents' marriage was most frequently mentioned, followed by incidents involving abuse which the young person had witnessed or suffered. Approximately fifteen percent of social workers were concerned that young people lacked information either about the identity of a birth parent, usually a father, or about the type of person he or she was. Social workers were often unsure what young people had been told about absent parents and were sometimes concerned that too negative a picture was being presented. Often related to this was a third issue, namely for young people to understand why they were in care or registered as at risk of abuse. Several social workers said that it was important for young people to enhance their knowledge of these matters because of the effect on their self-esteem but there was no evidence that the young people whom social workers identified as requiring more information had lower self-esteem than the others. In common with the sample as a whole, they divided equally between the higher and lower Coopersmith scores.

Similarly there was no difference in the Coopersmith scores according to whether or not parents identified young people as lacking understanding of an aspect of their background. The scores for self-esteem were, however, lower among the young people who *themselves* identified family issues they did not understand or wanted to know more about. Over half of these teenagers had low Coopersmith scores and none had a high score. These results were consistent with the view of Triseliotis (1983) that a positive self-image depends on people having an understanding of their background and how they have arrived at their current situation.

There were indications that social workers and young people had rather different ideas about what issues were important. As outlined above, social workers most frequently talked about the young person's need to understand past events. Young people themselves, however, spoke of wanting more information rather than understanding. In half the cases they wanted to know about their own paternity, the paternity of another family member or about the current circumstances of an absent parent. Two young people wanted to contact a parent they had lost touch with and were actively pursuing this. The remaining half wanted to know more about some aspect of their parents' earlier life, for example why a marriage had broken up or why they themselves had come into care.

Though obtaining information would ideally lead to more understanding and the young people and social workers possibly had the same aim in mind, their different perceptions may have contributed to the fact that, despite the high level of social workers' awareness of such issues, there were very few cases in which they had been openly acknowledged and were being tackled as part of the on-going work.

Parents' Views on Background Information and Continued Contact

The parents' responses illustrated some of the tensions and difficulties which can arise when dealing with issues of this kind. In a quarter of cases the parents implied that there was some aspect of family history about which the young person was either unclear, unaware or not fully aware. These were mainly related to areas of family reconstitution and in exceptional cases situations where the young person had been born outside marriage and the mother married someone other than the child's father. There were a handful of cases where the young person was still unaware that their 'father' was in reality a step-father or where this knowledge was only recently acquired. In one such case the mother remarked that her daughter was asking questions but 'I won't tell her because the circumstances are that I don't want her to know'.

In another case where the mother married her husband when the young person was only a baby, they still could not come round to tell him that his 'father' was his 'step-father'. They thought they might need some outside help before they would be able to do so. Shades of secrecy and evasiveness that were once associated with adoption were present within reconstituted family relation-ships and partnerships. In discussions, some parents began to wonder whether the young person's current difficulties reflected underlying tensions in the family. Other studies have highlighted how the impact of parents divorcing can be different for younger and older children (Wallerstein and Kelly, 1980).

A number of young people whose parents had split up, sometimes before the young person was of school age, still kept in touch with the non-custodial parent. This ranged from the occasional contact to the exchange of letters and/or birthday and Christmas cards. Sometimes there would be periods of intensive contact only to fade out for a long time and resurface again. As one mother remarked, the father would one year remember the young person's birthday but forget the next. Or a father would write to promise he would collect the child for a trip, but not turn up. Spurts of activity between a young person and a non-custodial parent presented some form of threat to the custodial parent or fears of the young person being let down and left to feel more bitter and frustrated. It was not unusual for young people to join a non-custodial parent only to return after a short period of time because things were not working out. Some of the custodial parents said they would have been glad if the arrangement succeeded, but others thought that the young person was only trying to exploit the situation by pitching one parent against the other.

Summary

The sample comprised 116 young people aged 13–17 at referral. Many of them had already received social work intervention before the current episode. Baseline data in respect of their health, education, behaviour and self-esteem showed that a high proportion of the teenagers had behaviour difficulties and school problems. Low self-esteem tended to be linked with a poor behaviour rating. The majority of young people were said to be in good health. For many, parents and friends were the main sources of support and also 'best helpers' in times of difficulty. Assessments of the quality of the young people's relationships with their close family and peer friends made by social workers were similar to those of the teenagers themselves. Nevertheless social workers were aware of only half the concerns raised by the young people about family background information, most often about absent fathers. Parents confirmed that issues relating to family reconstitution were problematic and the next chapter shows how some of the resulting tensions contributed to the need for care services.

3 Problem Definition and the Setting of Expectations

At the start of the study we set out to understand the parents', young people's and social workers' perspective on the reason for the most recent episode of intervention which resulted in formal or informal supervision/care measures. We also examined the expectations each party had of these measures at the outset, in order to establish in which situations subjective expectations were fulfilled or not at the end of a year. Inevitably, because some of the young people had experienced a supervision/care episode before, their views and those of their parents were coloured by these events. As already pointed out, the social services deal with only a small number of teenagers each year who are new entrants to the system. Most of the rest have been known to the social services before.

Harris and Timms (1993), who interviewed Social Service Managers, field and residential social workers and children, take the concept of narrative from Peterson and McCabe (1983) to describe the idea of possible differences in perspectives. They liken the interviewees to narrators who are 'variably "truthful" no doubt and variably aware of complexity, but all telling their tales not as reliable or omniscient reporters, but as actors in the drama itself, each offering a unique inflexion, a perspective which, though never complete, constitutes a necessary part of a complex whole' (p.103). The 'actors' in our own study were narrators who had a story to tell from their own perspective, and were trying to make certain that their point of view was understood and their definitions, concerns or interests prevailed. The centrality of their story was the young persons' actions, with all three parties viewing their manifestation in simple behavioural terms but having some similar and some different explanations for their origin or what was needed to be done about them.

The Circumstances that led to Intervention

It would have been easier and perhaps more useful, for comparative purposes at least, if we could use similar problem categories as those used by previous studies. For example, Packman *et al* (1986) classified the children featuring in their study into '*victims*', '*volunteers*', and '*villains*' whilst Farmer and Parker (1991) used a two fold classification using the terms 'protected' and 'disaffected' children. These categories, however, were not discriminating enough to express the complexity of circumstances which led to measures of intervention for our older, teenage group. Yet aspects of the circumstances identified by previous studies featured also in each of the categories used here.

Our first attempt at classification was to provide a table (Table 3:1) which reflects the frequency of problems mentioned by the 78 parents interviewed on behalf of 82 children, by the 105 young people interviewed and the 80 social workers who conveyed their views on 116 young people.

Table 3:1 Circumstances necessitating measures of supervision/care as presented by the parents, the young people and social workers

	Parents		Young People		Social Worker	
Frequency	N	%	N	%	N	%
Behaviour in the community, including offending and drug related	54	66	45	43	39	34
Difficulties in family relationships	47	57	39	37	35	30
School problems, incl. non-attendance	36	44	20	19	26	22
Other problems at home (parents not coping, abuse etc.)	18	22	28	27	21	18
Other	16	20	7	7	–	–
Total responses	**171**		**139**		**121**	

The problems that dominated the social workers', parents' and young people's thinking and experiences fell into three categories: (i) offending, (ii) difficulties in family relationships and (iii) school issues, though each brought to them a different perspective (Table 3:1). There were many overlaps between all of the three main problematic areas. For example, though chronic non-school attendance might have been the predominant problem, this could trigger off wider offending behaviour and sometimes domestic conflict. Similarly tensions and conflict within the family could often lead either to non-school attendance, to offending or both. Only in a tiny number of cases did the young people simply need another family to care for them because of their own families' circumstances. There were also only two cases of *repeated* abuse, which reflects the concentration of the study on teenagers instead of younger children. There had been suspicion of sexual abuse in relation to a further ten girls and seven boys. Many of the problems identified were symptomatic of the rapid social and economic changes taking place, particularly the changing role of the family and the instability and conflict created through separation, single parenthood and re-constitution. In addition young people had to cope with school failure, unemployment and other economic problems.

Table 3:1 also shows that, compared to young people and social workers, parents identified more problems. They referred to an average of 2.1 problems for each young person compared to 1.3 by young people and 1.0 by social workers. This was in line with the parents' description and comments which indicated much more concern, anxiety and stress over the various problems, compared to social workers and young people. They put most emphasis on undesirable behaviours outside the home followed by tense relationships within the family. Young people, whilst acknowledging past negative actions, tended to move the emphasis from past behaviours to future events. Social workers on the whole, appeared to underestimate the extent of the problems, particularly undesirable behaviours outside the home. One explanation for this was their tendency to define problems in terms of personal needs rather than deeds. We return to this point when considering expectations.

The incidence of offending was significantly higher with respect to boys than girls with 58% of boys and 37% of girls having been involved in offending. Concern over drugs and alcohol abuse was frequently mentioned. In contrast to parents, social workers mentioned physical and sexual abuse far more frequently, but young people confirmed this in only six cases. Physical abuse had been a problem in the past for less than a quarter of both boys and girls but a far higher proportion of girls had been sexually abused in the past (35% compared with 4% of boys). Drug taking seemed to become a concern at around the age of 15 with social workers indicating the use of drugs by over 40% of those aged 15+ compared with less than a fifth of 13 and 14 year olds. In contrast 40% of 13–15 year olds caused worries about their use of alcohol while this was a worry in just over a quarter of those aged 16+. It may have been that by this age drinking was not really seen as a cause for concern. A higher proportion of young people from intact families than from other types of family structures, had school-related problems. Half of those where school problems had led to intervention were from intact families, though such families accounted for only 22% of the sample.

In their accounts of what had led to the recent reception into care, social workers indicated that the young person's behaviour had been a precipitating factor in 39% of cases, that school was a problem in 16% of cases and that home related problems contributed to 45% of admissions. The main factors relating to new supervision orders were:

young person's behaviour	42%
school problems	36%
home based problems	14%
other reasons	8%

Now each of the three categories of problems will be dealt with in turn.

Problems in Families

Rapid changes in family structure and uncertainty among parents on how to relate or handle their teenage children's behaviour often led to the family conflict and strife which resulted in care arrangements or supervision. According to young people and social workers, relationship difficulties led more frequently to care than to supervision at home. Sixteen young people saw relationship problems as the only reason for them currently being in care and at least one family-based problem was mentioned by 80% of young people in care. Over half the young people from reconstituted families spoke of family difficulties compared with approximately a third of those living with a single birth parent and of those living with both parents. Similarly one in every four parents said that the main problem necessitating measures of care or supervision were long-standing disputes and conflict between themselves and the young person.

Girls and boys were equally likely to acknowledge relationship difficulties, with age being more important than gender in this respect. Of those in care and aged 16 or over, 80% identified family relationship problems, including rejection, compared with less than half of the 13–14 age group. This may have reflected the fact that older and younger teenagers face different types of problems or it may have been that, as they became less dependent on their parents and more mature, young people were more willing or able to acknowledge the extent of family problems.

The Parents' Perspective on Family Problems

Most of the disputes and conflicts were between the young person and parental figures, including step-parents/partners. Though some partners said they did not to want to be involved, they were instrumental in influencing events indirectly by, for example, threatening to leave or refusing to have the young person in the home. Many parents felt under considerable stress and sitting down and crying after failing to control a teenager was not an unusual response. To make sense of the subsequent moves and of the measures taken, it is necessary to understand first the position many parents found themselves in. Some felt hopeless, useless and tired. Typical comments from them included:

> 'shattered and depressed'; 'being at breakdown point';
> 'feeling drained and a failure'.

Despondency and disaffection is one way of describing what many parents saw as their impatience and frustration, made worse by not knowing how to tackle the problem. One divorced mother felt like 'going off the rails' or 'cracking up' adding that she was driven to drinking. A number of parents referred to their deteriorating physical or psychological health, attributing it entirely to the young person's behaviour. Mothers, whether alone or with a partner, seemed to take the brunt of the young person's behaviour either because there was no father, the father was at work or a step-parent wanted to have nothing to do with the young person. One mother illustrated her plight, as she saw it, by saying:

> 'I was going through all this and I was getting very little support and I was ill.'

A couple of single mothers became so fearful of the tempers and destructiveness exhibited by their children that they thought of moving out of the house to a new address and leaving them alone. Another mother said that, if it was her husband who was behaving towards her like this instead of her son, she would have left and gone to a Women's Refuge. With obvious exasperation she added: 'Because it is my son doing it, there is nowhere I could go.'

Parents involved in separation/divorce and/or reconstitution were aware that their children were harbouring resentment or hostility about the separation and mothers often felt unjustly blamed for what had happened. Comments made by young people would make mothers feel 'guilty', 'upset', or 'incapable'. A number of partners had already made it clear that the young person could not expect to return home once out of care. At times young people themselves took the initiative of influencing events. A common way of highlighting domestic tensions was by the young person arguing, running away or trying to move out. Typical phrases and words used by parents to describe what they saw as the young person's intolerable behaviour included:

> 'running away and beyond control'; 'violent tempers';
> 'destructive behaviour'; 'argumentative';
> 'disappearing for one or more days'.

Whilst parents would easily refer to poor relationships as being at the root of many of the difficulties, there was no acknowledgment of possible rejection being felt by the young person. Poor relationships could be accompanied by days of non-communication between the young person and parental figures. Clearly many parents saw themselves as victims of their children's behaviour and the latter as victims of family discord and sometimes of bad company. As a result, parents expected most change to come from the young person with less acknowledgement of their own possible contribution to the situation. Many parents tended to project a simple picture of the young person as villain, with rarely any positives being expressed unless pressed by the interviewers. Some young people would reciprocate by viewing parents as restrictive, rejecting, uninterested in them or even oppressive. The older the young person, the more likely it was for them to see moving out independently as a resolution to the difficulties. Social workers, on the whole, saw the multifaceted nature of problems, but parents and young people tended to offer a more unicausal explanation.

The Young People's Perspective on Family Problems

Taken together, conflict at home and other household related problems constituted the young people's main concern. Like their parents, many teenagers experienced the home as a stressful and sometimes rejecting place. Unlike offending and drug taking, the home situation was the one issue around which they demonstrated both concern and feeling. Many of them spoke in detail about the kind of family tensions they had experienced. Several specific problems seemed to recur and difficulties in accepting step parents were very common. Some resented having to share their birth parent with someone else and accept the authority of a new parent. This seemed to be particularly difficult if the young person had been close to one parent and their relationship had been based largely on mutual equality. One girl's comments illustrate both these points :

> 'Since my mum married again we just didn't get on, the three in
> a house just didn't get on because I'd been with my mum since
> I was six years old. Then when I was twelve it changed – the
> whole thing with another guy in the house and we just didn't get
> on the three of us . . . It was *my* house. Me and my mum's
> house anyway until he walks in and took over and telling me
> not to watch television and things like that.'

In this type of situation, teenagers are able to make demands on their parents or to take action to change their home situation in ways which are not available to younger children. In some instances it was clear that, as young people became less dependent or less afraid of their parents, the balance of power between them had changed. Parental threats to 'put them in a home' could be replaced by young people defiantly leaving if they were unhappy with the situation. One girl explained her leaving home by saying:

> 'She (her mother) always threatened to throw me
> out anyway so I done it and she got a fright.'

We would, however, not want to give the impression that all teenagers in the study were in control of their families or that decisions to leave were made calmly and logically. Young people could also be at the receiving end of abuse either from parents or occasionally from older siblings brought in to control them.

Several young people acknowledged that they had been seeking an alternative to life at home but had no clear idea except that they 'wanted a way out' of their problems. Whilst prepared to take some responsibility for their actions they did not see themselves as the aggressors as their parents often did, neither were they prepared to make all the accommodations. The young people were generally frank about their misdemeanours though they did object when all the blame was put on them. A typical comment was:

'I must admit some of it was my fault and I will
always admit that, but what I don't like is when
people say it's my fault and nobody else's.'

Social Workers' Views of Family Problems

Social workers conceptualised family problems in a somewhat different way
from parents and young people. The families tended to concentrate on
behaviour whilst social workers sought explanations that went beyond this.
For example, they would refer to the relationship as being unbalanced or
inappropriate in some way. In some cases parents were felt to lack control,
while in others they were seen as too restrictive or rejecting. Sometimes parents
were seen as remote or uncommunicative with their children but others were
considered too close to allow the young person space to grow up. A few tried
to become a 'friend' rather than a parent. In a number of cases social workers
referred to parents expecting to meet too many of their own needs in the
relationship with their son or daughter.

There was also an ambiguity concerning the social workers' role vis-a-vis the
whole family. In the interviews with social workers several indicated that the
existence of offending legitimated their involvement in a case whereas, if the
case was judged to be a family matter, it would be considered to be the
responsibility of psychological or psychiatric services. The impression is that
some social workers feel less confident about dealing with adolescents'
family-based problems.

Behaviour Outside the Home

The Parents' Views

Forty-five (or 57%) of the parents made reference to at least one problem
occurring outside the house which led to measures of supervision/care. The
most common problem was stealing followed by the use of drugs. Sometimes
the stealing was for money to finance the purchase of drugs. The drug most
often mentioned was cannabis, though solvent abuse and, less frequently,
heroin were also referred to. 'Joy-riding' was also not uncommon. Some of the
behaviour, particularly stealing, was not always confined to outside the home.
Parents gave vivid descriptions of the behaviour and of their own bewilderment
at such behaviour, with drugs and glue sniffing being a major concern.

'I know that he's not alone, most of the children round
here are, not maybe hooked on, but they've all experienced
some trouble with it. There's drug dealers all over the place.'

Like drug taking, most stealing took place in the company of others, sometimes older than the young person in the study. In contrast to conflict at home which was usually blamed on the young person, parents on the whole, would blame 'bad company' rather than their own child. A typical comment was:

> 'Someone else talked him into stealing.'

The Young People's Views

The second most frequently mentioned reason for care reported by the young people and the major reason for supervision was their behaviour in the community. This most often referred to offending but could include running away, taking drugs and being out of control. As previously noted, several problems could occur together. Running away from home could lead to offending, which could reinforce very tense home situations. A cycle had sometimes developed which was difficult to break:

> 'I mean I never done any burglaries or anything like that
> while I've been at home. It's always been when I've been
> on the run.'

One notable feature of the young people's attitudes to offending was that they were generally willing to accept responsibility for their actions. They described in some detail their involvement in car thefts, burglaries, theft and assault. Unlike their parents, very few blamed the influence of their friends or others. Supervision or care was seen as the price you pay for this kind of activity. When asked whether this social work intervention could have been avoided, the most common response was to say that they could have avoided it by stopping offending and when asked who could help them stop the offending they most often said only themselves.

Whilst young people were ready to acknowledge their misdemeanours, they would not necessarily accept that they had a problem, nor were they all motivated to end their involvement in crime. For some the 'problem' was dealing with the consequences of crime rather than the fact that they themselves had offended. In many ways, they did not see themselves as bad children or as 'villains' but as young adults doing ordinary adult things. Less than half of those with a criminal record said that offending was a problem they would want to tackle in the coming year.

The attitudes described above were not true of all young people who had committed offences. Several worried about their lack of control over their temper, particularly when they were likely to hurt people or destroy property. While many viewed taking drugs such as cannabis or ecstasy as normal behaviour to which the authorities or parents over-reacted, a few were worried about their drug abuse, particularly one boy who had started to use heroin.

The Social Workers' Views

Social workers identified about a third of the young people in the sample as having been involved in some form of offending and/or drug related episode. The severity of offending varied. In some instances it was the central problem while for others offending was peripheral to other difficulties in the family or in relation to school. A minority of offending was thought to be taking place within the home mainly taking the form of stealing money. Outside the home, offending took several forms including: burglaries, assaults, joy-riding, shop-lifting and a small number of stabbings.

Though most interventions relating to offending were initiated by the courts or Children's Hearings, in a number of cases involving stealing from home, parents had asked for a service. The slight underplaying of offending by some social workers could be explained by their adopting a welfare rather than justice orientation, that is considering *needs* rather than *deeds*. This approach was sometimes misunderstood by parents and young people. This orientation may also explain, as we shall see later, why in some instances behaviour such as offending did not figure much in the setting of expectations, even though it may have featured in other statements.

School Based Problems

Non-attendance at school and disruptive behaviour in school are subjects of considerable public concern and have been widely analysed and written about. Official responses to such problems differ and have been found to be somewhat arbitrary (Carlen, 1976). Whether a legal or therapeutic path is followed depends partly on local policy, services and attitudes. Factors such as class and gender can also influence how individual pupils are treated. We found considerable variation in practice across and within the five agencies. Even if policy guidelines had been issued, the professional response in individual cases reflected differences of opinion among staff. The debate often centred on whether school based problems were seen as reflecting difficulties in the school setting or more fundamental tensions within the individual or family. The extent of co-operation between Education and Social Work/Services Departments also influenced the nature of the service provided.

With the introduction of the Children Act 1989 in England, a care order can no longer be granted on the grounds of non-attendance at school and children can be made subject to Education Supervision Orders which are implemented by Departments of Education. Under the Scottish Children's Hearing system, non-attendance at school remains a valid ground for deciding that a child is in need of compulsory measures of care. In both countries parents remain legally responsible for ensuring that their children receive education.

The Parents' Perspective

Many parents showed considerable exasperation about non-school attendance. In their view one third of the young people were having serious
schooling problems including chronic non-school attendance, school fights,
and exhibiting destructive or other offending behaviour at school. One parent
said:

> 'She wouldn't get up and get ready or she'd go out of the door,
> you know, so sometimes I thought she was at school,
> but lots of times I knew she wasn't. I think she lost
> that much schooling she didn't want to go back.'

Although the problem might start as one of non-school attendance, in some
cases it would not be long before it was accompanied by stealing, drug taking
and other offending. Mostly school non-attendance emerged during the early
parts of the secondary school stage, though a few had shown signs of this
happening during the primary school years. In a number of cases parents put
the blame for this on school size or on intimidation, whilst others had no
explanation to offer. Reflecting on the stresses of coping with secondary
schools, one mother remarked how it was a kind of 'sink or swim situation
with big classes and the teachers not having the time to give individual pupils
attention'.

No early warning system could be identified that would alert parents, social
workers and especially secondary schools of surfacing school difficulties.
Except for a few cases where teachers went out of their way to help some
children manage the transition by, for example, making use of halfway day
schools, there was little evidence of any constructive early responses to the
problem. Attention would usually come after the problem had been going on
for some time and when perhaps more drastic measures were unavoidable.
There would then be frantic activity on the part of the school. The parents,
having failed to get the young people back to school themselves, now pinned
all their hopes on outside professionals, mainly social workers. It was because
they felt so strongly about the importance of education for their children's
future that a number of them were prepared to consider residential solutions.

> 'You know it's not asking a lot. I don't want him to
> grow to be a brain surgeon or somebody like that,
> just as long as he can get a job and not go on the dole.'

Though only a small percentage of parents indicated that they had made
planned visits to schools to find out how the young person was getting on, the
general feeling of many was that there was little they could do.

The Young People's Views

The young people who did not attend school by choice were not a homogeneous group. There were some who found going to school very unpleasant, often for reasons they could not specify, but their aversion to school was nevertheless strong:

> 'I hated it. You don't want to stay with something you hate.'

Others described how not attending school had been an unintended result of other circumstances or difficulties:

> 'At first it was sort of to get back at my mum and dad "I'm not going to school" and then I started missing school work. It got harder and then I just started missing school more and more.'

Young people not going to school were well aware that they were legally required to do so. They accepted social work involvement or care as an inevitable consequence of their actions. Their behaviour appeared to them rational at the time. One boy explained this clearly:

> 'Well if you stay off school that's going to happen to you and I don't think I'll go back so I'll just have to put up with it anyway.'

Some of them said that their misbehaviour in class was the result of not being able to do the work whilst others referred more to their behaviour or ability to get on with staff. The 'solution' in their view was to find a form of schooling which they could tolerate and which would satisfy the authorities. This might involve part-time schooling or day attendance at a specialist unit. These were regarded as preferable options to being admitted to a residential school which was feared as the most drastic action the authorities could take.

Social Workers' Views on School Problems

School related problems were judged by social workers to be the third most common reason for care or supervision. In one case a young girl beat a teacher up, but such behaviour, though dramatic, was very rare. Social workers believed that school problems were the only reason for involvement in ten cases but it was more usual for them to overlap with family difficulties or offending. In some cases it was clear which problem predominated or had come first but it was sometimes more difficult to determine this. An assessment of this to some extent depended on the theoretical model from which the matter was considered.

Managing Difficulties

Parents used a range of methods to control or influence the young person. The most common method they said they used was to indicate disapproval with an act and/or try to reason and talk things over. However, many parents found that this was of no use as the young person 'would not talk' or 'go quiet' or 'withdraw'. As one parent put it 'I tried to reason but it was no use' or 'she won't reason' or 'she will not talk'.

To a lesser extent parents also used threats such as reporting the young person to the father, the social worker, the police or key worker or even of sending them away, to which at least a couple of young people responded that they wanted to be sent away. Confining a young person to his or her room was sometimes used, until some parents realised that far from it being a form of punishment, some young people enjoyed spending long periods of time on their own. Rewards and praise were tried by more than half of the parents but often didn't seem to work.

Perhaps it was not unexpected to find that many parents used physical punishment as a means of control when the teenagers had been younger, but it was surprising to find a number who were still doing so. With childhood over though, most parents had stopped the use of physical punishment. Quite characteristic was the comment of one parent who said 'If I did this now he would break the house down' or of another who stated that her daughter threatened to report her to the social worker if she touched her. Another one viewed her physical punishment as moderate:

> 'If his father was here he would be walloped you know,
> had a good hiding or something, so I undertook this myself,
> and of course it wasn't long before G. (son) started to fight back.'

A father who 'belted' his offending and abusive 13 year old was told to f . . . off and was struck on the nose. One mother who had stopped hitting her children since they were small found herself doing so recently for the first time.

Seeking Help

When problems arise between the family and the state or between parents and young people, social workers are expected to mediate as 'experts' with little certainty about their skills and knowledge. Harris and Timms (1993) comment how social workers are trained to see themselves as 'experts' and yet 'they regularly encounter situations beyond the scope of their influence; their expertise frequently fails to find a pathway through the thicket' (p.67). This theme will be recurring in subsequent chapters with parents particularly questioning the knowledge and expertise of social workers and of other professionals.

At the time of the first interviews many of the parents seemed defeated and sometimes ashamed for being unable to resolve the difficulties with the young person. This was particularly the case where outside control and their own efforts had proved inadequate with the problems often getting worse rather than better. The chronicity of many problems raised the obvious question of what was done before to help parents, including those when the difficulties had started in childhood. In many cases, the young person was already known to the social services from previous episodes of supervision/care and the parents were aware of probable sources of help. Therefore they had important views about the responsiveness of the social services and the help offered. Those with no previous contact with the social services expressed a badly felt need for access to some form of counselling/advisory service. Typical comments included:

> 'get some counselling early or to get to the bottom of things';
> 'opportunity to discuss together, to compare';
> 'have constructive psychological advice'.

The absence of early accessibility to sources of help was found to be frustrating. Yet in spite of their need for help, some parents had mixed feelings about involving the social services, either because of previous experience or of the images they had about social workers:

> 'Once you start with social workers you never finish.'

According to the parents, when they turned to social workers their responses varied. The parents' main criticism was of not being seen as a priority or of social workers saying that there was nothing they could do. Such criticisms were made for each of the authorities in the sample. Several parents complained that when they first approached the agencies with these problems, they had been told that social workers could only intervene if the young person was on a Supervision Order or committed an offence. Typical comments made by frustrated parents included:

> 'The emergency team didn't bother.'
> 'I was told the time to start worrying is when your son
> is chucking bleach over you . . .'

The absence of detailed policies for preventive work with teenagers means that some social workers may well respond uncertainly, hesitatingly and sometimes off-puttingly to requests by parents for help. Unsurprisingly, parents were themselves left uncertain and frustrated from not knowing what to expect. There was a further problem though which had to do with the image parents had of the social services and of social workers in particular. Unless they had previous positive experiences, most parents did not automatically associate social services as the place to go to when having problems with their teenager. Perhaps with child abuse being in the forefront of child care work, the promotion of preventive work with teenagers is increasingly taking a back seat.

Expectations of Measures of Intervention

We now move on to concentrate on the setting of expectations by each party to allow us to establish to what extent subjective expectations at the start had been fulfilled a year later. When each of the parties was defining the problem earlier, this was seen as largely arising from some circumstance or need, as perceived by each of them. Though not all young people acknowledged that they in fact had a problem, when they did they generally attributed it to circumstances and events, such as the relationship with a step-parent or parent, with the school or the police. Their perception of need arose mostly out of a pre-occupation with their current problem. There was no evidence that they linked it to some sense of personal deficiency. This was in contrast to social workers who tended to explain the problem in terms of internal needs, such as low self-esteem, lack of confidence or lack of controls. Parents in their turn, saw it mostly in terms of the need for controls and discipline and occasionally for greater maturity. The expectations each party set arose mainly out of these perceptions of need and they formed the basis for establishing in later chapters the relationship between needs, the deployment of services and outcomes. The divergence of expectations confirmed the well-known distinctions of felt, expressed and expert-defined needs (Bradshaw, 1972).

Social work literature strongly supports the view that a social work agenda for action should be preceded by discussions with other interested parties to develop a shared view not only about the problem, but also about expectations from intervention and the means for achieving them. The concept of partnership and parental participation and of children being actively consulted and listened to when drawing up care plans and finalising agreements is also in the spirit of the Children Act 1989. It is not assumed that all parties to a situation will have exactly the same expectations, but differences should be acknowledged and recorded. Most of our initial interviews took place just after the introduction of the Children Act 1989, so it is very possible that the concepts outlined above had not yet been fully assimilated and acted upon. Our discussions with agencies about two years after the introduction of the Act suggested that jointness, partnership and participation were seen to be good practice.

Expectations could be viewed as being of three kinds:

a   altering the precipitating problem (eg reducing family conflicts, altering aggressive behaviour or increasing a young person's self-confidence);
b   arranging environmental changes (eg new school, different placement);
c   working towards termination of supervision/care.

They also had three types of focus:

1   *Centred on the young person* eg
    appropriate schooling;
    more emotional security, increased self-esteem;
    time out from family conflict;
    to leave care as soon as possible/be with family;
    training for independence.

2   *Focused on family relationships* eg
    improved relationship between teenagers and parents,
        including step-parents;
    modifying especially the young person's behaviour within home;
    support the family to become a social base for young person.

3   *Reflecting adult wishes for conformity* eg
    modified attitude to offending and other anti-social
        activities eg drug-taking;
    unacceptable behaviour at school, control of temper tantrums
        and aggression.

To start with, a significant number of young people were unaware of what social service (work) departments offered and as a result were uncertain of what to expect from social work intervention. Not surprisingly, perhaps, one in seven said that they expected 'nothing'. The rest placed some of the expectations on themselves and some on parents and/or social workers.

Table 3:2 provides a rank ordering of expectations as defined or put across by each of the parties. When outlining expectations, each of them placed importance on what they thought were priority needs to be addressed. What Table 3:2 also highlights is the considerable disparity in priorities set by the three parties, particularly by social workers on the one hand and young people and parents on the other. Such disparities raise obvious questions about the extent of jointness and participation in the setting of expectations.

In order of importance, social workers identified for attention the young person's developmental needs (self-esteem, confidence, origins, maturity, better expression and general support), followed by improvements in family relationships, the education of the young person, support towards independence and the wish to see a reduction in offending, drug taking and other similar 'anti-social' behaviours. Unlike social workers who put developmental needs top, first priority for young people was the wish to stay where they were, usually at home and sometimes in a foster home or the wish to return home from care. This expectation reflected immediate anxieties and preoccupations either about being moved from home or not being returned home quickly enough. As a result some could not think beyond this expectation. This was followed by the wish to improve their education, stop/reduce offending and substance abuse, move to independent living, improve family relationships and lastly personal developmental needs. Whilst social workers put the ceasing/reduction of offending/drugs as sixth in priorities, young people and parents had it as third.

Table 3:2 Rank ordering of expectations

Expectation	Social Workers	Young Person	Parents
Personal Development	1	6	4
Family Relations	2	5	1
Schooling	3	2	2
Independence	4	4	5
Stay/return home/placement	5	1	–
Offending/drugs	6	3	3

The parents' expectations reflected the concerns they outlined earlier in this chapter. Following from this, they attached importance to behavioural outcomes, preferably within a short period. As a result, they put about equal emphasis on improved family relationships, less aggression within the home by the young person, attention to schooling and a stop or reduction in offending and drug-taking. Where conflict was a dominant feature within the family, a frequent comment was that supervision or care would help the young person to control his 'behaviour', 'impulses' or 'destructiveness'. Unlike social workers, parents stated very few expectations around the young person's developmental needs. On the whole though, the parents' expectations involved change by others and rarely by themselves.

Overall, two major points emerge. First, the absence of jointness and participation in the setting of expectations which leads to the second, that is a fundamental difference in orientation between social workers on one hand and young people and parents on the other. Social workers, probably reflecting their 'welfare orientation', put the main emphasis on personal development, the parents on behaviours and the young people on practical concerns. To a large extent it was like operating from different agendas. Yet it would be wrong to conclude that social workers were not interested to address practical and behavioural issues. Stated expectations, after all, are about intentions and they do not tell us what exactly goes on when social workers and young people meet, as we shall see in a later chapter.

The Social Workers' Expectations and Aims

Social workers' expectations from the care/supervision measures put the main emphasis first on the youngsters' personal needs, as they saw them, followed by attention to family relationships, education, support towards independence, placement support and on stopping/reducing offending and other similar forms of anti-social behaviour. They were also keen, in a few cases, to address needs that mostly concerned the parents, such as housing or health problems. Social workers rightly perceived many young people as having a low self-image and a low opinion of themselves which called for something to be done. The enhancing of the young person's view of himself/herself was expressed in terms of:

> 'help raise his low self-esteem'; 'let him know someone cares about him'; 'for him to develop and mature'; 'help integrate his sense of self'; 'develop capacity for relationships'; 'make sense of his life and family rejection'.

When the young person was away from home, social workers generally were expecting that much of the initiative with regard to some of his or her practical and personal needs would be dealt with by the carers (foster or residential) and that the care arrangement itself would have the most impact. For example, foster carers were expected to talk to the young people in their care about relationships with their original families and key workers in residential establishments to deal with the personal concerns of the young person. In one authority 'alternatives to custody' workers were also said to be dealing with family issues. Though social workers appeared clear as to who would be meeting at least some of these expectations, the young people and particularly parents did not seem to have the same clarity as to who was meant to be doing what.

The second most frequent expectation set by social workers, was an improvement in relationships within the family, usually between the young person and parent(s) and not infrequently a step-parent. Most social workers had recognised that problems in family relationships required attention, because they had a bearing on the problem, but the response to these differed widely and lacked consistency. When they talked of what was needed to resolve family difficulties, social workers saw themselves as mediators, 'achieving a balance', 'compromise' or 'accepting limits'. What was required, as some suggested, was to negotiate a settlement which allowed each party enough of what they needed or wanted. Sometimes they would say that a change in the balance of the relationship would help relieve the problem. Some planned to offer support to a needy parent themselves in order to lessen the demands on the young person, while others wanted to help young people and their parents learn how to negotiate more effectively with each other.

Individual social workers seemed to have some idea of what a 'balanced' or 'appropriate' relationship between a parent and a teenage child should be but it was not clear that there was a shared view or consensus about this. Balancing the needs and demands of the various parties could prove very difficult and it seems that neither social workers nor parents have clear guide-lines about how rights, responsibilities and power can or should be allocated in families with teenagers. Some social workers saw it as their main role to deal with this, either with the young person directly or with the parent(s) and sometimes jointly. In this respect an important expectation was to work on family relationships not only for their own intrinsic value but also to make it possible for the young person to continue living at home or return to live there. Typical comments signifying these expectations included:

> 'getting everyone to recognise that family rows do
> not need to lead to permanent rifts'; 'sustain her at
> home'; 'parents to listen more to young person'.

In situations such as the ones described above, high skills of family work, including mediation and conflilct resolution, were usually required to achieve a satisfactory solution, but later evidence will show that in spite of the intentions for family work, these were not usually deployed.

Other social workers, though identifying the need for family work, did not set expectations around it. They believed that it was too late or too difficult to attempt to alter family relationships. This could be because it had been tried in the past and failed or because of a perceived lack of motivation by family members or the absence of resources and skills. In at least four cases, intervention was meant to protect the young person from abuse by family members in the form of 'beatings' or sexual abuse, involving mostly step-fathers.

Almost one in every five expectations set by social workers had to do with concern for the education of the young person. This was seen as of considerable importance and therefore meriting special attention. The most common aim was to improve school attendance through support. In other cases it was to encourage the young person to get maximum benefit from schooling or continue their education beyond the statutory school-leaving age where appropriate. The choice of a residential school for placement was often done with the educational needs of the young person in mind and was usually arranged for young people with a long record of non-school attendance or with disruptive behaviour in class sometimes leading to expulsion. Educational expectations were explained in statements such as:

> 'school attendance is a priority'; 'sow the idea of school';
> 'seek residential school for her education'.

Plans to support the young person to become more independent at home or move to independent living in the community or to continue there featured in 16 per cent of the cases. This had mainly to do with helping the young person to obtain accommodation and/or a job, to manage his/her day to day living and cope with possible isolation and loneliness. As a result, part of the plan and expectations were 'to prepare for independence', 'try to secure work for him', 'training for independent living'.

Anti-social behaviour had been foremost in line in the definition of the problem, but when it came to expectations was relegated to sixth position. The stopping or reduction of offending did feature in a number of cases with comments such as: 'steer him away from offending' or 'keep him out of prison'. However, the young person's anti-social behaviour in the community and the social workers' expectations in this area were not always closely matched. Social workers, even if they had these in mind, prioritised other areas for attention and change. For example there were young people who were involved in stabbing or burglaries, but paying attention to offending did not occur explicitly as part of the aims. Yet irrespective of the arguments surrounding the notions of justice and welfare, there is an expectation that measures of intervention will also contribute to the reduction of offending, where present. Possibly some social workers believed that direct challenge could prove counter-productive and that by focusing their expectations and attention on other areas, usually practical and developmental ones, it would result in enhanced self-image contributing also to a reduction in offending. The findings lend some support to this notion but a focus on personal needs does not dispense with the need for young people to know what is going on.

Looking at similarities and differences between agencies, social workers in Agencies C and E were more likely to stress work around family relationships than Agency A or B. Also social workers in Agency C were far more likely to stress expectations about the personal needs and development of the young person. On the other hand, social workers in Agency C put much less emphasis on stopping or reducing offending as part of their explicit expectations. Looking at expectations in relation to gender, the biggest difference found was in offending. Whereas 58 per cent of boys and 37 per cent of girls had been involved in offending, when it came to expectation around the area of stopping or reducing offending and associated behaviour, 87 per cent of the social workers responses were in relation to boys and only 13 per cent in relation to girls.

Parents' Expectations from Intervention

Parents in their expectations put top priority on the reduction of observable undesirable behaviours at home and on an improved school record followed by stopping or reduction of anti-social behaviour in the form of stealing, drug taking etc. (Table 3:2). They attached much less importance than social workers did to the young person's individual needs and also placed less emphasis than social workers did on young peoples' bid for support towards independence.

By far the most frequent expectation by parents was for the young person to behave at home in ways more acceptable to themselves.

'Better tempered'; 'change attitude'; 'open up'; 'be nicer at home'.

Their own part in such an improvement was played down, fuelling some young people's urge to move out of the parental home or to want to go into care.

Reference has already been made to the importance parents attached to the young person getting a proper education and their awareness that, without education, the young person would be socially disadvantaged in later life. They said things like: 'Priority is to get her back to school', or 'school is the urgent thing'. In terms of behaviour outside the home, the parents' expected social workers, residential staff and foster carers to provide the controls on the young person's behaviour which they had not been able to provide themselves. A minority of parents voiced additional more generalised expectations of social workers, mostly in the form of availability, support and counselling. For example, they hoped that social workers would provide opportunities to examine family conflicts, facilitate communication between them and their children, but also be contactable during times of crisis. Even when sceptical, parents wanted to feel that the social worker was in the background if problems arose again, or that they would keep in touch or be accessible. They expressed this wish with comments such as:

'able to contact him (social worker) if problems arise';
'have an opportunity to discuss things together';
'get some counselling'.

The Young People's Expectations

Young people who set expectations, framed them mainly to reflect their most recent concern or preoccupation (Table 3:2). Not surprisingly, perhaps, the wish to stay or return home, and sometimes to stay in the foster home, topped their expectations and wishes. The second most frequent response (20%) was to improve their education. Far from young people with school related problems not being interested in their education, this group attached much importance to it. Almost a fifth of the responses were aspirations that a change of school or particularly care in a residential school would help improve their school attendance record and their general educational prospects. These comments did not always come from those with the worst non-school attendance record. It included some on supervision who were hoping their social workers would help them get access to further education or that by helping straighten out family problems they would then be able to concentrate on their education. Their hopes were encapsulated in statements such as:

'get back to school'; 'pass exams'; 'go to college'.

Like their parents, some but not all teenagers welcomed residential schools as offering a solution to the school problem and perhaps enabling them to get some benefit.

As already noted, some youngsters did not see that they had a problem, did not believe that anything could be done or simply did not know what to expect. If some young people do not see that they have a problem, then the question of expectations does not arise. Nevertheless, occasionally a few would add as an after-thought some expectation such as: 'help to get a job', 'become independent' or 'be out of care'. More girls were likely to say that they had no expectations or required 'nothing' compared to boys. On the whole, however, this group of young people did not define or perceive problems in the same way as their social workers or families did. If their behaviour was a problem to others, they did not appear to see it that way or did not want to. Typical comments included:

'no problem'; 'nothing I can think of';
'will make no difference'; 'running away is no problem for me';
'not my problem'.

Saying that they had no expectations because they had no problems or that there was 'nothing wanted' seemed to make some of them still feel in control and in charge. Harris and Timms (1993) also point out in relation to young people in Secure Units that feeling in charge, even if illusory, was possibly the only thing that some of them felt they had left. Overall, these youngsters were prepared to pay the price for their misdemeanours but also wanted to be left alone: 'nothing is needed'.

Another expectation which was again mixed with considerable anxiety was the hope of making it on their own independently of their parents. Whilst some pondered about finding jobs and housing, mostly they tended to dismiss possible difficulties in case they were deflected from their resolves. Though many young people had identified family conflict as a major problem, not many set expectations around it. Instead they tended to seek the solution elsewhere, such as in care or independent living. Those who viewed care as offering them the opportunity of a respite from family pressures would say:

'give me a break from home'; 'a break from hassles';
'easier to build relationships with mum when not together'.

Seeking for solutions outside inevitably reduced motivation for investing in the resolution of difficulties within the household. Only a minority (11%) were hoping or expecting that the measures might help in improved relationships all round, making it possible not to have to go into care or be able to return home from care. Typical comments included:

> 'get on better with dad and stay living at home';
> 'get on better with parents'; 'stay at home, if mum lets me';
> 'get things sorted out with mum'.

Like their social workers, some young people viewed stopping or reducing offending and/or drug-taking as important but they did not give it much attention or at least it was not always foremost in their minds. Some though would acknowledge the need for help in this area and said that the measures taken would help them:

> 'stop offending'; 'stop buzzing glue'; 'keep me out of trouble';
> 'help accept authority'; 'help see things differently'.

Levels of Congruence or Overlaps

The analysis tried to identify how the expectations of each of the three parties coincided or overlapped. To call it levels of agreement might be seen as rather too strong, because there was little evidence of commonly agreed goals and expectations. This applied irrespective of agency, including the one agency that had a general expectation of contracts being drawn up with young people on supervision or in foster care.

Where responses were available from all three parties (N=82) the highest levels of overlaps between the three or as twosomes were first the need to pay attention to the young person's educational needs, then to improve family relationships, followed by attempts to stop or reduce offending and drug-taking. Higher levels of congruence were achieved in dyads, that is between social workers and young people, young people and parents or parents and social workers. These ranged from 25% to 41%. The stated expectations of the three parties overlapped in only 13 per cent, or about one in every eight. The following is a rare example of matching expectations between all three parties:

> *Young Person:* 'Get on better with dad (step-father) . . . not have trouble at school.'

> *Social Worker:* 'Sustain her at home, work on relationship between her and parents, reduce tension; get her to school.'

> *Parents:* 'She won't go to school; she has to stop drinking and there are all the arguments at home.'

The following is another of a few examples of the young person and the social worker having similar expectations:

> *Young Person:* 'Get off drugs, keep out of trouble and get a job.'

Social Worker: 'Steer him away from offending and drugs.'

The expectations set out above are predominantly about problem-solving involving support, discussion and some direction and were not seen as incompatible by any of the three parties. However, incongruencies between the parties also abounded as the following example demonstrates:

Young Person: 'No problems; the only problem is having had nowhere to stay.'

Social Worker: 'Help his personal growth; review relationship with father and prepare for independent living.'

The Parent: 'Non-school attendance; out of control behaviour; stealing.'

Though it is proper that social workers should have a number of expectations in mind, these findings suggest a greater need to prioritise them in consultation with young people and their parents. Full agreement will not always be possible, especially between parents and young people about what needs to be done, but even highlighting where the differences lie could help to reduce the gap. Addressing both personal, practical and behavioural concerns are not incompatible, provided each party understands what is happening. Furthermore, it is not always necessary to talk about issues such as confidence and self-esteem in order to promote them. Whilst personal development may be an ultimate objective, attention to practical and behavioural concerns could be a means to that end. Holding firmly to the idea of a contract setting out in writing the perceptions and expectations, including priorities, could perhaps help to reduce the gap found providing more direction to the work undertaken. Morris and Beverly (1975) writing on the same theme raise the dangers involved of the supervisor defining the situation and the problem and then proceeding 'to try and put things right' (p.132). We would add that if, for example, the social worker identifies developmental needs these should be discussed with the young person (and parents) in order to decide the best way to address them, rather than they should feature solely in the social worker's plans.

How the Measures of Supervision or Care were expected to work out

Social workers, parents and young people were asked during our first interviews to say how they envisaged the next 6 to 12 months would work out. Their responses were grouped into optimistic, pessimistic and uncertain/neutral (Table 3:3).

Table 3:3 Social workers', parents' & young people's views about the next 6–12 months

	SW (N=116)	Parents (N=82)	Young People (N=105)
Optimistic	54%	66%	86%
Pessimistic	16%	12%	3%
Uncertain/neutral	30%	22%	11%

More than half of both social workers and parents felt optimistic and hopeful about the immediate future, but this went up to 86% when it came to the teenagers themselves (Table 3:3). Over half of social workers believed that the main outcome of the care episode would be an improvement in the young person's behaviour or circumstances. This could come about in various ways such as greater stability in life circumstances, development of new skills, or more maturity and understanding.

Given the early stage of the new intervention, it is not surprising that many social workers used words like 'hopefully', 'uncertain' and 'depends' rather than offering confident predictions. Where social workers were optimistic this was often based on the beginning of progress at school, the young person settling well in a new placement or a new relationship being established. Otherwise they were acknowledging that some problems were fairly intractable, whilst the alleviation of others was contingent on resources and events outside their immediate control, like the provision of a foster care place, action by the education department, a court/panel decision or the availability of training and employment opportunities. The attitude and circumstances of the young person could be vital too. The social workers' pessimism about the future was present in one in every six cases and had mainly to do with continued offending such as: 'he will end up in prison' or because of 'peer group influence' or 'the tense home situation'.

As shown in Table 3:3 two thirds of the parents expressed cautious optimism about how the measures would work out, with about a fifth being uncertain or non-committal and one in ten being definitely pessimistic. Characteristic predictions with varying degrees of optimism included:

> 'if I keep a tight rein on him he will be alright';
> 'should benefit from schooling at the residential school';
> 'I am very confident in her now'.

The percentage of parents who expressed cautious optimism may appear high in view of their strong disillusionment with many of the children and the more negative appraisals given of the social work service they had experienced before. It is possible that by the end of the interview when this question was asked, having perhaps ventilated what to them were important feelings, they now took a more optimistic view. It is equally possible that without such a perspective it would be difficult for them to face the immediate future.

Like the social workers, parents often indicated that change relied on a number of factors which were outside their own control. Central to these was the young person's attitude and behaviour, but some also emphasised the absence of know-how on the part of social workers and of other professionals or the lack of what they saw as 'specialist resources'. As one parent put it:

> 'I don't think anybody really knows. I think
> that's the problem with the social services.'

The high optimism of young people (Table 3:3) may seem incongruous, but it is consistent with the attitude of some of them that they could not see that they had a problem, or that home or school was the problem or that once independent things would be 'alright'. Their optimism about the future was only partly related to the benefits they expected to get from the care/supervision measures and more to faith in their own efforts or their infinite belief that things would turn out well in the end. Such undue optimism might also make it difficult for social workers to discuss plans in any detail or support them to confront aspects of their behaviour such as offending.

Many young people felt confident and in control, whilst a few were unsure or saw themselves as prisoners of external forces like the courts, parents, schools, carers and occasionally of social workers. Optimism was expressed with comments such as: 'have a job, be independent', 'get a flat look after myself' or 'with girl-friend, be independent'. More of them were hopeful about their educational prospects adding 'be at home and at college', 'get A levels and go to college', 'do well at school and forget the past'. A few indicated their unhappiness of being away from home and were hopeful of returning there: 'be back with mum and dad', 'be back home', 'get on better with mum and dad', 'be back on the right track'. Other young people hoped that they would still be with their foster carers or a foster home would be found for them.

Summary Points

This chapter set out to define the precipitating problems and to identify each party's expectations from intervention. Offending, family conflict and school related problems were the dominant issues leading to referral to social services and the three were closely interrelated. In the absence of specific preventive policies for teenagers and their families, social workers were uncertain how to respond to requests for voluntary help, leaving some parents feeling frustrated and helpless. When it came to defining the problem, social workers, compared to parents, were more likely to underplay anti-social behaviour outside the home and the extent of domestic conflict.

Needs as perceived by each party, were translated into expectations, setting the scene for establishing the relationship between expressed needs, the deployment of resources and outcomes. Whilst there were a number of similarities, there were also significant differences between the parties on the nature and prioritisation of expectations, depending on each party's orientation and outlook. Whilst social workers put priority on the developmental needs of young people, teenagers and parents put the emphasis on more concrete, immediate and observable changes, either practical or behavioural. Concepts of partnership, jointness and participation in the definition of the problem, its assessment, the setting of goals and the sharing of the process were not much in evidence as demonstrated by the many disparities found.

4 Service Provision During the Year

Introduction

As might be expected there was wide variation in the events of the year and range of services experienced by young people. It has been a common criticism of social work research and programme evaluation more generally that it has sought to assess what does or does not work, but has neglected to document the precise nature of the intervention being assessed (Scheirer and Rezmovic, 1983; Cheetham *et al*, 1992). Therefore, we tried to understand in some detail both the actual components of the social work intervention and how these had been combined to form the service programme for the year. In this chapter we describe each type of service provided and outline the pattern of service provision for young people during the year. In Chapters 5, 6 and 7 we consider how the services were evaluated by the young people, their parents and social workers.

We begin therefore by outlining the range of services available and go on to consider ways in which they had been combined to form the 'care package'. We use the term 'care package' to refer to the combined provision during the year, though in few instances were the services planned as co-ordinated 'packages' from the start. Instead services were provided as they became available or were needed in response to the young person's changing needs. Several services might be offered together or provided in sequence during the year. In this chapter we consider both types of package and finish by outlining how the year developed and ended for the teenagers. The shape of individual care 'packages' depended on several factors, notably the young people's circumstances and resource availability. As we chart the young people's moves we have also identified some of the factors which prompted change, influenced access to services and contributed to the formulation of care programmes.

The Nature of Services Provided

Firstly we consider the direct work provided by social workers, the only service received by all the teenagers. Our focus then turns to substitute care services, supervision, group work, befriending and other specialist services, which were arranged by social workers but provided by others.

Social Workers

We have used the term 'social worker' to refer to the main caseworker interviewed in each case, because nearly all were social workers by designation and training. However, a few did not hold social worker posts or qualifications and of course some of the residential carers were also social workers, but we have considered them separately as carers.

There were only 80 different individuals interviewed in the study, since about one third of them were responsible for two or more cases in the sample. The vast majority were basic-grade area team social workers (69). Nearly all had a social work qualification and 90% held a CQSW. About half of the whole sample were graduates. Most had been in post for between 1 and 4 years, though one quarter had more than 5 years experience in the same post. We did not ask about prior experience so this gives an indication of recency in post rather than overall experience, but evidently the young people in this sample were mainly receiving a service from trained and at least moderately experienced workers.

Since many of the cases concerned new forms of intervention (though not necessarily recent referrals), it was to be expected that at the start of the study many of the workers would have only quite recently become responsible for the work with the young person. This was indeed the position, with just under half having been the young person's worker for less than 6 months and about one fifth for 2 years or more. However rather more than half had been the young person's social worker before the current circumstances which led to them being in the sample. Even so, a number of young people were negotiating a significant change in their care career (such as a placement move or transition to independent living) with a new social worker whom they were just getting to know.

Social Workers' Contact with Young People

Most social workers reported at follow-up that they had seen the young person at least once a month and two fifths met at least once a fortnight. Once or twice per month was the typical pattern:

every 1–2 weeks	39%
every 3–4 weeks	28%
less often	33%

In the main, social workers' claims about frequencies of contact were confirmed by carers and teenagers themselves. If closed cases are excluded, two thirds of the young people said they had seen their social worker within the last fortnight:

in the last 2 weeks	69%
in the last month	9%
over a month ago	22%

The statutory or voluntary nature of the intervention seemed to have no bearing in itself on the frequency of contact. Overall young people living away from home were seen as often as those at home. However a few individuals had noticed that they saw their social worker less often after admission to care, eg 'since I came here, my social worker hasn't come to see me hardly at all'.

Over half of the teenagers normally saw the social worker on their own and most of the rest did so sometimes, though one tenth of the sample said they had never seen the social worker alone. These were mostly young people who had been supervised at home throughout the intervention, but surprisingly four young people who had been in care said they had had no private contact with their social worker.

For three quarters of the young people, contact with social workers had usually been in the family home. Approximately 30% had normally seen their social worker at the office but in almost two thirds of these instances there had also been some contact at home. About one in ten spoke of being taken out by their social workers and a few saw them at school. Understandably, in the main it was those in care who saw their social workers away from home. Some arrangements for those on supervision appeared not to be well planned or communicated. For example, one young man said the social worker had been out to see them a few times 'but so far she hasn't caught us in'. Occasionally, the purpose of contact seemed to have escaped the young person altogether – 'To tell you the truth, I don't know why I do have to visit the social worker'. This accorded with what was reported in the previous chapter about the young people not knowing what to expect of intervention.

Aims and Nature of Direct Work with Young People

Social workers were asked at the end of the year to state what they now saw as having been their main aims in their direct work with the young person. Many described the overall case plan rather than confining themselves to direct work. The most common aims were, in order:

> Assist in moves to independence
> Improve family relationships
> Deal with school issues
> Assist in adjustment to placement
> Reduce offending/avoid custody
> Facilitate return home
> Give advice, befriending, counselling

Other goals included help with finding work, aiding self-protection, preventing removal from home, improving self-esteem and temper control. It is interesting to note some of the discrepancies between the expectations set at the beginning and the actual content of intervention described a year later. There were some differences between agencies. For instance, working on family relationships was an aim for over a third of cases in Agency C, but in none of the Agency D cases and less than one fifth of the Agency A cases. As expected, preparation for independence was most prominent for 17–18 year olds, but family work was concentrated on those in their mid-teens.

In order to ascertain which specific aims had been attempted and how successfully, a set of closed questions was put to social workers and young people. The overall pattern of responses was similar from both, though social workers indicated there had been more *unsuccessful* attempts to improve family relationships while young people accorded social workers more *success* in helping them stop offending than social workers themselves acknowledged. Social workers' responses were as follows:

Table 4:1 How social workers tried to help young people N=101

	Achieved	Tried Unsuccessfully
talked with young person about problems	56	21
spoke up at court or panel	48	6
kept young person out of care/custody	36	14
helped get on better with family	35	32
helped get on better with others	29	9
helped with school problems	28	25
helped to control temper/fighting	22	22
helped to stop offending	21	26
helped prepare for independence	17	19
helped get accommodation	16	11
helped get a job/training	13	14
helped control drugs/alcohol abuse	12	16

The actions which seemed to be proportionately most successful were advocacy in legal settings, preventing care/custody and improving social relationships outside the family. All the other actions did not have a large difference in the numbers of workers who had been successful and unsuccessful in their efforts. The tasks which were most likely to be unsuccessful involved tackling offending, drug/alcohol abuse and employment.

British social workers appear to be more reluctant than those in North America to label their ways of working in terms of a specific model (Hill *et al*, 1993). This was borne out in the present study. First of all we asked workers to describe their model of work, but this proved unsuccessful. A few did specify their approach eg behaviourist, task-centred, individual counselling, but most denied using any model or gave vague formulations like 'tried to work with him and his family together'. Therefore the question was altered to ask about particular roles undertaken in the case.

The social workers claimed that their work included a focus on the family in rather fewer than half the cases and some form of individual counselling in about 60% of cases. Other roles were each adopted in roughly half as many cases:

individual counselling	60%	enabler	28%
family counselling	42%	service provider	28%
case coordinator	33%	advocate	26%
mediator	29%		

Of course, often several roles had been taken on in the same case. Five claimed to have carried out all of them! There was only a slight tendency for family counselling to have been undertaken more often when the young person was living at home throughout the year. There were no significant variations according to agency or legal status.

It may be helpful at this stage to consider what type of work social workers were referring to as individual or family counselling. There is no agreed view about the nature of counselling, this largely being dependent on the theoretical and value orientation of its adherents (Hill *et al*, 1990; Brower and Nurius 1993). A range of approaches was included in the work described as 'individual counselling'. It might involve 'talking around' school, family or behaviour difficulties with the social worker listening, debating and encouraging reflection. Only rarely was the focus exclusively on intrapersonal concerns. Some social workers said they would use challenge and confrontation, particularly in relation to offending or non attendance at school. This discussion might go alongside the social worker intervening in other ways, as mediator, resource provider or co-ordinator. In social work, insight giving usually occurs in combination with other roles (Hill *et al*, 1990).

There were relatively few examples of focussed counselling involving the whole family. In one such instance the social worker described the purpose of the weekly meetings as:

'Examination of the dynamics in the family. Understand
what events and behaviour produce the crises, see what
games the parents have played and challenge and
confront both parents.'

More usually, 'family counselling' meant that the social worker discussed issues with parents as well as the young person, sometimes meeting together and sometimes separately. In cases where family meetings were planned and purposeful, most social workers indicated that young people also needed some time on their own to receive individual support.

We asked the teenagers what they had talked about last time they saw their social worker. Several could not remember. The recollections of the rest mostly included their current behaviour and progress, especially in relation to school, or else future plans which were mentioned by about one third. Surprisingly in view of some recent commentaries on social work practice, a lot of attention did seem to be given to educational issues, whilst family relationships were not often prominent, at least as far as the teenagers themselves recalled. Perhaps understandably, only a minority referred to discussion of problems caused by their own behaviour (like offending and drug-taking).

The social workers were invited to say more generally what was the main focus of their discussions with young people. Usually several things were mentioned in each case and several pointed out that conversations depended on what was happening at the time and the young person's own agenda. By and large, they depicted the conversations as problem-focussed and task-centred, though some had attended to emotional issues, insight development and boosting self-esteem. They also referred to family relationships far more than was apparent from the young people's recollections. Possibly this was because it had been more of an issue earlier on in the year or maybe it impinged less on the young people. Whether the young person was living at or away from home, relationships with parents apparently often remained high on social workers' agendas. Schooling and the young person's behaviour were the other most common topics:

Table 4:2 Social workers' reports of the main focus of their discussions with young people N=108

Topic	% Mentioned
Family relationships	44%
Schooling	35%
Offending/drugs	20%
Placement issues	13%
Work	12%
Other behaviour	9%
Peer relationships	8%

Parents' Contact with Social Workers

When an adolescent is living at home, work with parents is likely to be crucial. Research in several countries has shown that social workers' engagement with parents and other relatives has a major impact on the success of young people leaving care, whether that involves returning home or a move to supported or independent living (Colton and Hellinckx, 1993).

The frequency of contact which parents reported they had with social workers over the year ranged from 'almost daily' to never. Most commonly it was every 2–4 weeks, sometimes tapering away as the year progressed. If we consider just open cases, only a handful of parents were in contact every 1–2 weeks by the end of the year, compared with about a third of young people. At that stage 40% of parents were being seen less than monthly and 22% of young people. In about half the cases there had been a similar frequency of contact with parents and teenagers, but in a substantial minority of cases social workers admitted to devoting less time to the parents than to the teenagers themselves:

saw young person more often	39%
saw parent more often	7%
saw both similar frequency	53%

This is the reverse of the normal pattern of social work intervention with families in relation to younger children, when change-oriented work is mainly directed at the parents. More direct contact with the young person can be seen as appropriate to the greater independence of teenagers, although as we shall see this did not always accord with parental wishes. In some instances, however, the focus on the teenager in his or her own right reflected the reality of a total breakdown in the relationship between parents and offspring. Nearly all the parents saw the social workers at home and indeed often that was the only place they met. Sometimes there was also contact at the office or in residential establishments for reviews.

Separate meetings with the young person or parent were more common than joint contacts. In a third of the situations there had been no joint contact at all throughout the year. According to social workers the frequency of meeting with at least one parent and teenager together was:

every 1–2 weeks	8%
every 3–4 weeks	12%
less often	49%
not at all	31%

Parents confirmed that they usually saw the social worker without the young person there or just sometimes jointly. Only a few reported seeing the social worker always with their son or daughter also present.

When it did occur, joint contact was not always part of agreed and planned family work, but either arose by chance or occurred when social workers and parents visited establishments together, often for reviews. For example, a few social workers noted honestly that it depended on who was home when they called. Separate discussions were sometimes part of a deliberate strategy for negotiation and compromise to avoid the heated conflicts which ensued when everyone was together. This was not always welcomed by parents, however. Mr and Mrs G. thought their difficulties with their daughter would have been resolved more quickly and effectively if the worker had seen the family together, rather than acting as a go-between.

When social workers met parents separately from their children, the discussions centred on their relationship with the teenager in over half the cases. This was also the most common topic in contacts with the teenager alone but, in contrast with the conversations between social workers and young people, it seemed that school was seldom discussed (4 families only). In a minority of cases time was spent discussing family or individual problems unrelated to the young person (eg to do with money; the parent's addiction; another child). Occasionally, parents wanted help for themselves but this was not forthcoming. It was stated by one social worker that Mrs K. wanted help for her own needs, but such a service could not be provided because the priority was to help her son. When the young person was away from home, not infrequently the social workers took on the role of informing the parents about the young person's progress.

Just as discussions with the young people about their behaviour normally involved attempts to get them to change, social workers mostly appeared to be getting parents to alter their ways of treating their son or daughter. In spite of what some young people thought, the social workers were usually trying to get parents to respond in a more flexible or understanding manner and were not allying themselves with parental disapproval. Mrs. T's worker had encouraged her to show more interest, consistency and acceptance towards her sons. Aims in other cases included helping the parents to see positives in their children, to agree rules and limits more clearly and to stop colluding with anti-social behaviour.

Turning to social workers' meeting with parents and the young person together, the focus was again mainly on the interaction between family relationships and the young person's behaviour. This could mean little more than monitoring of progress, as in relation to home leave, but in some instances involved more active change-oriented work. For example, the intention in one case was to get the parents and young person to listen more to each other's viewpoints and be more constructive in their responses. One worker spoke of assisting the family to put their problems in perspective. Progress could be difficult. In the D. family, conversation was stilted as parent and child were frightened to upset each other. Either party could seek to control the communication. G. disliked her mother talking to social workers about family problems, whilst B's social worker said that the mother would 'go off the deep end if she suspected I was taking B's side'.

For 25 young people contact with a social worker was the only type of service they experienced, but most of the teenagers were either in some form of care provision or in receipt of additional services while living at home. We now turn to examine the nature of these other resources.

Substitute Care

Residential Placements

The quality of residential care for young people has been the subject of a number of investigations in the last few years, following several disclosures of ill-treatment. Some investigated the immediate circumstances of abuse (eg Levy and Kahan, 1991) whilst others took the form of a more general enquiry (eg DOH, 1991a; Scottish Office, 1992). These reports have confirmed that residential care remains the principal form of substitute care for teenagers. The importance of residential provision as a positive care option has been reaffirmed but each report has recognised that residential services for children need to be more generously resourced if they are to provide an effective service. There has been particular focus on the training required to equip staff for the job.

As noted in Chapter 1, the term 'residential care' can apply to a wide range of settings (Berridge, 1985; Kendrick and Fraser, 1992). The young people in the study who experienced residential care were in a variety of placements including the following:

- **small units** catering for 6–20 children and young people. A few provided only reception facilities but the majority were 'multi-purpose';
- **resource centres** with approximately 40 residents. Some provided only assessment while others also offered longer term care. Education was normally available on the premises for a temporary period;
- **residential schools** managed by the social work department, education department or independent management;
- **secure units**, some were separate institutions and others were located within a residential school;
- **semi-independent units**, some self contained, others located in children's units or attached to a residential school;
- **reception unit** providing psychiatric assessment.

Numbers were too small for useful examination of the differences between each type of placement but, where appropriate, a distinction was made between residential schools and other units. The primary reasons for admission to residential school were school based difficulties, offending and family problems. Each applied to approximately a third of the residents. In contrast almost half the young people in residential units had been admitted to care because of family tensions while school problems were a precipitating factor in only 13% of admissions. Behaviour problems were predominant in a third. Residential schools were a quite distinct resource in that they aimed to care for and educate the young person in the same setting, usually for a period of a year or more. They are a specialist educational resource as well as a care placement and are considered within both contexts in this chapter. In the following section, however, the term 'residential care' is used collectively to refer to residential schools and other units.

Social workers were generally less enthusiastic about residential units than other types of care. Whereas most foster homes and residential schools were rated as providing 'good' emotional care, this applied to only 40% of other residential homes. Residential care was often viewed as a last resort and it was not unusual for social workers to define their aims in terms of avoiding or curtailing a period in residential care. This may reflect the failure of residential units to specify what they can offer. In all 55 young people had experienced a total of 78 residential placements in the course of the year:

first living situation	44
after first move	17
after second or subsequent move	17

Moves into residential care might be from home or from other placements. Less then a third of the residential placements ended with the young person returning home and a quarter moved to another placement. Six young people moved into independent living and the remaining 28 were still in residential care at the end of the year. Most placements had lasted less than a year and at least 10 young people had lived in two or more residential units in the course of the year. Placements in residential schools were more durable than those in other types of residential care. Over half the young people who began the year in a residential school were still there compared with only 16% of those teenagers who were in residential homes.

Foster Placements

The role which foster care should take in the placement of teenagers is unclear and contested. On the one hand, there is a view that most teenagers in care prefer residential homes and would resist settling into a foster home (Kahan, 1979; Berridge, 1985). It is argued that most have either had very negative experiences in their original families which has made them mistrustful of family settings or conversely have long established loyalties to their own family and do not want a second one. Moreover, many are at an age when growing autonomy from the family is normal, so it is the wrong time to start establishing new quasi-parental relationships. On the other hand, teenagers can be successfully fostered, including some over the age of 16 with major difficulties (Hudson and Galaway, 1989; Hazel, 1990). Some agencies have pursued active policies to place all children in families (Cliffe with Berridge, 1991). It may be noted that the UN Convention on the Rights of the Child, which covers everyone under the age of 18, expresses an implicit preference for family placements (Article 20).

In none of the agencies in the current study was there an expectation that teenagers would normally be placed in foster care, but practice ranged from one agency where foster care was seldom considered for adolescents to others with special schemes for teenagers. A remand fostering scheme was in operation in Agency A. The project staff were often providing intensive support to placements, in some instances having daily contact for several weeks. Apart from this scheme for offenders, virtually all young people who had foster placements were in care primarily because of family difficulties.

At the start of the study 17 young people were in foster care, including two who also attended residential school and spent vacations in a foster home. Two of the foster placements were private. Arrangements for teenagers to stay with family friends or neighbours had become formalised, partly to enable payments to be made. Of the original 17, seven were still in foster care at the end of the year. Three had stayed in the same placement all year, one had left then returned and three had moved to different foster homes. By the end of the year six of those who had left foster care were living in community settings (5 back to parents and one on to independent living) and the other four were in residential care.

Ten young people came into foster care in the course of the year, of whom four remained in placement at the year end. Overall, 27 young people experienced a total of 37 foster placements during the course of the year:

first living situation	17
after first move	10
after second or subsequent move	10

All but a few of these placements were in two agencies, A and C. Nearly half of all foster placements ended with a return home to parents after a matter of months. We did not interview the foster carers, so do not have detailed information on their perspective. However, three quarters (12) of foster carers at the start of the study had returned a self-completion questionnaire. Although some were part of a specialist scheme (4) and a few more had received training (3), others had had no training at all (5).

Supervision

At the start of the study 55 young people were being supervised while living at home. In addition 24 young people who started the year in care were supervised on their return to the community so that during the year a total of 79 teenagers had been supervised at home. In only 25 instances had supervision solely involved contact with a social worker, the majority having also had access to additional services such as group work. Later in this chapter we describe some of these services and outline their availability. Here we concentrate on the main characteristics of the social worker's support to young people living at home. As outlined in Chapter 1, there has previously been relatively little examination of the nature of home supervision by local authority social workers and for that reason we devoted particular attention to this aspect of the service.

Reasons for being supervised at home were varied and for half of the young people more than one reason applied. Anti-social behaviour such as offending or drug taking had precipitated two fifths of the home supervisions. For just over a third family difficulties had been serious enough to require social work intervention and a fifth had been referred because of non-attendance at school. The contact was on an informal basis, often following referral by a parent, for approximately a third of teenagers supervised at home. Non attendance at school, offending and previous or current lack of parental care were the main reasons for the remaining two thirds being subject to a formal supervision order. The majority were living with their parents but 15% were offered support in an independent living situation. (More detailed information about services for young people living independently is provided later in this chapter).

In order to focus specifically on the social worker's input during supervision at home, we examined closely the nature of the contact with 44 young people who had had no experience of care during the year. We identified few significant differences between what social workers offered teenagers while on supervision and while in care. Frequency of contact with the social worker was not substantially different. A third of those being supervised at home met with the social worker every week and only a quarter had contact less often than monthly. Perhaps surprisingly, social workers did not meet more often with parents when the young people were at home, though this in part reflects the inclusion of some young people living independently. However social workers more often indicated that they had worked as a family counsellor when young people were living at home.

When they identified the aims of the supervision a third of social workers indicated they had set out to make an impact on school related issues. The objective might be to change attitudes towards school, to increase attendance or to obtain suitable educational provision. Other aims included:

provide support in independent living	25%
improve family relationships	25%
reduce offending behaviour or drug/substance abuse	22%
provide support in obtaining employment	19%
improve self-esteem/communication skills	13%

Of course these aims were not mutually exclusive. One social worker believed that obtaining employment would raise self esteem while another was convinced that family tensions would ease if the young person was not at home all day. Supervision was characterised by the provision of support, practical help or advice with the aim of promoting the young person's personal development. The aims set for supervision of one young man on the fringes of delinquency illustrate this well:

i   to introduce a service provision for youth such as would initially help the YP to rediscover & continually realise his own potential;
ii with a similar aim a school transfer had been sought & secured.

When we asked social workers what in fact had been the focus of their meetings with young people on supervision they indicated that there had been discussion of family and school difficulties with almost half the young people. Anti-social behaviour such as offending or drug taking had been discussed with a third of the young people, the majority of whom were on formal supervision as a result of offending behaviour. Some of the young people faced serious practical difficulties and needed help, for example to find accommodation, obtain money or find work. Almost a third had received practical help or information and a further 10%, all female, had been given advice about personal matters such as health-care, contraception or handling relationships with partners. Not surprisingly, the last two forms of help most often applied to older teenagers.

The wide ranging nature of discussions during supervision is illustrated by the social workers' accounts of the topics covered:

> 'His mother, his drug taking. I try to talk about what happens at home . . . try to get him to acknowledge how he feels.'
> 'Talked "around" school. Some discussion about whether he would stay with his mother or father when parents split up . . . Generally talked about offending.'
> 'School issues . . . contacts, who his pals are, what he is doing . . . His mum, how things are going at home.'
> 'Self-care, personal safety, health care and contraception. Importance of education, encourage her to have home tutor.'

According to social workers discussion of family issues was prominent but when young people were asked what they had talked about during their last meeting with the social worker no young person on supervision mentioned family problems. They provided less detail than social workers and were more inclined to describe the conversation as a general chat about school and future plans. Perhaps surprisingly, a third could not remember what they had talked about at all. In contrast, only one in six young people who spent part of the year in care was unable to recall their last meeting with the social worker. This may indicate that young people viewed meetings while on supervision as less important.

With parents the most common topic was their handling of the young person. Social workers offered advice on how to respond in particular situations and in general seemed to encourage parents to treat young people fairly and consistently. Almost half the contacts with the social worker had this focus which often included discussion of family relationships, in particular the appropriate allocation of power and control between family members. Over a third of parents had been given help in their own right. This might involve practical help, for example with benefit claims or advice about personal or emotional difficulties.

Social workers' particular descriptions of being asked what they talked about with parents included:

> 'How she parents her children . . . how she disempowered T.'
> 'Need for parent to control P., not to be manipulated as she raised the emotional stakes. To be consistent.'
> 'How mother's life style affects the children. Effect of tensions on them.'
> 'Practical assistance for mother, help with filling out forms etc.'

Parents' comments about the content of meetings were generally consistent with social workers' accounts, though they placed more emphasis on the young person's need to change and less on developmental needs or the parents' own behaviour.

While all young people on supervision had a social worker, the majority also had access to other services such as group work and befriending. We now move on to examine the nature of the main additional services.

Groups and Specialist Services

The availability of different kind of services to supplement supervision or care showed marked agency differences. In particular, Agency E provided a wide range of group work, whereas in Agency A befriending and outreach was common. Both were offered infrequently in the other 3 authorities.

Groups

Just over two fifths of the young people said they had been offered the opportunity to attend a group during the year. Curiously, there were often discrepancies between the teenagers and social workers about whether a group had been offered. Over three quarters of those who had the chance did attend, although for a few this was once or twice only. Eight had attended more than one group. The types of group attended varied considerably in nature and in the breadth or narrowness of focus. They included:

> groups for young people in care
> leaving care groups
> groups for solvent or drug users
> youth justice groups
> alternative to custody schemes
> intermediate treatment
> group for school non-attenders
> young women's group
> youth club

Nearly all the groups were organised within social services or juvenile/youth justice systems, although a few young people had used general youth facilities. Of course the nature of the group closely affected what happened there. Some concentrated on activities, often including outdoor pursuits like horse-riding and cycling. The majority mainly involved discussion, with varying degrees of structure and formal input. Most young people said they had both talked and engaged in activities, games or outings at their groups. Some groups appeared to be primarily promotional, aiming to enhance young people's awareness and self-confidence, whilst others were closer to the preventive or behaviour management end of the spectrum (Bottoms *et al*, 1990). The in-care groups followed the former pattern, discussing topics like preparation for reviews, assertiveness and methods of changing the care system. In other settings, groups tackled such things as school problems, offending, social skills, sex, family relationships and use of self. Several groups were quite specialised (eg therapy for victims of sexual abuse; vehicular activities for offenders).

There were major differences amongst the agencies as regards availability of groups. Agency E has a clear strategy of supporting youngsters in the community with an emphasis on a wide range of intermediate treatment and group work. Hence four fifths of the youngsters in E had been *offered* a group, compared with only one fifth in Agency C. The other three authorities were in between, though in none had more than half of the teenagers been offered a group. Over half had *attended* a group in Agency E, compared with one tenth in Agency C. As a result most of those who would have liked a group but did not have the opportunity were in C.

Although group work and intermediate treatment have been seen as vital elements of prevention or diversion, young people who had been in care (whether for a period or continuously during the year) were as likely to be offered group work as those who had been at home on supervision. This reflects the recent development of groups set up for children in care and care leavers, some under the auspices of NAYPIC and Who Cares? Indeed the highest rate of group attendance (half) was amongst the teenagers admitted to care at the beginning of the study, followed by those placed on supervision (one third). Only a few of those who were in the study as a result of a move in care or out of care had attended a group during the year.

Rather higher proportions of younger than older teenagers had been offered group work and taken advantage of it. As Intermediate Treatment in particular has been criticised for being 'male-oriented', it was perhaps surprising to find that the proportion of girls who had attended groups was the same as that of boys. This was largely accounted for by the fact that well over half of the females in Agency E had attended. Also all the girls who attended a group had done so whilst in care or as part of after-care. Nearly half of the boys but none of the girls who had been supervised throughout the year had been to a group. Group work had been experienced by smaller proportions of teenagers when the original problems had centred on domestic issues than if they revolved round the teenagers' own behaviour.

Special Projects

A number of the teenagers, particularly the older ones, had been referred to specialist projects, which might offer help by means of groups, on an individual basis or a combination of both. For example, P. had come off drugs with the help of a Drug Advice centre.

In Agency A there were two projects which offered programmes as an alternative to custody. These offered a range of services including group work, befriending and individual counselling. Seven young people in the study had attended at least one part of the programme which imposed varying demands, ranging from twice weekly group attendance to daily contact with a project worker. One of the projects provided a weekly opportunity to help a group of children with learning difficulties ride Quad-bikes at a local track. Staff in these programmes worked closely with workers in the Youth Justice teams and together they provided a flexible, accessible service which young people and their parents appreciated. Agency B ran a special programme for young offenders, providing those who had missed a lot of schooling with some of the basic skills needed to obtain and hold a job. A range of methods were used including group work, activities and individual counselling.

Befrienders/Outreach

A befriender is an adult who takes a special interest in a young person, normally engaging in enjoyable activities to gain co-operation and trust. This role can be taken by a volunteer or someone employed partly or mainly for that purpose. When carried out by staff from a residential base and with a residential care background, then it is named 'outreach'. One of the areas in Agency A has an outreach team working from one of its residential units, but otherwise befriending seemed to be available largely on an individualised and *ad hoc* basis.

Twenty people had been offered a befriender or outreach worker (all but two aged 15+) and two thirds of these had taken up the offer. Most of these were in Agency A, where half the sample had been offered befriending. In two of the agencies (D and E) nobody had received a befriending or outreach service, which in the case of Agency E reflects the policy that group work is the preferred form of assistance for teenagers. Normally the contacts had involved out-of-home activities like swimming, fishing, pool, ice-skating, canoeing and hiking. These were provided both to compensate for limited opportunities at home and as a means of gaining the youth's trust. In Agency A befriending was primarily available to young people in care, sometimes to help relieve the pressure on residential or foster carers as well as to benefit the young person. Elsewhere, befrienders also assisted young adults living on their own, but only a minority of people in that position were offered a befriender. Usually, group work and befriending appeared to be alternatives rather than combined, but eight teenagers had received both services.

Psychiatrists and Psychologists

Nearly one third of the sample had been offered the chance to see a psychologist or psychiatrist and one quarter of the sample had actually done so. Most commonly this meant an educational psychologist or a psychiatrist specialising with children and adolescents. A few people had been referred to drug or alcohol counsellors. Some teenagers had been referred by a court. A small minority had wanted to see a psychiatrist or psychologist of their own accord, because they were frightened and puzzled by their own behaviour. One went 'because of my temper. It's really bad and I don't know what comes over me'. Another said 'I was cracking up'. A few youngsters who had experienced sexual abuse or rape had been referred for therapy.

Mostly psychologists carried out assessments in relation to schooling or behaviour difficulties, psychiatrists worked with individuals or families together and specialist counsellors offered individual or group work. Frequently contact was quite brief, either because the main task was assessment or because the teenager/family stopped attending.

The proportion of young people who had actually seen a psychologist or psychiatrist ranged from 13% in Agency E to 36% in Agency C and 50% in Agency D, although here information was available about only 8 cases. Nearly all were aged 14–16. Half of the girls had been referred, but only one third of the boys, with the result that slightly more girls had been seen, despite their considerably lower representation in the sample. It might have been thought that those with more psycho-social problems would be seen as in need of this kind of help, but as many with medium Rutter scores had been referred as those with high scores, whilst a few of the small number with low Rutter scores had also been referred.

Specialist Educational Services

Though education is not a social work service, it was a key aspect of the work with many young people to ensure that education was provided. School related problems were common. Approximately two thirds of young people in Agencies A, C and E had significant school related difficulties during the study year. We considered school problems to be significant if suspensions, exclusions, non attendance or other difficulties had led to the provision of specialist measures or to young people receiving no education for one term or longer. School problems could have wide repercussions. It was not unusual for social workers to attribute the success or failure of a placement in care to the availability of suitable education and some teenagers had been placed in residential schools because they did not attend school. Of the 97 young people who were still officially attending school at the first interview, 39 (40%) received some form of specialist education during the year.

All agencies operated within a policy framework which aimed to keep young people within main-stream schooling if possible. This principle was most clearly articulated in Agencies C and E where policies had been developed jointly between the Social Work and Education Departments and a joint administrative system set up so that responsibilities for pupils with difficulties might be appropriately shared. In contrast arrangements were much less formalised in the other agencies where social workers were often required to negotiated on an individual basis with school managers and boards of governors.

A variety of resources were provided for specialist education within and outwith mainstream schools. In Agencies C and E there were day units run jointly by Education and Social Work staff. Specialist services provided within the mainstream school included attendance at school based units, provision of a support teacher or after school classes. The range of specialist services was more limited elsewhere. The specialist educational services taken up by the teenagers during the year included:

- home tutors providing individual tuition;

- day specialist education (within or outwith a mainstream school);
- day units within residential schools;
- residential schools run by local authorities;
- independent residential schools.

In addition some children's units provided temporary schooling on the premises.

The extent of provision varied between authorities, most notably between Agencies A and E. Although the level of school problems was similar in both authorities, half the young people in Agency E, but less than a quarter in Agency A had received some form of specialist education. In Agency E nine young people had boarded at a specialist school and five had attended a specialist unit on a day basis. Only two young people had residential school placements in Agency A and a further 3 received the services of a home tutor for a few hours each week while living at home or in care. Some residential units provided schooling on the premises and this had provided temporary education for two young people. It seemed that the higher level of service provision in Agency E may have helped prevent long term absence from education. While a similar number of young people in each of these authorities had 'significant' school problems, the proportion who had received no or virtually education for a year or more was 10% in Agency E and almost 50% in Agency A.

Combinations of Services

The services described so far were the individual components of the care programmes provided for each teenager who took part in the study. Variation in both young people's circumstances and resource provision ensured that each package of care was unique. However it was possible to divide the sample into three groups according to whether young people only received a social work service while in care, had experience of both care and supervision during the year or were only supervised while living at home. We shall consider briefly the pattern of service provision for each of these groups.

Care Only

Over half the 36 young people in this group had placements solely in residential care, a sixth had only been in foster care and the remaining 30% had experience of both. One quarter had lived in 3 or more placements during the year. Additional services had been provided for 40% of the group, though the proportion increased to two-thirds among young people who had had three placements or more over the year. The most extensive use of additional services for young people in care was in Agency A, usually in the form of outreach or befriending. During the year 15 (43%) of the school age teenagers in the 'care only' group had received their education in a residential school or with a home tutor.

Supervision and Care

Of the 55 young people who started the year on supervision, 12 were admitted to care during the year. Conversely 24 young people were supervised at home after leaving care. Thus a total of 36 teenagers had experience of both care placements and home supervision during the year. Three quarters of them had only one placement in care and only one person had more than two. Experience of residential care predominated, though seven had only been in foster care and three had had experience of both.

The highest uptake of additional services was by young people in the sub-group experiencing care and supervision. Of this group, fourteen school age teenagers (45%) had received specialist education, though for two this involved only short term teaching in the school of a residential unit. Overall two thirds received group work, befriending or specialist support, the highest proportion (80%) being in Agency A. Sometimes these additional services were provided in an attempt to avoid care but they might also be offered while in care or constitute after care support. Supervision offered support in the transition to independent living for six of those who moved out of care.

Supervision Only

Over a third of the young people in the sample had no experience of care placements but were supervised for the whole year while living at home. Some young people were on 'alternative to custody' schemes, in which case, social work supervision was one part of a clearly defined programme including group work, activities and befriending. For over half supervision involved only contact with a social worker. Others used additional services as follows:

attendance at a group	8
befriending/outreach	2
befriending/outreach and a group	2
service from psychologist or psychiatrist	3
group and psychologist or psychiatrist	3

Thus almost half of supervisions involved at least one service in addition to contact with a social worker. Group work was a common feature of supervision in the community, particularly in Agency E where it was taken up by half the young people in this category. Though befriending/outreach was widely available in Agency A for young people in care it was included in the supervision programme of only three of their twelve young people who were supervised at home all year. Only 9 (30%) of school aged young people on supervision attended a specialist educational resource.

Movements During the Year

While the provision of a particular service could be crucial, social work intervention was not necessarily a major influence on the course of a young person's life throughout the year. Some young people moved house, changed carers or left school with only passing reference to a social worker. We were keen to have a picture of this wider experience in order to have some appreciation of the context in which the various services had been provided. At the follow-up stage we obtained information from the social worker about all the moves young people had made during the year. Inevitably there was some degree of flexibility in defining a 'move' for teenagers who were going backwards and forwards between various addresses and some short or over-night stays were likely to have been overlooked. Nevertheless it was clear that frequent changes were a feature of many young people's lives.

By the time they were followed up, two-thirds of the young people had moved from where they were living when the study began. In the majority of cases the young people who moved did so once or twice, but 30% had 3 or more moves during the year. Exceptionally, one social worker carefully recorded 14 moves for a 16 year old youth and in 4 cases the full number of moves was not known. There were no overall differences amongst the 5 agencies between those who moved and those who did not, but more young people in Agency A moved 3 or more times. The majority of moves for young people who moved once or twice were related to care situations – admission, discharge or new placement. Subsequent moves increasingly took place more often among those living in the community but the numbers became quite small. However, a few of the most mobile teenagers ran the risk of going (back) into care after doing the rounds of family, friends or other types of residence in the community.

Inspite of all the difficulties which had led to contact with Social Services, living at home with a parent provided a better chance of continuity of residence during the year than placements in care. Even so, more than half of the young people who were living at home at the start of the study moved away during the year, although some returned and 72% were resident with a parent at follow-up. The temporary nature of much residential care is emphasised by the fact that only 16% of teenagers stayed in the same unit throughout the year and nearly three-quarters were living in other types of residence at the end of the year. While foster care remained stable for only a quarter of the young people placed there at the beginning of the year, two-fifths were still in this type of placement a year later. Nearly two thirds of the young people in residential schools were still resident there at the end of the year but half of those who remained there had spent a substantial period of time on home leave.

Attempting to chart the reasons for the various moves was complex and the list grew longer with each subsequent move however much we tried to summarise the reasons. For example, when we listed the 5 main reasons for the young people's first move, which accounted for 86% of first moves, we found that these reasons only covered 59% of second moves and 54% of third moves (Table 4:3).

Table 4:3 Five main reasons for moves during the year

Reason for move	1st Move N	2nd Move N	3rd Move N
return home from care	19	8	5
rejection by parents or family	15	9	4
new placement in care	13	3	1
breakdown of placement	12	6	3
independence	8	0	0
	67	26	13
(% of all moves)	(86)	(59)	(54)

The unsettling effects of criminal behaviour became more apparent as the total number of moves increased. Thus, among those experiencing a first move, 4% of moves were because of sentence, remand or release. Of those with a second move, 7% were related to court appearances. By a third move, 25% were determined by the courts. Although there were no new second or third moves into independence, some of the young people living independently had to move elsewhere because they could not cope or were subjected to harassment. Each time there were a few moves which were to new addresses with no other 'cause' and also some 'respite' moves to a temporary address.

Rowe et al (1989) commented that a straight counting of moves was 'potentially misleading' as it did not take into account the differences between 3 nights in a Children's Home and a move after a long-term foster home breakdown. We therefore examined the length of time the young people who moved spent in each place before moving on. It was evident when comparing young people who moved 3+ times with those with 1–2 moves that the more mobile group spent a shorter time at their original residence. At the follow-up less than a quarter of those who moved 3+ times had lived in their current place of residence for more than 3 months compared with 69% of those moving less frequently. This was not related to the type of place where they were living.

Routes through Care and Supervision

At the start of the year 61 young people were in a care placement and 55 were being supervised while living outwith the care system. For the majority the first placement or service was only the first element of the care package for the year. In addition to examining the services which had been provided we were keen to understand the process through which young people had moved into new situations or gained access to specific services. It was not feasible to consider each episode and transition in detail; instead we considered the circumstances in which the first placement or period of supervision had ended, indicating where the young person moved to at that point. We then moved on to the end of the year and reviewed the position at the time of the second interview. Table 4:4 indicates the distribution, according to agency, of placements at home or in care at the start of the year:

Table 4:4 Placements at the initial interview

Type of Placement	Agency A	B	C	D	E	Total
Foster care*	6	0	8	1	2	17
Residential unit**	8	3	9	7	4	31
Residential school***	1	0	6	0	6	13
Supervision at home	18	5	11	2	19	55
Total	**33**	**8**	**34**	**10**	**31**	**116**

* Includes one private fostering and one placement with family friend as a condition of Children's Hearing Supervision Requirement.
** Includes one placement in a psychiatric unit for assessment
*** Includes two secure placements

In terms of age the distribution was as follows:

Table 4:5 Age distribution according to placement at the start of the year

Age	Supervision	Residential unit	Residential school	Foster care	Total
13–14	22	10	8	11	51
15	17	12	4	3	36
16–18	16	9	1	3	29
Total	55	31	13	17	116

In each age group the majority of young people were being supervised while living at home. The proportion increased with age, with 43% of the youngest but 55% of the oldest age group starting the year living in the community. Similarly, only a fifth of young people aged 13–14 were in a residential unit compared with a third of teenagers aged 15–18. In contrast, 13–14 year olds took up two thirds of placements in foster care and residential schools, though this age group accounted for less than half the sample.

Young People who were in Care at the Start of the Year

There were 34 boys and 27 girls in care placements at the start of the year. Of the young women, nine were in foster care as were eight of the young men. All but three of the foster placements (82%) were in Agencies A and C. Social workers indicated that the main difficulties which had made admission to care necessary were:

family based difficulties	45%
young person's behaviour	39%
school related difficulties	16%

Several young people had faced more than one type of difficulty.

The Continuing Placements

A year later, 15 (25%) of the 61 young people who were initially in care remained in the same placement. The 15 placements which had lasted the whole year were:

foster placements	3
residential unit	5
residential school	7

Of those who remained in the original placement all year, 11 were boys and only 4 girls. This in part reflects the fact that the residential school placements lasted longer and were generally for boys. According to social workers, in only three instances was the continuation of the placement contrary to the original plan, though in another three the planned duration of the placement had not been clearly defined at the initial interview. When placements had been unexpectedly extended the social workers gave sound reasons for this, for example that the young people had not been ready to move on as the original plan had envisaged. They indicated that the plan had been delayed for good reason rather than altered or prolonged simply by drift and did not attribute the extension to lack of resources. Nor did they consider that the young people's future prospects had been adversely affected by the change in the plan.

When asked what factors had helped sustain the placements, social workers most commonly cited the relationship between the young person and carer(s) as the key to the placement's success. This was true across the three placement types. At the initial stage it had been anticipated that 9 residential and 12 foster placements would last for the whole year. Of these placements only two residential and three foster placements were in fact continuing so that only a quarter of each type had worked out as planned. In contrast, over 60% of residential school placements which had been expected to last were continuing. In some cases there was a planned reduction in the amount of time spent at school so that a few young people were spending as little as one night per week there.

The Completed Placements

The proportion of placements which had ended in the course of the year was approximately three-quarters in each agency. Residential schools were the most durable with only 6 of 13 placements having ended. In contrast 83% of the young people who were in other residential units or in foster placements at the first interview had moved on in the course of the year. Their destinations on leaving the first placement are indicated in Table 4:6.

We see that while only a third of the young people who left residential units returned to the parental home, this was the destination for all but one of the young people in residential school. This reflects the fact the teenagers in residential schools had more often been truanting or offending rather than in dispute with their families. Farmer and Parker (1991) also found that the families of young offenders were relatively stable.

Table 4:6 Moves from initial placements

Initial placement	Parent/ Relation	Foster Home	Destination Res. Unit/ school	Indep/ Supp. Accom	Custody	Total
Res Unit	9	3	6	7	1	26
Res School	5	0	1	0	0	6
Foster Home	6	4	3	1	0	14
Total	**20**	**7**	**10**	**8**	**1**	**46**

Twelve of the 20 returns to parents were planned moves home, the other eight occuring in haste, usually because the young person and/or their parents started to push for it. One young person decided he would be better off financially if he returned home from foster care and another family brought forward the return home because of the timing of a family holiday. Social workers thought that the young person's behaviour or attitudes had influenced almost half of the decisions to return home on a planned basis. This influence could be positive or negative. For example some young people were getting on better with their families or seemed more able to cope on their own while others simply wanted to leave care, though basic problems persisted. L. and his social worker both described the changes which had made return home possible for him:

> SW – 'The offending has stopped and behaviour at home is better. Life at home is much more settled – Father is not drinking and the family has moved house. This has reduced the risk of L. offending.'

> YP – 'I was doing good at school and in no trouble with the police.'

T's situation was an example of a return home for less positive reasons:

> SW – 'T. wanted to go home and his parents were prepared to have him. Staying on in care would probably not have made much difference. It had made little difference so far.'

> YP – 'There were too many restrictions in the Home and I got fed up . . . Too many rules like I was not allowed to do boxing or other self defence activities.'

> Parent – 'They (Social Services) were always too keen to have him home too soon. They always wanted to build up the time at

home much too quickly. In the end I said "well it [care] has been no help so far, we might as well give it a try [at home]".'

T's planned return home lasted only a few weeks and since leaving home he had been homeless or living with friends. Despite these difficulties, he had not returned to Social Services for help and no specific service had been offered. All but three planned returns home were from placements which were considered by social workers to have lasted as long as originally planned and/or as long as needed. However this did not necessarily imply that the young person was returning to an improved situation. A quarter of the placements which ended in a planned return home were considered not to have met the placement aims nor to have conferred any significant benefit. For 5 young people social work contact ended on returning to their home or to live on their own but the remainder had had some follow-up social work support.

While nearly two thirds of moves out of care were planned, this applied to less than half the moves to another destination within care. Approximately half the moves into foster care or independent living had been planned but only one of eight moves to a residential unit. Most moves to independent living were from residential units rather than foster care. The majority of *planned* moves within care were made on a positive footing with hopes that a foster placement would go well or that a step along the road to independence was a sign of progress. Other transfers were planned for administrative reasons, for example because the residential unit was closing or because the foster placement was time limited. Understandably young people viewed these moves less favourably.

In a third of cases the social worker believed the young person's behaviour or personal difficulties had prompted the move from the initial placement. However, in these instances, the young people often presented a different perspective, citing problems in their relationship with the carer. According to the social workers, difficulties in the relationship with previous carers had prompted a further third of transfers in care and all but one of these was from a foster home. Most of the young people agreed about this with the social workers.

Four of the seven moves into a foster family were made by young people already in foster care, in most cases because they and the original carer were not on good terms. The change of placement sometimes turned out to be very beneficial, though in other cases the young person regretted moving on. One young woman was very angry that she had been moved for administrative reasons from a temporary foster home she liked. In other cases, going along with the young person's wishes seemed to deprive the teenager of an opportunity to work on the problems which were causing the difficulties. Thus whereas J's social worker explained that she had been moved to a new foster home because she did not want to live with her sister and wanted to move closer to her father's home, J. herself, described the problem in terms of relationship and communication difficulties.

> 'I was not getting on with the foster mother. I was used to having responsibility for my younger sister [aged 4] and didn't like it when [other child in foster home] tried to take over with her. The foster mother didn't understand this.'

J. had been very unhappy in her second foster home, and when interviewed at the follow-up stage, was having little contact with her sister. She said she remained very mixed up about what had happened in her first placement.

The decision to transfer the young person to another placement often resulted from a combination of 'child' and 'resource' factors. It was sometimes acknowledged that the first placement had been unsuitable. Several social workers had recognised at the first interview that small children's units with low staffing levels could not be expected to give either the emotional support or structure which some young people needed. When disruptive behaviour resulted, the young person moved either to a more structured unit with more resources or to foster care. This occurred most often in Agency A. In other cases the expectation that the young person would benefit from short term care proved wrong. One young person persistently absconded from her first placement but settled quickly when transferred to a setting which provided nurturing rather than problem solving. Yet another move followed serious vandalism of a children's unit by the residents, most of whom were subsequently dispersed.

In almost two-thirds of completed placements the impetus to end the placement had come, at least in part, from the young person. However at the follow-up more than a quarter of the young people doubted whether this decision had been right. Not surprisingly there were regrets when subsequent foster placements proved worse than the first or returns home resulted in homelessness. However all but three social workers still believed the decision had been right.

Young People who were on Supervision at the Start of the Year

By the end of the year 23 (42%) of the 55 young people who were being supervised while living at home were no longer in regular contact with a social worker. This included 6 who had moved into forms of independent living. Supervision continued throughout the year for 20 (36%) while 12 (23%) were admitted to care. However six of these twelve were back at home at the follow-up stage.

Significant family problems were faced by virtually all the 12 young people who entered care during the year and in several instances social workers also cited offending or drug abuse as reasons for the admission. Services such as group work or outreach had been provided for them all to help avoid admission to care but this preventive approach had not been successful. Although in general we found that young people received limited support from the extended family, for a few the opportunity to have a short 'time out' period with relatives had been very important in helping prevent entry into care. Some relatives and friends had provided very useful short-term respite and on occasion had accommodated young people on remand. Young people who were supervised in Agency C were much less likely to be admitted to care during the year than teenagers being supervised in the other authorities. Only one of the twelve admissions was in Agency C. We provide information later on the combinations of services likely to be most effective with those on supervision.

The End of the Year (all cases)

At the end of the year, the circumstances of young people who had spent at least part of the year in care were very varied. Of the 44 who had started the year in residential care, 17 remained in some form of residential care, and 3 were in foster care. One young man's care was shared between a residential school and foster home throughout the year and another was in custody. Eleven of the original residential care group had returned to live with parents or relatives while the remaining twelve were in some form of independent living. This ranged from the relative security of having one's own tenancy to temporary arrangements which included living in Bed & Breakfast accommodation or with friends. Of the 17 young people whose year started in foster care, 6 remained in a foster placement, 4 were in residential care and 5 had returned to live with their parents. The remaining 2 were in a form of independent living. Half the twelve entrants to care during the year were back at home at the follow-up stage, 4 were in residential care and one in foster care. One young man was in custody. Thus of the 73 young people who spent at least part of the year in care, almost half (35) remained in care at the end of the year. A further 22 had returned to live with their parents or other adult relatives and 14 were in some form of independent living. Two young people were in custody.

As might be expected, age was an important influence on where the young person ended the year. Whereas three quarters of young people aged 13–15 remained in care at the end of the year, only two fifths of 16 year olds and one young person aged 17 were in this category. Similarly, while three quarters of 16 year olds were living with their parents or relatives at the follow-up stage, only a third of those aged 17 were still at home. Interestingly, for those aged 16 and over, the proportion living with parents was the same among young people who had spent part of the year in care and those who had been supervised in the community. Almost half the 26 young people in the sample who moved to independent living did so from supervision which highlights the need for preparatory schemes for those on supervision. Only one young person had recently been in foster care and the rest came from residential units.

The fact that teenagers have the option to move to independent living introduces a dimension to work with teenagers which is not present in work with younger children. We conclude this chapter on services by examining how young people were helped prepare for living independently then were offered support in the early stages of setting up home on their own.

'Independent Living'

There are obvious grey areas in what constitutes independent living because of the diversity of semi-independent provision and the fact that few teenagers will be completely self sufficient. Indeed the term 'interdependent' is now preferred by some, indicating that young people living alone still need to be part of a support network (Aldgate *et al*, 1989). However the phrase 'independent living' has become so entrenched in practice that it seems necessary to adhere to it. Our definition of 'independence' was that the young person had left what was seen to be their 'permanent' household, including local authority care, and moved either to a separate home as a tenant, joined a relative other than a parent, or went to live with friend(s).

A number of previous studies have drawn attention to the needs of young people leaving care and without a social base to return to. Attempts to set themselves up independently with or without social services support have run into many difficulties, often ending in failure and further disappointment (Stein and Carey, 1986; Garnett, 1992). The plight of some young people leaving care has been linked to subsequent homelessness, offending and general poor management of their situation. Though young people in the general population normally choose to leave home when they feel ready, young people who are involved with social services often have independence thrust on them either by their families or the local authority who have been responsible for their care.

No single agency is responsible for providing a total service to young people trying to set themselves up independently. The Social Services (Social Work) Departments have certain responsibilities particularly towards young people who have been in their care. The Children Act 1989 (England and Wales) imposes a duty on local authorities to advise, assist and befriend children they ceased to look after, whether returning home or living independently. Some of the assistance may be in kind or exceptionally in cash, but this is left to the discretion of the local authority. The Children Act 1989 Guidance and Regulations (Department of Health, 1991–92) also states that 'each SSD should provide a written statement of its philosophy and practice on the preparation of young people for leaving care and the provision of after care support. It is a requirement of paragraph 1(2) of schedule 2 that each local authority must publish information about services provided by them under section 24'. In addition to providing a written policy statement to care leavers, each SSD 'should provide an easy to read guide to its services for young people when they leave care' (Department of Health, 1991).

If a number of criteria are fulfilled, the local authority Housing Department is responsible for providing accommodation. The Children Act 1989 (England and Wales) gave local authorities powers to provide for young people up to the age of 21, even if they have not previously been in local authority care. The present position in Scotland is less favourable than in England and Wales, but new proposals aim for greater parity. Young people leaving care may also qualify for local authority accommodation under housing legislation, if considered both 'homeless' and having 'priority need' because they are 'vulnerable' (Bannister et al, 1993). The Code of Guidance advises that young people who have left local authority care may be considered vulnerable if they have no one to support and assist them. It also provides that the housing authority should where appropriate co-operate with social work departments in assessing vulnerability.

Formal, corporate arrangements between Social Services (Work) and Housing Departments did not exist in the agencies covered in this study. One authority gave general priority to single homeless people, including those who have been in care, but this policy was recently abandoned. In another of the agencies, the supported accommodation team had an informal arrangement with their local housing department, which managed to house six of the seven young people featuring in the sample. Besides council housing, some young people were living in rented accommodation or with friends, including three who were living with partners. Some were still waiting in the hope of securing local authority housing. A number of young people when faced with a housing crisis would go to live with a friend or relative such as an aunt or a sibling, but this only worked for a short while. Relations and friends proved to be a source of support during a crisis or emergency, but on the whole they were not a long term solution.

The Department of Social Security provides a limited range of benefits, mostly discretionary, particularly for those aged 16–18. Employment agencies and training schemes are also frequently involved as so few young people have jobs. There is no evidence that these various departments and services co-ordinate their work in relation to young people. Setting up home requires a range of skills and competencies which young people may need to acquire quickly. These include securing and maintaining accommodation, managing money and dealing with agencies such as Gas and Electricity suppliers. Some young people may need to learn to cook for themselves or wash their own clothes and to cope with all of this while building up new relationships with partners or friends.

Preparation for Independence

Social services departments have a number of schemes for training young people towards independent living. These can vary from specially designed activities within the residential establishment where a young person lives, to a move to an adjacent or distant 'hostel'-type accommodation where the whole emphasis is on skill development as a preparation for independent living. For others still this task may be delegated to foster carers, community carers or landladies. More recently, one agency in the present study has developed what it describes as a 'through care programme' which is meant to involve more explicit preparation for adulthood. This includes providing support and after care from specialist workers. Less clear is what is being done for those on supervision in the community who may require such training because their home situation indicates that a move to independent living might be necessary.

Social workers estimated that, compared to other young people of the same age, six out of ten of these young people could look after themselves from quite well to very well and only about one third could not do so. Many of them were seen as having improved in this respect over the year and only two got worse. At the same time 44 per cent were still seen as requiring help now or in the future to develop more practical skills such as cooking and budgeting. Social workers identified a much higher proportion of girls in the relevant age group as being prepared for independent living than boys. Forty one young people identified themselves as requiring some form of preparation for independent living.

Table 4:7 Preparing young people aged 15 and over towards greater independence

Amount of Preparation	Social Workers' Responses		Young People's Responses	
	N	%	N	%
Steps taken	45	48	8	9
Not tackled yet	19	21	33	39
Not an issue	27	29	43	51
Other	2	2	1	1
Total	93	(100)	85	(100)
Not asked	2			

Social workers said that for 45 (48%) out of a total of 95 young people aged 15 or over at the time of the follow-up interviews, steps had already been taken to prepare them for independence. For another 19 (21%) the matter had not been tackled yet and for 27 (29%) it was not seen as an issue (Table 4:7). There was a big discrepancy between the percentages identified by social workers as being prepared for independent living and what the young people themselves said. While social workers said that 45 young people were being prepared, only 8 young people, six males and two females, confirmed this. It seems that either programmes were not working in accordance with the arrangements social workers had made or else they operated in an informal way which young people did not recognise as 'preparation'.

The 8 young people who did acknowledge having been prepared for independence said this had been provided by key workers/residential staff, social workers, one foster carer and a Housing Association worker. Four of these young people were also attending a preparatory group or class. Half of them were expecting their worker to keep in regular touch but the rest were uncertain. Preparation involved:

> 'lots of cooking'; 'manage budget';
> 'help around the house'; 'taught how to iron';
> 'help us manage money – just getting us ready'.

Two thirds of the young people were said by social workers to be helped mainly by residential staff within existing units or foster homes whilst 13 (or 29%) had been moved on to specialist schemes or units. Preparation varied from the planned to the informal. The more planned approach was carried out mainly in separate 'independence units' or attached to existing residential establishments, in separate flats, or what were called 'steps to independence' projects. Specialist units were not very common, but where they existed the emphasis was on cooking, ironing, domestic chores and budgeting. Where the preparation was left to mainstream residential establishments it seemed to be less organised and less planned. Though mention in both types of preparation was made of practical skills, there was little reference to the kind of survival skills young people needed like making friends, applying for jobs, or avoiding HIV/AIDs. These may have been part of the specialist units' package, but neither social workers nor young people made reference to them. For those in foster care there were no special programmes but reliance was placed on foster carers preparing the young person for independent living. This was typified in comments such as:

> 'foster carers to help him develop skills';
> 'foster placement involves preparation';
> 'foster carers introduced him to handling bills,
> budgeting and saving'.

An apparently successful arrangement was that of a foster carer who owned a second house next to their main dwelling and rented flats to young adults whom they had fostered. The young people lived on their own but with foster carer support available, if needed.

In over half the cases which they identified as involving an eventual move to independence, social workers anticipated that the people helping the teenagers to prepare for independence would keep in touch with them after they had moved on. When all those young people who saw themselves as requiring some preparation for independent living were asked to say who they expected to help them find somewhere to live, a third of them expressed the hope that their social worker would help and a small number referred to Housing Associations. Almost one in every five expected a parent or relative to help but equally about a fifth did not know who might help.

With respect to the study sample, Agency C was claiming to be doing more preparatory work with young people in the relevant age groups, compared to the other agencies. Agency A identified itself as having the highest number of young adults where this need had not been addressed, followed by Agencies E and B. Young people looked after by Agency A agreed with their social workers in stating that their training needs for independence had not been adequately addressed. However a large percentage from Agency C were also of this view even though this agency claimed to be addressing these issues. Two of the sample agencies were closing down their specialist units preparing young people for independence. The intention was to integrate this task within generic type units. Yet it was within specialist units that, according to the young people, preparation was most consistent.

Support to Teenagers already Living Independently

At the follow-up stage, 26 young people were or had been living independently of their primary families. Over three quarters of these young people were in the age group of 17–18. Half of them were from single parent households (50%), another 36% from reconstituted and the rest from intact families. Over half of them were living alone, but about a third were living with peers. Girls were far more likely than boys to be living on their own. Approximately two fifths of the young people had stayed in the same accommodation since independence, about a quarter had moved once and the remaining third had moved two or more times. One young person returned to live with her parents because of the accumulated debts and harassment, and she was about to give up her local authority tenancy. Some of the difficulties faced by these teenagers and their views about trying to live on their own are considered in Chapter 6.

Social Work Support: Social work support varied considerably from being a highly valued life-line to almost non-existent. One sample agency agreed that once young people were given keys to their tenancies they were left to fend for themselves. There was generally no follow-up and no support. In another agency consistent follow-up or occasional follow-up depended on the workload of the area team. A number of young people, particularly in Scotland felt that the 'system' wanted to get them off their hands. On the positive side were social workers who would visit regularly, sometimes taking the young person out for coffee, a meal, going shopping, helping to sort out debts, or simply talking. Where there were money problems, social workers might provide some extra cash or other practical help but availability depended on the individual social worker and agreed practice within a particular agency or district. This variation in practice was acknowledged in discussion with managers. At other times social workers would get in touch with the DSS or fuel agencies to prevent disconnections on the promise of money to be made available.

Gaps and Deficiencies in Resources

a At the Start of Intervention

In relation to other client groups, the idea that assessment and planning should be 'needs-led' rather than 'resource-led' has now become so familiar it is almost a cliché. Yet, as we have noted in this chapter, few care packages were co-ordinated and planned in advance. More often the precise nature of service provision depended on resource availablity. Too often, very few options were available for consideration, especially when it came to placements away from home. At both the initial and follow-up stages, we obtained specific information about resource availability.

In the first round of interviews we asked about the resources available to social workers for responding to the problems and needs presented in the particular case under consideration. At this stage, many indicated that the resources had been adequate, but just under half reported difficulties in obtaining suitable resources. This frequently meant either inadequate placement options or else delayed access to a specialist agency:

- no placement locally;
- placement found was 'last resort' or only identified after much time and effort;
- no foster home available;
- low priority for a psychiatric clinic;
- problems in arranging special education or home tutoring;
- limited nature and duration of group work;
- absence of services at week-ends;
- no transitional setting for care leavers.

Even when a suitable placement or resource was found (and some considered this was largely a matter of luck), there could still be additional resources which might have been useful so somewhat more social workers mentioned things they would have liked to have access to:

- *home-based:*
  rehousing of parent or carer,
  more suitable school,
  activities in the community,
  drop-in centre,
  group work,
  outreach/detached workers;

- *care-based:*
  family placement,
  residential school,
  behavioural treatment,
  crash pad (for 'cooling off' outside the care system);

- *either care or home-based:*
  special day education,
  intensive IT,
  family therapy/psychiatry;

- *in relation to leaving care/independence:*
  money,
  befriending scheme,
  better training and work opportunities,
  caring landlady,
  baby-sitting.

The resources identified as desirable but lacking ranged from crucial to incidental. One worker described how the girl's unhappiness and deterioration at school were due to the lack of a local foster home or children's unit. Quite often it was a delay in obtaining resources which prolonged the young person's problem or uncertainty. Several workers in more than one authority bemoaned the difficulty of finding foster placements for teenagers at the point of reception into care and pointed to bullying, stresses and delinquent influences in residential establishments. Delays did not always concern family placements, however. One worker regretted the 3-month wait for a place in the local assessment/treatment residential unit. Whilst many would have preferred a less institutional setting if available, two workers thought that gradually going up the scale of restrictiveness had been counter-productive and that an earlier move to secure accommodation would have made the young person's oppositional behaviour less entrenched.

When workers wanted more access to community-based preventive options, their ideas were usually circumscribed by agency norms. They usually asked for services which were already quite common in their own agency, but not available in that area or for that child. In other words, they wanted extended coverage of a resource they were familiar with. Only rarely did they consider different kinds of provision used more in other agencies. Thus staff in Agency E were inclined to ask for intensive IT groups, which is that agency's favoured resource for those at severe risk of removal from home, although its geographical availability is restricted. This highlights the fact that such services need to be local and easily accessible. In Agency A, workers were more inclined to mention the more individualised outreach and activity-based work which is common there, although preventive group work was also mentioned. One worker remarked that preventive group work had stopped since the establishment of juvenile justice teams with an emphasis on diversion, yet such a group would have been helpful.

Given the high incidence of school-related problems, it is not surprising that the main resource difficulties outside the SSD/SWD concerned education. Commonly there was a need for non-residential schooling with approaches which differed from mainstream school where the teenagers had failed to cope.

Carers were also questioned about needs which the placement could not meet. The principal deficiency of residential placements was seen to be the absence of a family atmosphere or individual attention:

> 'we can't be P.'s natural family';
> 'a real family surrounding and individual caring';
> 'family – love, togetherness, belonging, continued care
> after placement ends';
> 'a home atmosphere and parental controls and affections'.

One fifth of the residential staff argued that the teenager they were concerned with would have been better placed in a foster family placement, if it had been available. Other provision which carers thought would have been helpful included – referral to psychologist or psychiatrist; better staffing in the unit; more local activities; an independent living group.

b *Resource Issues During the Year*

In the follow-up interviews we did not ask a specific question about gaps in resources, but the interviewers extrapolated information about weaknesses in provision from a range of answers across all 3 interviews. For young people living in the community, the main deficiencies were:

- group work not available;
- outreach/befriender not available or not considered;
- no special day schooling;
- lack of employment;
- no after-care planning or follow-up.

The most frequent problem in relation to placements away from home was distance from the young person's home. Next most common was the limited choices of placement, including the small chance of obtaining a foster placement. We explored the factors affecting placement choice in some detail in our second interviews, since we were aware from the initial stage that alternative placements were seldom available. According to social workers there had been a choice of placements in only 20% of admissions and 42% of moves. Young people were even less aware of different options and only 10% said they had been offered an alternative placement.

Availability of resources was seen by social workers as influential in affecting placement choice with respect to 84% of placements; the young person's personal characteristics or needs were seen as important in two thirds and policy decisions in one third of placements. Other factors such as geographical considerations or the wish to keep all family members together were taken into account in a quarter of the placement decisions. Although availability of resources nearly always influenced placement choices, social workers rated the personal characteristics of the young person as the most important consideration in 63% of decisions and availability of resources in only 47%. In only 15% was agency policy rated as most important.

The thinking by the social worker which had gone into C.'s placement illustrates the combined effects of these key factors:

> *Personal*: 'C. had disclosed abuse and needed a
> supportive, protective placement to work through
> the consequences of that for herself.'
> *Availability of resources*: 'I became aware of a foster-
> carer who was just right. This availability was
> fortuitous.'
> *Agency policy*: 'Agency policy would have pushed in
> the opposite direction, more towards independent
> living. Requesting foster care for a 16 year old was
> almost against agency policy but was seen as
> necessary in this case.'

Deficiencies in substitute care resources varied among agencies. While in Agency A there could be delays of up to several months for a placement in their more specialised Children's Centres, in Agency E there was a particular scarcity of foster placements, even for young people for whom a family was the obvious choice. An example was N. whose social worker explained why foster care would have been ideal but was not provided:

> 'At the start he was no problem – there was no indication that he
> needed residential care but there were no families for him. To
> seriously pursue the application is pointless – it only exposes him

to the risk of further disappointment because the chance of finding a family is virtually non-existent.'

[N.'s behaviour had seriously deteriorated while in residential care.]

By comparison with the other two main agencies, social workers in Agency E referred less to the personal needs of young people and more to agency policy when explaining constraints on placement choices. This is consistent with the fact that in Agency E there were clearer policy guidelines and more management monitoring of decisions. However there was no indication that young people in Agency E were less happy about decisions than their counterparts in other agencies. The majority in each agency were in favour of the decision, though most also felt they had little option.

Other difficulties identified in relation to placements were:

- failure to review reasons for placement breakdown;
- unqualified staff out of their depth;
- lack of support worker for foster carers;
- lack of specialist help for suicidal repeat absconder.

A few workers noted that intervention had come too late. Failure by Education and Social Services to agree had meant that one teenager lost several years schooling. Several repeated that the absence of resources to handle people with school problems (eg day units) had necessitated placement away from home.

Similarly, now and then it seemed that in retrospect there had been too great an emphasis for too long on keeping the young person at home. The intention of preventing family break-up had only served to defer breakdown or make problems worse. In one case a psychiatric assessment had recommended removal from home some years earlier, but the child had been left at home and there were still major concerns. Another teenager was now doing well in residential school, but the social worker stated that a plan 'to keep her in the community at all costs' had led to 2 years wasted effort.

Occasionally the failure to reallocate a case when a social worker left caused difficulties. For instance, V. was unhappy about aspects of his placement and review plans, which was made worse by the fact that he had no worker to share his feelings with.

Summary

In this chapter we described the range of resources available and outlined their take up during the year. The movements and progress of young people during the year were also examined with particular reference to the factors which prompted change and influenced access to resources.

All young people in the study had a social worker for at least part of the year. Residential placements were provided in a range of settings which included small children's units, residential schools and secure accommodation. A total of 78 residential placements were experienced by 55 young people in the sample. Foster care was provided almost exclusively in Agencies A and C. Overall 27 young people had been placed with foster carers during the year. The total number of foster placements was 37 ie roughly one third of all placements away from home. In all 79 young people had been supervised while living at home for all or part of the year. In most instances supervision involved meeting with the social worker and contact with at least one other service.

Additional services were provided for young people living in care and at home. These included group work, befriending and referral to a psychiatrist, psychologist or other specialist service. Of those who were still of school age at the first interview, 40% had also received some form of specialist education. There was considerable diversity in agency provision with some favouring group work and others developing befriending or outreach services.

Frequent changes were a feature of many young people's lives. By the time they were followed up two-thirds of the young people had moved from where they were living when the study began. Despite all the difficulties with parents, living at home with a parent had provided a better chance of continuity of residence than placement in care. At the start of the year 61 young people were in a care placement. A year later 15 of them remained in the same placement. Almost half of those who had left the original placement had returned home, the majority on a planned basis. The others had moved on to other placements in care or into some form of independent living.

By the end of the year 23 of the 55 young people who started the year on supervision were no longer in regular contact with a social worker. This included 6 who had moved into forms of independent living. For 20 teenagers supervision continued throughout the year. Of the 12 who were admitted to care during the year, 6 had returned home by the follow-up stage.

Almost half the 26 young people in the sample who moved to independent living did so from supervision which highlights the need for preparatory schemes for those on supervision. Only one young person had recently been in foster care, and the rest came from residential units. Over half were living alone but about a third were living with peers. There was limited monitoring of preparation for independence to ensure that young people were equipped to cope on their own. It was often difficult to obtain suitable housing and there was little evidence of joint working between the various agencies involved.

We now move on to examine how the services provided were received and evaluated by the young people, their parents and social workers.

5 Participants' Views of Social Workers and Their Activities

Our attention turns now from the analysis of the nature of social work intervention to consider how this was evaluated by the consumers and providers of the service. We begin with the direct work of the social workers themselves. This will be followed in Chapters 6 and 7 by participants' perspectives on the services arranged by social workers but provided by others.

Views of the Social Work Role and Activities with Teenagers

Social Workers' Own Evaluations

Among other things, social workers were asked to assess the ways they had tried to help each family and to state which had been successful or not. The activities described as most successful were advocacy in legal settings, preventing care/custody and improving social relationships outside the family. Each of these had a clear majority of social workers saying they had succeeded when using that approach. All the other actions had only small differences in the numbers of workers who claimed to have been successful or unsuccessful in their efforts. For instance, in two thirds of cases the social workers said they had set out to help the young people get on better with their families. Half believed they had accomplished this and half admitted they had tried but failed. The tasks said to be least often successful were tackling offending, drug/alcohol abuse and employment.

Typically the degree of success was explained in terms of the responsiveness or resistance of the young person or parents. In particular, ineffectiveness was attributed to such things as unwillingness to take advice, hostility, inability to change, continued offending. Only occasionally was the insufficiency or inappropriateness of the input by the social services or social worker referred to. Effectiveness was described mainly in terms of outcomes, including greater understanding or self-confidence, successful return home, more independence and responsibility by the teenager.

In the main, workers seemed satisfied with their chosen approach to the case, since only one in ten said that with the benefit of hindsight they would have chosen a different way of working, whilst two thirds would not. The rest were unsure. Amongst the suggested changes were more structured/authoritative work and earlier placement in residential school or foster care.

Young People's Views on the Helpfulness of Social Work

In the follow up interviews young people were prompted by a list of social work activities to state which had been carried out successfully, unsuccessfully or not at all. Considerably more social workers were thought to have acted successfully than not. Substantial numbers of the teenagers reported success in each of the major social work roles – individual counselling; advocacy; mediation with family; practical assistance. Strikingly, in two thirds of the cases where it was an issue, the young people said the social worker had helped them stop offending – a remarkable level of success, given the pessimistic results of many evaluations of attempts to modify offending (McCord, 1990). Social workers themselves recognised lower success rates in this area. On the other hand, the teenagers largely concurred with social workers' opinions that they had least success with employment, addictions, fighting and tempers.

Fewer young people thought that their social workers had been helpful with the problems which led to intervention. A quarter each felt that the social worker had helped a lot, only a little, not much or not at all. Clearly most were not greatly impressed with the social workers' effectiveness in this respect. Of the teenagers who said that the social workers had helped a lot with their original problems, a disproportionate number were from Agency C:

Agency C	43%	Agencies B & D	36%
Agency E	15%	Agency A	10%

About 40% of the teenagers in Agencies A and E stated that the social workers had not helped at all or had made things worse.

When asked to explain their views about the helpfulness of social work, some young people simply described what had or had not happened, but others spoke in detail about the manner of social work intervention. Interestingly, the feature which was most commonly stated to be helpful was the social worker's counselling role – giving good advice, listening well, talking things over. Also important were practical assistance (which ranged from getting a flat to providing lifts to school) and family mediation.

When social workers had been seen as ineffectual, this was explained in terms of five main factors, only two of which related to qualities of the workers themselves:

infrequency of contact/lack of availability
young person's dislike or distrust of the worker
intractability of parents
resistance to change by the young person
young person changed by own efforts

About one in ten of the young people were at pains to emphasise that the problems were largely in their own hands – either they had sorted things out themselves or else they had carried on getting into trouble despite the social workers' attempts to change them.

Parents' Views on the Benefits to the Young Person of Social Work

Overall, just under half of the parents acknowledged that their son or daughter had benefited from seeing a social worker during the year, though not always substantially. Only three believed the social worker had made things worse, but the most common view was that the social work contact had made little or no difference. A quarter of those interviewed said the social worker had helped a lot. The pattern corresponded very closely to the teenagers' own opinions:

Table 5:1 How much had the young person benefited from seeing a social worker?

	Parents' View N=67	YP's View N=97
Not much difference/worse	52%	54%
A lot	25%	24%
A bit	22%	22%

In the main, parents and teenagers in the same family took broadly the same view. Hence the agency patterns were in line with each other. 70% of parents in Agency C thought that the young person had benefited from seeing a social worker, compared with fewer than 30% in Agencies A, B & D, with Agency E in between.

Several parents noted that it had been helpful for their son or daughter to have someone they trusted, could talk to or let off steam with:

'They've been a bit of a backbone for him.'
'She likes the social worker and can talk to her better than me.'

More than one confessed, though, that they did not know how the helping process had occurred:

'I know she had helped, I see an improvement in R., but I don't know what way she's done it.'

Sometimes, though, the benefits were described in terms of the whole family gaining something:

'The social worker has been good to us with our little problems.'
'The system has worked well for us.'
'We have become more of a family and I'm not under so much stress and strain.'

More specifically, one mother described how she had learnt to praise her daughter and show her greater affection.

In response to a check list, about two thirds of parents recognised positive things that the social worker had done to help. Just over one quarter of the parents interviewed said there had been help with each of – improving the young person's behaviour; school issues; family tensions; the young person's attitudes; the young person's maturity; arranging new activities (usually by referral to a group or outreach). Generally, the parents had found social workers helpful with more than one area, except that a number reported only arranging new activities. About two fifths thought the social worker had not helped in any of the key areas listed.

Parents said that a few social workers had helped encourage a youngster back to school, arranged home tuition or negotiated better arrangements in mainstream schooling, but just as many parents said that improvements in education resulted from placement in residential school or the commitment of foster carers. When parents felt that family tensions had been eased, this was also sometimes explained in terms of the young person having a break away from home. A few did acknowledge that they had modified their approach to the young person as a result of social workers' advice (eg by being firmer or making more allowances). A number of parents also recognised that their son or daughter had become more mature and a few of these definitely thought that talking to the social worker had helped.

Parents were asked to say what they would have liked social workers to do differently. Some replied that they were completely satisfied or that the workers had done everything they could. The most common wishes were for social workers to give parents themselves more attention and see things more from their point of view. Often they were simply wanting more contact, information and discussion, but in certain cases specific action was called for too, such as help with housing, finance, respite care. Some thought social workers should be more firm with the young people, but others felt that the worker had identified too strongly with their department or with carers rather than supporting the teenager.

Parents were mixed in their views about whether they personally got the help they wanted. Some were satisfied and a few thought they did not need help themselves. Others wanted more time, understanding or practical action. Mrs D. said it had really helped when the social worker enabled her to let off steam. Ms. F. appreciated help with debts which had been given attention independently of her son's difficulties. A few said they had benefited from a change in worker, so they had then received greater empathy or information.

The Quality of the Relationship between Social Worker and the Young Person

Overall Relationship

Most people like to be liked and it has been suggested that social workers are particularly prone to optimism when assessing their relationships with families (Mayer and Timms, 1970; Blom-Cooper, 1986; Fisher *et al*, 1986). When asked how the young person related to themselves *at the beginning of the year*, all but a handful of the social workers stated that they got on well (48%) or quite well (45%). Just two described the relationship as poor and a few others were uncertain. By and large, young people's own views confirmed the social workers' picture of mainly positive relationships, though a minority were more negative. Slightly under half reported getting on very well with their social worker but one in five said they did not get on very well or not at all – usually unbeknown to the social worker.

With very few exceptions, the same social workers or their successors continued to feel positively about their relationships with the young people they were working with *after a year* had gone by. The number describing the relationship as poor had doubled, but only to four. The others divided almost equally again between those stating 'quite well' or 'well'. Indeed, nearly half thought their relationship had improved over the year and only five thought it had deteriorated.

What evidence did they have after a year for these assessments of their relationships with the teenagers? Mostly they explained them in terms of the young person's communicativeness and attitude. They referred to such things as openness, willingness to listen, trusting with confidences. Another good sign was when the teenager always turned up to see the social worker as arranged. In some cases the young person had explicitly conveyed their positive feelings or demonstrated a wish for contact by frequently calling in uninvited. Some social workers observed that the teenager seemed more open or relaxed with themselves than with other people.

When social workers expressed reservations about the young person's relationship, they spoke of such things as superficiality, lack of motivation, lying or avoidance. Several also noted ambivalence. For example a few teenagers were known to resent the worker's authority or refusal to accede to every demand, but were also thought to respect the worker for not being too soft.

Regardless of their overall relationship, social workers stated what qualities of the young people had made them easy or difficult to work with. The responses corresponded closely with those expressed by carers in our self-completion survey at the start of the study. The characteristics which most commonly made the young person easy to work with were – pleasant manner, receptiveness to advice, open communication, sense of humour and intelligence. Conversely, obstinacy, uncommunicativeness, reluctance to change or listen and apathy were cited as reasons for difficulties in the work.

The majority of young people themselves reported in the follow up interviews that they had good relationships with their social workers:

Table 5:2 How did young people say they got on
with social worker? N=96

Very well	43
Quite well	34
Not very well	10
Not at all	7

In over half the cases, the two were in agreement about the quality of the relationship, but more than a quarter of the young people reported getting on worse than the social worker did, whilst in a few instances it was the teenager who was more positive.

There were no major differences amongst the agencies in these proportions. In Agency C, which had the poorest record at the start of the year, just over half the young people rated the relationship very good at the end of the year, which was more than in all the others except Agency D. One third of the females reported poor relationships compared with only one in nine of the males. Only a minority of the younger children said they got on very well with their worker, which may reflect the fact that more of this age group were supervised at home and so the relationship was less salient than for those living away from home. More young people related very well to their social workers when the arrangement was on a voluntary rather than statutory basis. The highest proportion getting on very well was in the group of care leavers. Perhaps their greater maturity and the paucity of other close supports accounted for this.

There was good correspondence between the teenager's personal relationship with the social worker and feedback about the impact of intervention. Over 90% of those who reported at the end of the year that the social worker had helped a lot with their original problems also said they got on very well with the social worker (and all the rest got on quite well). Likewise two thirds of those who rated the overall impact of social services intervention positively had got on very well. Of those who reported negative relationships with their social workers, three were nonetheless favourable about the intervention, largely because of positive placement experiences.

Qualities in Social Workers which Teenagers Liked

It was noteworthy that the young people mainly appreciated social workers who were doing things on their behalf (usually to improve their family/social environment) and paying attention to their views. This corresponds with the findings of studies of adult social work clients, who also value both positive action and feeling understood (Truax and Carkhuff, 1967; Rees and Wallace, 1982).

Many young people were pleased with their social workers. They could not always put into words why that was, but comfortable communication was usually central:

> 'I don't know what it is – I just like him . . . I can speak to him quite freely.'
> 'She's just easy to speak to.'

Feeling able to talk to social workers was clearly a crucial dimension by which they were judged. The contents of what social workers said were valued too:

> encouraging you
> saying helpful things
> telling you what was going to happen
> saying that offences are wrong

Popular social workers seemed to convey a commitment to the interests of the young person and a sense of fun. M. regarded his worker as being very much on his side – 'sort of a friend more than a social worker . . . Everything he's done, he's just trying to help me'. L. was similarly positive 'He's been a help just getting things that I need and just really understanding, because a lot of people just don't understand teenagers'.

Often the young people had already known several social workers and were able to contrast their styles and personalities. Respect and ease of communication were two key characteristics which were approved of. For instance, K. liked one man because 'he was actually an all right guy to talk to', but most of the others were seen as 'looking down at you'. H. valued his current worker who was interested in his progress and plans, to which she listened well, but the previous social worker 'didn't let us speak much, you know, she always cut us off'.

Social workers were also valued for having helped in practical ways eg to get a flat. Some appreciated their workers' protective/advocate role in a legal context by keeping them out of care (or jail in one case) and writing favourable reports. A change in circumstances, though, could modify how social workers were perceived. G. had changed her views about social workers since coming into care. Previously she had resented them as people called in by her mother and 'putting all the blame on me'. Now she was away from home, she saw the social worker as her own and someone to talk to without involving her mother.

Although personal liking for the social worker usually accompanied helpfulness, the two did not always go together. For instance, all of the young people on supervision who felt they had benefited from the intervention also had a good relationship with their social worker, but then so did some who felt they had not benefited. As one youngster put it – 'She was a nice person, but she didn't help things get better'. A few were like R., who was fond of her social worker as a person but felt neglected by her. She 'never comes to see me – maybe once a month'.

The same general approach could be seen as positive or negative by different youngsters. For example, some young people resented being told what to do or having the consequences of their behaviour pointed out. Others valued advice or said it was helpful to think through what would happen if they did not change. Presumably this depended on the attitudes of the young person and the communication style of the worker. R. described how 'he does not lecture you or say "You should do this or do that". He says "You may try this or that" '. He felt the social worker had been crucial in enabling him to stop taking drugs and keep out of trouble with the police.

Ability to Confide in Social Workers

In the first interviews when the intervention had just started, we explored with young people their ability to confide in social workers. It became clear that 'getting on well' did not always mean that the social worker was trusted with confidential thoughts and feelings.

Asked if they could confide in their social workers, the ones who said 'No' (54%) or were unsure (7%) outnumbered those who said 'Yes' (38%). There was a marked difference in the proportions who said 'Yes' to this question between Scottish (25%) and English agencies (56%). This may reflect the higher representation of statutory cases north of the border. Only two Agencies (A and D) had a majority of youngsters saying they would confide. At the opposite extreme was Agency C, where only 15% felt able to confide.

As might be expected, the teenagers who had been in care for some time and hence mostly had more developed relationships with social workers were more likely to confide in them (60%) than were those recently admitted to care or on supervision. Length of contact could foster trust, as in the case of J. whose social worker 'has been with us for years' and 'I really trust him – I think he's about the only person I really do trust'. It may be recalled that there were 26 social workers who were responsible for more than one teenager in our sample.

Several of these apparently had the trust of one, but not another, indicating that this was an interactive quality which might depend as much on the young person as the worker.

At the follow-up stage two thirds of the young people regarded their social worker as easy to talk to. Most of the rest found the worker difficult to talk to, though a few were unsure. Over 80% of teenagers in Agencies B, C and D found their workers easy to talk to, compared with half in A and 60% in E. When this is considered together with the pattern at the start of the study noted above, it seems that workers in Agency C had become far more trusted after a year, whereas elsewhere the reverse was sometimes true. Higher proportions of older teenagers found their social worker easy to talk to, which may reflect their greater skills and confidence. There was a good congruence between social workers' perceptions that they got on well with the young person and the latter's own appraisal of the worker's approachability:

Table 5:3 Relationship between social workers and teenagers

Easy to talk to (YP)	We Get on Well (SW)		
	Well	Quite Well	Not Well
Yes	85%	47%	33%
No	11%	50%	66%
Unsure/Varies	4%	3%	–

The teenagers were given the opportunity to say why the social worker was easy or difficult to talk to. They mentioned a wide range of qualities:

> **Social characteristics** – being young, of the same sex, having children
> **Communication** – listens, not pushy or critical, understanding
> **Attitude** – concerned, interested, respectful
> **Activities** – does things the young person enjoys
> **General manner** - easy-going, down to earth, friendly

Whereas some wanted a person they felt was like themselves as regards gender, interests, activities or life-style, others responded to an approach which showed empathy and commitment. Some described their social worker as 'like a friend'. Several were extremely fulsome:

> 'She's just great. I think of her like my Mum.'
> 'I don't know what it is, it's just the way she talks – she's brilliant.'

'The other social worker was good, but I never talked to him about what was going on at home. C. gets all that out. It's a help to me.'

The reasons for finding social workers difficult to talk to mainly centred on the young person feeling that the worker did not see things from their point of view, either because of lack of effort or a conflict in perspective:

infrequent contact
poor communication style
unreliable (breaks promises)
not interested
checks up/interferes
breaks confidences
doesn't listen

A few young people said they did not talk openly to anyone.

Dislikes and Complaints about Social Workers

Although over half were reluctant to confide in their social workers, considerably fewer teenagers admitted to actually disliking them – just over one in ten. Most of the social workers who were disliked would presumably have been surprised by this, as they claimed to be getting on well or quite well. It appears that a minority of workers overestimate the quality of their relationships with young people, although in some instances they may be discounting what they see as a more general resentment at authority figures. As with expectations, there is a need for better feedback to reduce the gaps in perceptions. In about half the cases where the social worker was disliked by the young person, the parents got on well or very well with the worker, so in relatively few cases was there shared hostility to the worker by parents and teenager.

There was a wider group of young people who made negative comments on their social workers. The most common criticism was simply to the effect that they were useless (one fifth of the sample). More specific complaints included not keeping confidences; not caring or listening; talking but not doing anything; nagging or threatening. A few simply disliked the fact of having a social worker at all. Although some whose own behaviour was the main focus of attention had come to appreciate being encouraged to take responsibility for their actions, others resented being blamed.

Among the more extreme disparaging comments was the statement by D. who had asked to change social workers because she saw her present one as 'just a big growler. She sits and goes on and on. She's just a bitch'. J. referred to his worker as 'a clown – I can't stand her'. His attitude to her was all of a piece with his generally aggressive manner towards adults (like the psychologist and IT worker) although he did praise his key worker and got on reasonably well with other staff in the unit. This demonstrates the value of having access to more than one adult helper.

Lack of trust and concerns about breaches of confidence were major considerations in some cases. One boy said he would not confide in his social worker in case she let it 'slip out' to his mother. Another remarked 'She blabs around'. A significant minority of young people complained about the infrequency of contact or lack of support from their social workers. This mainly applied to those living away from their parents. Some of those in care remarked that social workers did not come to see them often, came late or even did not turn up as agreed.

When youngsters in care were critical or even harsh, they often seemed to be wanting a much more peer-like relationship and not one in which they felt the worker was out of tune with youth or acting in a superior or autocratic fashion. H. expressed a not uncommon wish for someone younger – 'just somebody that knew the things we get up to'. Referring to a previous social worker L. identified his good points as not assuming a professional role – 'he was young and he wasn't like a social worker. He was like a friend'. Informal conversations and being taken out could aid the relationship. Gender might also be significant. B. had always known female workers and made it clear to the interviewer that 'I'd prefer a guy social worker' although he had never told his social workers of this preference. Although L. liked and trusted her social worker a lot, she admitted that there were certain things she could not discuss with him 'because he's a man'.

Comparisons of Teenagers' Perceptions of Social Workers and Other Professionals

These views about social workers may be compared with the information about how the teenagers felt about other professional helpers. At the start of the year we acquired data on adults important to the young people while compiling charts of their social networks. The inclusion of particular types of people depended on the young person's reports of whom they saw regularly:

Table 5:4 Teenagers' willingness to confide and dislikes in relation to important adults (other than social workers)

	Number seen regularly	% Can Confide in	% Dislike
Residential staff	31	81%	13%
Teachers/tutors	12	67%	–
IT/group & project workers	17	24%	6%
Psychologists & psychiatrists	27	12%	42%

Numbers are small, but Table 5:4 shows some interesting contrasts. The poor showing of psychologists is evident (see Chapter 6 for further details). To some teenagers, teachers were clearly important and well-liked confidants. Usually these were young people who had had considerable individual contact with a Head of Year or Guidance Teacher. H. contrasted her social worker unfavourably with her guidance teacher who was 'dead nice to talk to' and explained things carefully, whereas the social worker was seen as blunt. L. similarly felt more able to talk about private matters (like taking the pill) with her teacher, because she knew her much better. Other research has shown that it is usually more able students who confide in teachers (Galbo, 1986).

With a few exceptions, social workers were less important than other people in the teenagers' lives when it came to sharing serious personal issues like getting pregnant. When the young people were asked with whom they might discuss worries about sex, only 6 stated their social worker, whereas 8 nominated residential staff, 10 a doctor, 10 parents and 19 friends.

Another kind of comparison was carried out at the end of the year, when we gave each teenager sheets of words and phrases and asked them to circle those which applied to their social worker and, for those in residential care, key worker. Forms were completed by 94 young people, of whom 43 also had a key worker. The majority of young people circled mainly positive attributes for the two workers and the rank order of particular attributions was very similar for both. However key workers usually gained credit from an additional 10–20% of the sample compared with social workers.

The characteristics most frequently ascribed to social workers were general dispositions like friendliness and helpfulness. Four fifths were seen as friendly, as were nearly all key workers. Two thirds were deemed willing to listen, compared with over three quarters of key workers. Fewer teenagers depicted social workers as effective. Under half indicated that social workers 'gets things done' or 'gives you enough time'. Only one fifth indicated that the social worker 'Does what you want'.

The negative traits on our sheets which were most commonly circled for social workers related to availability and effectiveness – being too busy, forgetting promises and not getting things done. Even so, only a minority chose each of these. A fifth circled more personal criticisms like 'annoying' and 'interferes'. In general, slightly fewer young people assigned negative characteristics to key workers than to social workers. The exceptions were 'too tough', 'gets you into trouble' and 'never listens', although each of these was only circled by about one tenth of the respondents.

Just looking at responses about social workers, there was a tendency for a higher proportion of those aged 16 and over to be very positive about social workers. For instance, over half of them thought the social worker was 'good fun' compared with only one quarter of 15 year olds. Three quarters of the 17–18 year olds regarded their social worker as helpful. This may partly reflect the fact that more older people in the study were independent of their families and had a more direct relationship with the worker. Also at this age, there is less social pressure on social workers to encourage resistant young people to conform to adult expectations (eg about school). It was only amongst the 13–14 year olds that a majority saw the worker as not understanding young people nor giving them respect.

In other parts of the interview some teenagers compared their relationships with field and residential social workers. A few pointed out that residential carers had been more helpful on account of their availability or approach. J. asserted that she would go to residential staff before a social worker any day, because 'people can only help you if they really know you and you can't get to know someone if you only see them every couple of weeks'. V. saw social workers as *telling* you what to do, whereas residential staff *asked* what is the matter.

Group Consultation Findings

It was noted in Chapter 1 that we held group discussions in two of the same agencies with an entirely separate sample of 62 young people. They also filled in the self-completion questionnaires which we used later in the follow-up interviews of the main study. Reassuringly, these broadly supported the data from our main study (eg as regards what qualities of social workers were liked and disliked), but there were a few divergences. A higher percentage in the groups than in our interview sample appeared wholly negative towards social workers – just over one third. It may be that the groups contained more hostile youngsters than the main study or that peer influences in a group discussion encouraged bravado and expression of anti-authority feelings. In contrast to the main study, the most dissatisfaction was registered by those in residential schools. The groups also expressed much criticism of social workers' non-availability. Some explained this in terms of social workers having to help others, talk to many people or do a lot of paper work. However, some made dismissive references to them 'drinking tea', being on holiday all the time or sitting on their 'arses'. On the other hand, one third of the group participants were wholly positive about social workers and praised their helpfulness and understanding.

The forms used with the groups also included Intermediate Treatment workers and teachers. The former proved to be very popular like key workers, whereas teachers were the group who gained the most negative epithets – like 'boring' and 'annoying'.

The groups were presented with brief scenarios of problematic situations and asked who would intervene and who they would want to help. Mostly they did not expect social workers to get involved when there were conflicts with peers – that was a matter for friends, parents or police. Social workers were the most frequently cited people to intervene with domestic conflicts, however. In the main, it was thought social workers would and should mediate and try to reconcile the differences, but a few expected removal of the young person to be the actual or indeed preferred solution. Interestingly, friends were again often cited as relevant helpers in these situations and not simply as sources of trouble, which is sometimes the only way certain adults see them. There were individuals who saw teachers as sympathetic helpers who knew them much better than social workers and were easier to talk to. Conversely, some young people who were totally alienated from the education system were very hostile to teachers.

Parents' Relationships with Social Workers

Although a few parents had dissociated themselves from their children and the social workers, especially in cases where we did not have agreement to interview them, most of the parents we saw retained an active interest and wanted to be involved with the social work intervention. Parents usually viewed their meetings with social workers as an opportunity for discussion and sharing in an attempt to resolve the difficulties the young person was going through. They also wanted to obtain information about developments, have someone to express their emotions to and feel understood by. When this did happen it was experienced as supportive even if there was not much change in the young person's behaviour. Practical measures taken by the social workers were also valued. These could include arrangements for the young person to be involved in activities, arrangements with schools or housing. On the other hand a sizeable minority expressed frustration or disillusionment at the end of the year, because they felt their own views or needs had been largely ignored. A small group of parents wanted a social worker devoted to themselves, particularly to help with practical problems such as benefits, housing or other practical arrangements.

In the follow-up interviews, social workers usually reported that their relationships with parents were good, although frequently with qualifications, such as 'superficially', 'as well as can be expected', 'difficult to say'. Fewer said they got on very well with parents than did so with the teenagers. Quite often when there was statutory involvement, tension or resentment was reported, though sometimes this was thought to have diminished during the year or not to be focused on the worker personally. In several instances initially hostile parents were described as 'coming round' or 'accepting involvement now'.

In fact, more often than not parents were positive about their relationships with social workers, but nearly one in three were negative or equivocal. This was a higher proportion dissatisfied than amongst the young people. There had also been shift over the year towards more parents saying they did not get on well:

Table 5:5 Parents' views of social workers

	At the start N=82	After 1 year N=69
Get on very well	66%	46%
Get on well	21%	23%
Half and half	8%	16%
Do not get on well	5%	15%

Even so, nearly half of those interviewed claimed to have a very good relationship at the end of the year, although the proportion with a poor relationship had grown considerably.

There was no clear connection between the parents' and young people's views about their social workers. In several families, the parents had a good relationship and the teenager a poor one, or vice versa. For just under one third of the families where both were interviewed at the end of the year, they agreed on having very good relationships with the social worker. As would be expected, the great majority of the situations where parents thought the young person had benefited a lot from the social work intervention were those where both parties also said they got on very well with the social worker.

Social workers were liked when they enabled parents to unburden their worries, so they felt understood and supported. For example:

> 'T. says to me, if you ever feel like a chat or if you are feeling depressed, just give me a wee call and I'll try and be over.'

'She's a good listener. I mean I can phone her up at any time and I feel good after I've spoken to her.'

Ms. G. a single mother who had chronic difficulties in controlling her teenage daughter valued the support too:

'Very helpful indeed. Good to M (daughter) but extremely good to me as well when I needed it because I *did* need help . . . for a start they listened. I felt I was talking to somebody who knew what I was talking about. When the problems were getting really bad they were also there for me . . . '

The availability of what one parent described as 'a support system where you could have somebody to talk things through', seemed to offer reassurance and some confidence to parents in their struggles to cope. As another put it 'they've got the time they've had the patience they'll sit and talk to you and they'll sit and listen to you . . . and they try and help you as much as they can'. Several who were originally sceptical or hostile towards social workers came to value their advice or willingness to listen. This applied to one mother who had thought she was 'cracking up' because of her son's behaviour.

Being listened to and involved in plans were also of crucial importance to many parents. On the whole the majority of parents felt 'respected' and 'valued' by their social worker from the outset. Their views were being asked, they were offered relevant information and they were invited to reviews. They said things like we 'were never left out' or 'we worked together'. When relationships were good, it was sufficient to know that the social worker could be called on if need be:

'It was knowing that help was available if needed that mattered.'
'If I needed more contact I could pick up the phone.'

Over the year a composite profile emerged of the social worker who was well-regarded by parents:

- has a friendly, informal manner
- is available and accessible when a crisis occurs
- is seen to be trying to help, even if not successful
- keeps promises
- is prepared to listen
- provides information
- is not off-hand
- communicates well with the young person
- organises outside activities and opportunities for the young person

The best were seen to combine action, understanding and effective communication. For example, one was praised for having organised outdoor pursuits, given the teenager confidence, kept everyone in the picture and seen everybody's point of view. Some parents had been won round after a tricky start. One parent said she threw the social worker out of the house early on, but went on to say that by the end the worker felt 'like part of the family'.

Like the teenagers, parents tended to prefer people whose age or life stage was similar to their own, which was of course not always practical. Several parents felt an affinity with a worker whom they saw as having had experiences like their own:

> 'She's got a family, she's like myself, she's been divorced. She had a few problems with her own kids. She just understood.'

Some parents explained not only how the social worker was of help to them, but also how he/she was being of help to the young person. In this respect, it was important that the social workers were seen as impartial. Mr L. described favourably how his worker gave support to all the family – 'he's not just there for the child'. Many parents believed that if the young person were 'to open up' to the social worker then he/she would become more communicative at home. They also believed this would help 'to get to the root of the problems':

> 'He helped him with guidance and counselling, he helped him through a bad patch.'

Parents recognised the benefits of extra-curricular activities in facilitating communication and change:

> 'He is good with her (young person). He arranges meetings, takes her out for a cup of coffee . . . her behaviour is already changing.'

As far as we could tell, parental satisfaction with social workers largely related to the individual social worker and was not associated with particular agencies.

Fewer than one in ten parents held totally negative views about the social workers assigned to their children but when seen in conjunction with those who had mixed feelings bordering on the negative, the percentage increased to about one in five of all the parents. Critical comments illuminated parents' expectations of social workers and they were concentrated mainly on four areas:

i *Social Workers not Keeping their Promises or Being Unavailable:* As with the young people, a substantial minority of parents expressed dissatisfaction at the infrequency of contact with their social worker. About half of the parents were content they had seen the social worker often enough. Several wanted less contact, but considerably more would have liked it to be more often.

Parents who went to great lengths to be available or keep the young person at home for a social work visit were naturally dismayed when the worker arrived very late or not at all:

> 'She'd never appear. She'd make an appointment to come and see me and she wouldn't turn up.'

A single mother badly needed support when her son who was on supervision ran away and felt upset that it took well over a week before there was contact by the supervising social worker. Another exasperated parent stressed that help with crises needed to be immediate – 'we wanted them there that day to help sort it out'. Many of the parents featuring in the study were not on the telephone. To get access to their social workers, especially during emergency periods, involved considerable effort so there was immense frustration when the social worker was not available. They said things like – 'She was either always out or always attending a course' and 'She was never there when I needed her'.

Some seemed to blame the workers personally, whereas others explained that their availability was limited because social services were 'overstretched' or 'terribly undermanned'. A typical comment was: 'she's a good social worker but I still feel the social services haven't done enough, I don't think they are doing enough . . . they don't seem to have the time for individual cases'. One mother felt she had been discouraged from seeking help:

> 'I know they are grossly overworked but when you're getting things thrown at you like "We've got far worse cases than yours, I'm very busy you know", you don't like to trouble them.'

ii *Not Exercising Control Over the Young Person:* As in earlier research (eg Fisher *et al*, 1986) parents often wished that a firmer line had been taken about the young person's behaviour or education. Of course, the dilemma is that many young people would have resisted a more directive approach.

A lone mother found it difficult to resist her daughter's wish to come home, but thought the authorities should have insisted she stay away, because that was the only time she had any schooling. The parents with children who offended often wished that strong intervention had come earlier. One complained that her son had been let off too easily with cautions in his early teens. Two were glad that their sons went to secure units, only regretting this had not happened sooner. A few parents in England observed that the Probation Service had been more helpful than Social Services, because they were stricter or were more active.

A handful of parents thought that their social workers (and also some residential care staff) were not in 'control' or 'in charge' and that the young person was having his or her own way. Parents no doubt wished social workers could exercise some of the controls they were unable to exercise themselves. 'She was of no use to us', one father said, 'because she was not in control of the situation and L. was calling the shots'. Another man wished that the social services had insisted his daughter stay in care to ensure she attended school, as he knew he could not control her himself. V.'s mother saw the social worker as 'too much like her, rather than somebody in authority . . . He seemed more on the side of disorder than law and order'.

Whereas many young people were suspicious of psychiatric help, a few parents were disappointed that social workers had not heeded their requests for such specialist help.

iii *Attending Only to the Young Person:* Some parents felt excluded from participation and this failure to consider their point of view was understandably experienced as unhelpful. Mrs. D spoke for a number of parents when expressing the view that the social workers treated her son in isolation, as if he had no parents. Mr. T. believed that the social services sided with his son and 'ignored us'. One mother felt she was cast 'as the enemy' because the social worker was all for her daughter.

More than one step-parent felt marginalised on account of not being the biological parent. For example, a step-father remarked with justifiable exasperation that when he went either to the social worker or the police they cast him:

> '. . . as not being a father . . . but I am her legal guardian and I brought her up since the age of 3. As far as I'm concerned I am her father you know. It gets my back up.'

It would be disturbing if such messages were consistently conveyed by professional people to parents in non-traditional types of families, when at least one out of every five children lives in a reconstituted household.

We asked parents whether the social workers had explained what they were trying to do in their work with young people and themselves. The majority replied 'no' and many were critical of being given insufficient or inappropriate information. For example, Ms. F. said it had never been explained why life-story book work was being done with her daughter. Others expressed ignorance or puzzlement about the nature of direct work being carried out with the teenager, the aims of a placement away from home, the current legal position, a specialist project attended by the teenager and so on. However, some parents did feel they were fully informed, especially in Agency C, where comments included 'never felt kept out' and 'always consulted'.

iv *Lack of Confidence in the Social Workers' Capacity or Willingness to Help:* When asked to say whether they saw the social worker as someone who could help their son or daughter with his/her difficulties, two thirds said 'yes', but as many as a fifth said 'no' (the rest being uncertain or not in touch with the worker). A few parents had come to the conclusion that they wanted to have nothing to do with social workers either because 'they were useless' or 'a waste of time' or that 'they could do nothing'.

Some parents felt that too much responsibility was placed on them without enough support: 'It was me who had to sort everything out, that's how it just felt . . . She simply said "It's up to you to find a house for W."'. One remarked wryly on the provision of the Children Act 1989 – 'I thought it was rather unfair that my parental responsibility remains intact, in fact probably more so and that I should be consulted on everything . . . but when he last absconded I was not informed until after he was safely found and installed in another situation, so I was extremely angry about it'.

Many parents reported not feeling able to ask for help or not getting it when they had asked. Amongst the requests which had apparently gone unheeded were for: a bed so the son could stay at week-ends; respite care; a home tutor; help with accommodation so a son could return home. On the other hand, some social workers were highly regarded for being quick and sympathetic to respond to any approach for help. This had involved almost daily contact in one instance.

Conclusions about Perceptions of Social Work Intervention

Both the individual interviews of the main study and supplementary findings from group interviews demonstrated the wide range of opinions amongst teenagers who have experienced social work intervention. Some adolescents were very grateful for interventions they felt had helped them greatly. At the other extreme were those who resented the social controls which had been applied to them. In between were the majority who were reasonably satisfied with what had happened, but had some specific complaints which largely corresponded with those revealed in other studies (eg Buchanan *et al*, 1993; Fletcher, 1993). Most young people said they liked contacts with professionals or enjoyed activities, but fewer recognised this as having actually been helpful to them.

The teenagers valued practical assistance and advocacy, but the main role which the young people wanted social workers to fulfil was that of sympathetic counsellor. They placed great importance on social workers being able to listen to young people, understand them and keep confidences. Nevertheless, many did not see their social worker as their main helper or confidant, so in each case it is important to find out who the young person trusts and would like to support them. Even when an adolescent expresses hostility to most adults, there is usually at least one individual or category of person they respect (eg teachers, carers, IT workers).

Parents in the study were mostly positive about both the intervention and individual social workers. However a significant minority complained that social workers sided too much with young people or did not give parents themselves enough time and attention. Many parents wanted both social workers and carers to exercise greater control over the young person than was happening or than the adolescent would tolerate.

Social workers evidently do have to reconcile often opposing responsibilities. Society expects young people to conform; parents also often want improved behaviour as well as attention to their own problems; there is a legal and moral duty to take account of the wishes of adolescents themselves and progress is usually difficult without some co-operation from the young person concerned. Although social workers normally discussed family relationships with both teenagers and parents, it appeared that few saw their role as meeting with the family as a whole to seek to reconcile these differences, especially when the adolescent was away from home. Just as important was the need to explain to teenagers and parents the nature and purpose of their communication with the other party, which could otherwise be so easily misunderstood as taking sides.

6 Participants' Views of Supervision, Group Work and Specialist Services

The chapter begins with an examination of feedback on supervision at home as a distinct service, about which surprisingly little has been written. Here the input was sometimes made predominantly or even solely by the social worker, but direct work was also often carried out in tandem with other services, notably group work, befriending or referral to specialists. These complementary services are then dealt with individually, since they were sometimes provided to young people in care as well as those in the community. Placements and services exclusively for young people living away from home are considered in Chapter 7.

Home-Based Supervision

Assessments of Supervision and its Benefits

The majority of *young people* who had been supervised at home expressed contentment with supervision, but only a minority thought it had helped them significantly. Two thirds of young people on supervision said they 'liked' it whilst the rest were equally divided between those who did not like it and those who simply accepted it. Half of those on formal supervision found the social worker helpful but hardly any of those being supervised informally, most of whom were in Agency A. This may reflect the absence of clear purposes identified in court or at a panel when supervision was not formalised. It may also be that the status of supervision is less important than its content.

Teenagers mostly pointed to improvements in their own behaviour as evidence of the positive effects of supervision. Typically they referred to getting into 'less trouble' eg with the law or at school. K. declared that 'If I didn't have a social worker I would still be what I was like before, drugs, trouble with the police'. One of the consequences of being supervised at home which pleased several was that it helped to keep them out of care. Parents too usually considered the impact of supervision in terms of reduced law-breaking or improvements in attitude and behaviour at home or school:

> 'no trouble with law, no school truancy,
> less disobedience at home';
> 'no drugs, is home on time, follows rules,
> no thieving, somewhat better school attendance'.

Almost three quarters of the teenagers said that the pattern and frequency of supervision suited them. A few would have liked more frequent contact and rather more wanted to be taken out, sometimes simply because this was seen as a treat, but also in order to have opportunities for more informal communication.

The quality of the relationship with the social worker was particularly important for young people supervised at home since it was often the main element of intervention, in contrast to those placed away from home. All the young people who said they benefited a lot from supervision had seen their social workers at least once a month and said they got on very well with them, though otherwise there was no statistical connection between satisfaction and frequency of contact. Conversely, all the supervised youngsters who said their social worker was not easy to talk to also reported that supervision had been useless. As indicated in the last chapter, the main personal qualities of the social workers which contributed to positive supervision were:

- talking in a 'straightforward' or 'down to earth' way;
- taking trouble, putting themselves out;
- checking up and 'pushing you' without being 'bossy';
- showing they understood and were 'on the same wavelength';
- keeping confidences.

Criticisms of supervision took four main forms and were made by youngsters who were fairly satisfied as well as the minority who had resented it:

- *Only talking:*
  'I would have liked to be taken out sometimes. The last social worker took us on activities.'
  'She doesn't take me out – my sister's social worker takes her out and she is 18.'

- *No opportunity for private conversations:*
  'I would have liked to go out with her on my own as we used to do before. When she came to the house my mum was there and she only stopped for 5–10 minutes.'
  'I would have preferred the social worker to talk to me. She really came to see my mum.'

- *Lack of attention or concern, especially beyond the age of 16:*
  'I felt they should accept their responsibility and not try to get rid of me.'
  'The Department wanted to push me out and the Hearing concurred.'

- *Intrusive or stigmatising behaviour of the social worker:*
  'Nagging me all the time.'
  'Showing you up at school.'
  'Taking up your time.'

It was particularly the older ones who wanted more attention and private conversations, whilst the younger ones on formal supervision sometimes resented the opposite – too much talk and 'nagging'.

Social workers themselves were asked three inter-related questions about the results of supervision, which corresponded with those asked about care placements (see Chapter 7). Did the young person benefit? Did supervision help with the problems that led to measures of intervention in the first place? To what extent were the aims of supervision achieved?

Table 6:1 Supervision 'outcomes' based on social workers' views

	Amount of benefit/help		Help in relation to original problem		Achieved aims	
	N	%	N	%	N	%
A lot	8	16	6	12	10	20
Some	22	44	18	36	30	60
Not much differ/no help	19	38	22	44	10	20
DK/Other	1	2	4	8	–	–
	50	100	50	100	50	100

Whichever way the findings are looked at they suggest that well over half the young people were thought to have gained from supervision, including 12 to 20 per cent with substantial benefits. This left between one and two fifths who did not benefit or the original difficulties were still present. More social workers in Agencies C and then E said that the young person benefited or had some benefit from supervision than those in Agency A. Young people largely corroborated this view. Social workers, parents and young people indicated the age group of 15 years as including more who did well than either younger or older teenagers.

Social workers described the benefits of supervision mainly in terms of the young person's reduced problem behaviours and personal gains, eg:

> 'no shop-lifting and more mature';
> 'no glue sniffing, back in mainstream school';
> 'good adjustment; able to take responsibility for himself'.

In several instances the social workers' perceptions were confirmed by the family as in the case of R., where both he and his mother agreed that his offending was much reduced and that relationships at home had improved. Success in keeping the young person out of care was seen as a satisfactory outcome. Much less frequently reference was made to benefits for the whole family. For example, one social worker said she had enabled the family to work through difficulties and stay together.

The comments of social workers who placed almost half of the young people in the category of 'some benefit' were more guarded:

> 'Supervision not much help, except for helping him to change schools.'
> 'Supervision of limited help except put some check on his behaviour.'

According to *parents*, too, around one in five of the young people had benefited a lot. For example one parent noticed a general gain in maturity alongside improved behaviour which had contributed to the ending of the supervision order. However, parents were much more inclined than social workers to say there had been little or no benefit (60% of cases). As with young people, supervision was more often described as beneficial when the parent(s) had good personal relationships with the social worker. They also pointed to the importance of social workers being friendly, understanding and committed:

> 'I can really talk to her.'
> 'She let's me talk, let's me put my ideas and work out where to go next, what to do.'
> 'She goes out of her way to help.'

Agreement and Disagreement about the Effects of Supervision

Although supervision was seen as successful by a substantial minority of social workers, there were quite low levels of congruence between social workers' and young people's views. For example, in only one case when the social worker stated that there had been a lot of benefit from supervision did the young person agree. Similarly, when young people said that they had a lot of benefit from supervision, only once did the social worker concur. At the other extreme, there were 27 young people who said that supervision did not help at all or did not make much difference, when the social worker identified a lot of benefit for three and some benefit for fourteen.

There was somewhat more agreement between social workers and parents, who agreed on half of the people singled out as having benefited a lot. Likewise young people and their parents agreed on almost half of the cases where both said that the young person had benefited a lot from supervision.

The following is an instance where the social worker estimated that the benefits of supervision were moderate, whilst the young person and the parents thought that there was a lot of benefit, even if not all the issues were resolved:

Social Worker	Objectives partly achieved; no more offending and much better school attendance but still some arguments at home.
Young Person	Better all round. Talking to social worker things have improved; no problem with police and have been attending school regularly. Still some tensions with mother.
Mother	Of original three main concerns, trouble with the law and school truancy no more problems. Still some conflict and tension at home. (The mother was very pleased about what she described as considerable improvement).

The next example was more typical, with the social worker overestimating the benefits of supervision compared with the family. A 14 year old boy was placed on informal supervision for being beyond his mother's control, disobedient and destructive at home, truanting and having regular fights with the mother's partner. About nine months after the start of the supervision the boy had to be taken into care because his behaviour had deteriorated, including using drugs, running away and stealing from home. Both he and the mother asked for care because the situation was intolerable for both. At the follow-up each party described the impact of supervision as follows:

Social Worker	Fully benefited from supervision but home situation remained unchanged and N. found it difficult to adjust and had to go into care.
Young Person	Supervision was of no benefit at all and the original problems remained.
Mother	No change and no difference; N. still ran away, used drugs, stole and had fights with partner.

Reasons for Supervision Being Helpful

Often supervision involved a combination of counselling and practical action, so that it was not always possible to disentangle the main factor in any improvement. Practical help and arranging activities were most often mentioned by social workers as the reasons for progress. This included negotiations at school on behalf of the teenager or, in the case of older ones, assistance in getting a job. Sometimes such actions were not just ends in themselves but seemed to help develop more trust between social worker and young person leading to discussion of more personal issues:

> 'Having someone to support her, ensured that she had accommodation, food, someone to moan to.'

'Practical support to independence, form filling, applications, jobs, money, counselling.'

The young people who perceived supervision as helpful saw it as exercising a restraining influence on their behaviour or helping to sort out problems by listening and talking:

'I could talk to her (social worker) if I was in trouble or if I thought I was going to go pinching.'
'If there are any problems the social worker was there to listen.'
'He helped me understand things better. There was always someone at the end of a phone.'
'Not made much difference but it was good to know he was there.'

They also concurred with social workers that practical actions were helpful:

'helped with school';
'help over job, money-budgeting';
'organising activities'.

One of the roles of the social worker that received considerable approval from parents, was the organising or linking the young person to clubs, outreach and other similar activities, even though involvement in such activities was not noticeably correlated with success. Parents believed these services diverted their children from 'undesirable friends' or from boredom.

Reasons for Supervision Regarded as Not Helpful

When supervision was seen as ineffectual, it was important to identify the perceived causes of this. Social workers ascribed the lack of impact of supervisory measures to three main factors. Firstly, some young people were too committed to a pattern of crime, drug-taking or school non-attendance. For instance:

'He gets a real buzz from fast cars . . . '

In addition or instead, some found the young person difficult to engage with personally in the supervisory relationship. Appointments were not kept or the social worker felt unable to get through to the young person. One confessed to being at a loss 'to anchor him down and sort out what is going on in his head'. Thirdly, the parents or whole family were seen to have a negative attitude. In one case the worker regretted that he was only used as a threat by the parents. A different family was described as too erratic. Thus, social workers explained the failings of supervision almost entirely in terms of defects in the responsiveness by the teenager or family. As resistance is to be expected, it must be wondered whether the situations were indeed 'unhelpable' or whether different approaches might have worked better.

Often the young people agreed that the fault lay with themselves or their parents. Several were open and frank that their behaviour outside the home contributed to their failure to benefit from supervision. Their strong involvement in a particular life-style or with a particular group of friends was a more decisive influence on their lives than the contact with social workers. When the problem was more concerned with domestic conflict, several teenagers saw their parents as being both at the root of the difficulties and hard to change:

> 'The social worker couldn't change my dad. He was better
> for 10 days after she spoke to him but then he started
> up again and was just as bad as ever.'
> 'When she (the social worker) came, we came to an
> agreement and calmed down but as soon as she left we
> were arguing again. It didn't even get better for a day.'

Where some young people parted company with the social workers was in pointing to defects in what the latter had done or not done as being responsible for the ineffectiveness of supervision. Several teenagers indicated that they did not trust the social worker to be truthful, reliable or understanding:

> 'I took no notice of her (social worker). She told lies and
> never did what she said she would.'
> 'They (social workers) never done nothing.'
> 'I don't like her. They (social workers) stick their nose in too
> far, try to put ideas into your head.'

Like the social workers, parents normally attributed the absence of benefits to one of the other two parties and not themselves. Just as the teenagers sometimes expected all the changes to come from their parents, so the latter believed it was up to the young people to conform to their wishes. They often simply pointed to the continuation of the problems:

> 'Still disobedient and destructive (at home) and expelled
> from school.'
> 'The drug problem got worse. He stole all my jewels.'

Parents spoke with a mixture of regret and relief about a small number who had to go into care or prison because of continual offending:

> 'He was running totally wild. Police were never away.
> He spent most of the year in prison.'
> 'Problems got worse, offending, stealing cars and running off and
> taking drugs.'

Six out of every ten parents said that there was little else that social services could have done. The rest either wished social workers could have given more time to the young person or wanted them to organise more activities as alternatives to bad company and boredom.

The Impact of Supervision on Specific Problems

Besides looking at the broad effects of supervision, respondents were asked about its impact on some of the particular problems which had been identified as significant in the first round of interviews. These revealed a positive picture and suggest that young people and especially parents who could be quite negative about supervision in general were willing to acknowledge that it had been useful in certain particular respects:

Table 6:2 Proportion of each party responding that supervision had helped in relation to specific areas

Area of concern	Social Workers % said it helped	Young People % said it helped	Parents % said it helped
Family tensions	56	11	27
Offending/drugs	36	32	31
Schooling	29	23	31
Maturity/independence	34	32	21

There was reasonable concordance in the responses of all 3 parties, except markedly with respect to family tensions when social workers recognised gains in over half the cases, but young people in only one in ten, with parents' estimates in between. In about one third of cases there were thought to have been improvements in school work or attendance, the young person's behaviour or maturity.

It must be borne in mind that each issue asked about had not been a problem in every case, so we examined in more detail those cases where each item corresponded with a difficulty recognised by the family *at the beginning of the study*. When only those with *educational difficulties* at the start are considered, as many as half were helped with school issues according to both social workers and teenagers, although fewer parents recognised change. Nearly all of the successes with schooling were in Agencies C and E, which had joint policies between Social Work and Education Departments. As an example, both M. and his mother stated that the social worker's liaison with the school had been crucial in achieving better school attendance. The social worker thought that the school's willingness to negotiate had also been vital in keeping the lad in mainstream education. Another parent remarked: 'Without negotiations with the school D. would have had no education'. In other instances, pursuit of a different more suitable school had been helpful.

Looking again at only those youngsters who were identified at the start of supervision as having *behaviour difficulties,* each of the three parties identified about half as having stopped or reduced anti-social activities. This represents a considerable achievement. Young people's own explanations for these improvements gave prominence to their social worker's counselling and advice. For example:

> 'She told me I had will power. I should say "No" more times and not be bothered what anybody else thinks.'

The teenagers appeared to internalise the words of the worker as forethoughts which discouraged further wrong-doing:

> 'The social worker tells me what would happen if I kept getting into trouble.'
> 'He made me realise what could happen, it gave me a fright.'
> 'By talking to me about what would happen if I kept getting into trouble.'

Evidently the prospect of severe sanctions played a constructive part in such conversations. Yet, others on supervision had been very critical of their worker being intrusive or 'nagging'. Presumably, in the more successful cases, either the young person was more receptive or the workers had managed to gain the youngsters' confidence and talk over the consequences of their behaviour in an acceptable manner. Some young people and parents also said that the opportunity offered to the young person to take part in group work or activities helped to keep them out of trouble.

Nearly half the supervising social workers thought they had been effective in easing *family tensions,* but unfortunately the actual family members agreed with them in relatively few cases. For example nine social workers in Agency E said that supervision had helped to reduce family tensions, but no young person corroborated this. In only a third of the cases overall did the young people agree that lowering of tensions had happened. Both parents and young people recognised least progress in this area with respect to girls. The few young people who reported that supervision had helped to reduce family tensions appreciated the help offered by social workers through mediating in family disputes:

> 'It helped through talking to all of us in the family. I could hear my parents' point of view.'

Several parents also recognised that they had been helped to handle their son or daughter more effectively. For instance, they said they had learned 'how to talk to L.' or 'how to respond to M. when he was cheeky'.

Interestingly, although young people and parents had been less inclined than social workers to mention *personal development* as an aim of intervention, considerably more accepted that this had been a gain from supervision. Also a higher percentage of young people in Agency C than other agencies said that supervision helped them to become more mature or independent and this is the same agency where social workers put a lot of emphasis on intangible needs (Chapter 3). All three parties agreed that more girls than boys had gained in this way. The social workers explained that supervision assisted maturity when the young people gained insights from their conversations which enabled them to 'understand about communication', 'recognise other people's feelings' or 'learn to control his behaviour'. Young people themselves spoke of 'listening to advice more' and being helped to see things differently through discussion, talking and support.

There was broad agreement among the three parties that nearly half of those on supervision had been helped by being introduced to *activities* such as clubs, outreach schemes or IT groups (see below for further details). This applied particularly to boys and to those aged 15–16. The teenagers and their parents were usually positive about these arrangements, without necessarily believing they had exerted much influence on the problems which had led to supervision.

Supervision, Self-Esteem and Adjustment

The ratings on the Coopersmith scales provided an independent measure of the effects of supervision. They showed that young people on supervision had the same range of self-esteem as the rest of the sample both at the start and the end of the study. There was no support for the hypothesis that those with high self-esteem would benefit more from supervision. None of the young people who said they benefited a lot from supervision had high esteem scores.

Similarly young people who began the year with low, medium or high scores of disturbance were all equally likely to benefit or not from supervision. On the Rutter Scale, six teenagers on supervision moved towards improved adjustment in the three-fold categorisation and only one deteriorated. Taken together these findings indicate that there is no reason to use low self-esteem or high levels of disturbance in themselves as reasons for excluding anyone from the potential benefits of supervision.

Resource Issues

In social workers' spontaneous accounts of why supervision had worked or not, it was clear they thought this depended mainly on the way the family responded, rather than the manner in which the service was provided. However, when asked directly almost half admitted that there were potentially helpful resources which had not been available or were not used, which accounted for this relative lack of success. Social workers identified three key areas where better or different provision was required to meet the needs of those on supervision. These were:

i *Day educational facilities* for those with behavioural difficulties, particularly boys;
ii *More group and outreach activities*;
iii *Suitable accommodation* for older teenagers away from home.

The lack of suitable resources was mentioned mainly in Agencies E and C but not in A which had the highest unsatisfactory outcomes as far as supervision was concerned. Since Agency A had reasonable access to group work and outreach, it may have been the precise way these facilities were used which accounted for the relative lack of success.

The Necessary Components for Successful Supervision

Drawing together our different sources of data, we concluded that the following components are required to make supervision more effective:

- joint strategies between social services, education, housing and other agencies
- planned individual *and* family work based on a shared definition of problems and expectations
- attention to practical and personal needs, as well as behaviour
- establishment of positive relationships within which young people are challenged to 'own' and modify their behaviour
- frequent joint reassessment of goals and progress
- access to a range of groups and outreach activities
- access to specialist and other flexible day care resources, including short-term respite facilities.

Group Work, Befriending and Specialist Services

As we have just seen, these services could be a vital component in supervision, but were also important for children away from home too.

Feedback on Groups

Generally, the young people liked the people running the groups and found them easy to talk to. Only a few were ambivalent or negative. Group workers were usually seen as approachable, because of their youth, openness, informality and friendliness.

The sports and outdoor pursuits undertaken by several of the groups were generally enjoyed. Youngsters with little else of interest in their lives acknowledged that it was 'something to do'. Whereas some younger teenagers simply enjoyed the activities, many also valued the opportunity to talk with others in a similar position about problems. A few young offenders found it helpful in occupying their time constructively, eg:

> 'It kept my mind on other things and made me think more about what would happen if I did offend. It helped me see stealing cars as really pointless.'

It was also noted that they could not get into trouble while they were there.

A number of the teenagers in the alternative to custody projects of Agency A said they had very much enjoyed the combination of being able to help others (children with learning difficulties) in addition to receiving support and advice themselves. D. and his parents thought the alternative to custody scheme had been the most helpful part of the social services intervention. This was mainly because he got on so well with the worker who put herself out a lot for him, as he had not engaged well with the group work itself. It was true more generally about groups that some teenagers thought they mostly benefited from their relationsionships with the group workers and the advice they gave, whilst others valued the peer interaction more.

Although the groups were popular with the teenagers, they were not often seen as very effective in tackling the problems which led to social services intervention. Only a handful of young people who had attended said the group had helped a lot in this respect. For instance a young man said it had helped him a lot to talk about drugs, express his anger and learn how to handle his aggression better. A teenage girl said that group discussions had helped put into perspective her parents' restrictions on her freedom, whilst the social worker felt it had given her a sense of direction and greater self-worth. The majority of group attenders said the group had not helped at all or only helped a little. Several admitted that the group had not affected their law-breaking or school non-attendance at all. Of course some of the groups were not intended to tackle those problems and small reductions in the problems may still be helpful.

Social workers also indicated that in only one quarter of cases had the group made a significant difference:

helped a lot	24%
helped a bit	26%
not helped much	18%
not helped at all	32%

Although numbers are small, there were noteworthy agency differences. In Agency A only two out of the ten teenagers were thought to have been helped by the group they attended, compared with five out of twelve in Agency E and nine out of ten in Agency C. Social workers said groups had helped by providing support, improving relationship skills, sharing anxieties and assisting the teenagers to voice their opinions. It was also commonly observed that the groups were enjoyable and fun.

Social workers accounted for group experiences which were unhelpful mainly in terms of lack of commitment and non-attendance by the young person. In a few individual cases, other drawbacks were more related to a mismatch between the needs of the teenager and the aims or composition of the group. For example, one young person needed to work on family matters but the group was focused on 'in-care' issues, whilst another was marginal to the main target group (addicts). Occasionally there was a poor mix of group members and a few individuals were rejected by the group. One young woman was said to have enjoyed getting out of the house, but had got easily bored because she was older and brighter than the rest of the group. In contrast, a teenage boy was seen as not intelligent enough to comprehend what the group leaders were getting at.

It seemed that sometimes group work had been arranged without a clear purpose and not as part of an overall plan co-ordinated with social work input, especially in supervision cases. One worker admitted that she had done 'very little one to one work – I leave it to the group'. Another said that apart from arranging attendance at a group, his own contact with the family was mainly by phone. It almost goes without saying that group work is less likely to be effectual when it is arranged as a substitute rather than a complement to other forms of help to the family.

Usually parents spoke positively about groups. They confirmed that these were fun for the teenagers and could also help the young person's development. They pointed to such things as learning to mix better, acquiring skills and being able to talk about worries. Two parents stated that IT groups were a really good thing, but would have been more helpful if they had run for longer rather than in short bursts:

> 'It helped when he was at groups and they were actually doing something. But groups were only once a week and lasted for only six weeks.'
> 'He very much enjoyed the activities – swimming and venture. He got on well with the leaders. I would have liked it if the groups had run longer.'

Group Non-Attenders

As noted in Chapter 4, the majority of the teenagers who were not given the chance to go to a group said they would not have wanted to go to one. The reasons for not wanting to go included general apprehensiveness, preferring to be with friends and seeing a group as boring or useless. However there were a few young people who did feel they had missed out in not having the opportunity to attend a group.

Social workers were more evenly divided in their opinions on whether the young people who had not gone to a group would have benefited or not. In half of the cases, the social worker thought that a group would have enabled the teenagers to improve their social skills, assertiveness or understanding. Unfortunately these social workers did not know of any suitable groups. There were examples in all five agencies of social workers saying they would have liked to arrange group work, but none was available in an appropirate form as far as they knew.

In the other cases, social workers gave both positive and negative reasons for thinking it was not worth offering a group. Some young people were seen as having satisfactory social relationships or indeed a busy social life. Occasionally there were seen to be no major problems which a group might help with. Some teenagers were seen as strongly resistant to groups. Several others were described as 'withdrawn' or 'not a group person'. Now and then, the young person's life circumstances were too unsettled to permit regular attendance.

Feedback on Befrienders and Outreach

Nearly all of the teenagers said they had got on well with the befriender and found him or her easy to talk to, although a few qualified this by indicating they did not feel able to confide in them. Most befrienders had gained the teenager's trust by being 'friendly', 'normal' and 'down to earth'. One girl appreciated different qualities in her befriender and social worker. She appreciated the befriender for 'having a laugh' and talking 'dead straight'. At the same time 'I wouldn't talk to her the way I talk to my social worker', who was seen as softer and more accepting.

As with groups, most young people were inclined to think that having a befriending or outreach service was good fun and had helped them, but only a little. Several simply noted that they enjoyed going out and this had kept them occupied. A few reported more substantial gains, eg 'When I talked to him, it helped me calm down, made me think about what I was doing'. The befriender of one young man in a residential school had helped him complain about police harassment – 'It's good – they tell you your rights'.

Social workers also stated that befriending had helped a number of the young people with the problems which led to social work intervention and sometimes there had been benefits in other ways. In a few instances, the energies of youngsters with behaviour problems had apparently been successfully diverted into positive activities. Several were said to have enjoyed the activities, but not opened up or had their lives significantly altered. Not uncommonly, the teenagers co-operated irregularly or for a short while only.

Parents too saw the main value of outreach consisting in opportunities to take part in enjoyable activities. One or two could not see the point – 'What good did it do her going to the beach?'

Teenagers Not Offered Befriending or Outreach

Some of those teenagers who had not had the chance to spend time with a befriender were attracted to the idea of exciting activities and more personal attention. One or two were envious of friends in care who had such opportunities. Those who were not interested usually explained that they were content going out with their friends.

Social workers explained not offering befriending in various ways. In Agency B, it was reported to be against agency policy for children in care when there was family contact, whilst in C a few workers were unaware of the existence of such services. Workers in Agency E stated that it was a rare resource – 'you can wait for a year for one', 'there has been a shortage'. Quite often it was thought to be unnecessary because the young person's social needs were being met or their problems dealt with by several professionals already. It seemed that for some the idea of a personal befriender was associated negatively with an outmoded model of a voluntary visitor to younger children in care. Several commented that the young person was too old, although in North America people in their late teens leaving care or with major problems at home may be allocated volunteer 'mentors' with support functions.

Although the social workers who had not arranged befriending usually felt that there was little need, a few did believe that the teenager would have benefited from an additional interested person and opportunities to develop leisure pursuits. Gender was sometimes an important consideration. K's social worker thought she would have gained from having a 'mother-figure', someone to go shopping with. It was said that two teenage boys would benefit respectively from a 'male role model' and 'a father figure'.

Feedback about Referral to Psychological and Psychiatric Services

Leaving aside those whose contact was too brief to comment on, half who had seen a psychologist or psychiatrist said they got on well and found it easy to talk, but half said the opposite. Descriptions included:

'She is understanding and supportive, but can be a bit
unreliable.'
'He was helpful and listened to me.'
'You could tell she had been trained to get people to talk to
her.'
'She was a nice person but did not help.'
'I thought he talked rubbish.'
'She makes me feel weird.'
'He doesn't make much sense.'
'He kept interrupting.'

Much more often than with social workers, group workers, carers and befrienders, the style of communication mystified or alienated the adolescents. For
instance:

'He was a weirdo – he should have his own psychiatrist. He didn't
talk straight, came out with words I'd never heard of.'
'He kept on and on. He was just getting on my nerves.'

As a result nearly all those who saw psychologists or psychiatrists said they did
not confide in them and nearly half were actively disliked. This probably had
as much to do with the nature of the contact (divorced from the teenagers'
everyday lives and focusing on their personal problems) as the communication
skills of the professionals. Nevertheless it casts some doubt on the value of
referrals to these particular specialists to deal with 'deeper' issues, if young
people are much more likely to pass on confidences to carers and teachers.

Several young people felt they had benefited, but the majority said the referral
had not altered their behaviour as intended or had made things worse. Social
workers, too, only recognised the service as very helpful in a small minority
of cases:

helped a lot   4
helped a bit   10
not helpful   15

Social workers' reasons for the lack of impact of the referral included shortage
of resources to fulfil the assessment recommendations and the teenager's
reluctance to attend or open up. When the referral had been helpful, social
workers said this was due to such things as the young person finding the
sessions supportive, assessment leading to a suitable placement and the
problem behaviour ceasing.

Very few of the adolescents who had not been offered a referral to a psychologist or psychiatrist would have liked to see one. Anxiety and prejudice was
often expressed about the idea – 'I don't like the idea of head doctors'; 'I'm
not mental'; 'They make you feel daft'. A few had seen psychiatrists before and
regarded it as a waste of time. When a referral had not been made, social

workers normally also did not see a need for such specialist help. Only occasionally did they think that in retrospect it might have been useful. For instance, two teenagers from different families had serious emotional problems related to rejection by their mothers which the social workers believed could have been ameliorated by a psychiatrist or psychologist.

Conclusions

On the whole, feedback about home supervision was lukewarm. All parties agreed that approximately one in every five or six young people were helped a 'lot' by supervision and the majority were helped only a little. The outcomes were particularly low in one agency. Nevertheless in about half the cases where behaviour or educational problems had been an issue, all three parties agreed that this had reduced or stopped during the period of supervision. Important factors seemed to be a good relationship with the social worker who offered counselling sometimes helpfully combined with practical assistance, group work or organised activities. In particular gains were achieved with regards to anti-social behaviour when young people were helped initially to express a clear commitment to change and when social workers gave advice in a persistent but non-threatening manner about the likely negative consequences of continued 'trouble' with the law, parents or schools.

Both groups and befrienders/outreach were usually regarded very positively by those who had experience of them. Many enjoyed the activities and discussions, but few thought they had had a major impact on their lives or behaviour. Whereas group workers and IT workers were widely liked and respected, most of the sample appeared quite resistant to help offered by psychologists or psychiatrists and only a handful of those who had been referred found this at all useful. It would seem that use of these high status 'experts' should be sparing and prepared for in a way which demystifies some of the prejudices about them. In most instances young people responded better to workers who were more informal in language and approach.

7 Views of Services for Young People Living Apart from Their Families

We now focus attention on evaluations of the services provided to young people who had experienced being in care. As we have seen, social workers made direct contributions to the experiences of this group and some received other services (like group work), but the 'service' likely to have the most impact was the placement itself. In contrast to the inputs so far described, placements normally constituted 24-hour a day living environments, with almost inevitably a more pervasive influence for better or worse. We shall consider in turn residential and foster care, followed by an evaluation of services for young adults seeking to manage on their own after a period of care or supervision.

Care Placements In General

Before examining the specific types of placements, it is important to describe the criteria used to assess all placements and to identify some of the overall patterns. As described in Chapter 4, not every placement in sometimes complicated sequences could be evaluated in detail, so we concentrated on (a) the initial placements and (b) the most recent placements.

Researchers have moved away from a simple division of placements into those which broke down (failures) and those which continued or ended on time (successes). It is recognised that placement outcomes are often more subtle and more mixed. Hence we posed a range of questions to tap different aspects of 'success', including several derived from the study by Rowe et al (1989). Both social workers and young people were asked:

- to what extent did the young person benefit from the placement? What were the benefits?
- to what extent had the placement helped with the original difficulties?

Parents were asked if the placements had helped the young person and, if so, how. When placements had ended, further questions were put to all three parties:

- did the placement last as long as planned?
- did the placement last as long as needed?

In addition we asked social workers:

- were placement aims met? Fully, partly or not at all?
- how satisfied were they with how the placements turned out?

Besides these general questions, there were specific ones about the impact of the placement on different aspects of the young person's behaviour and situation.

All the answers helped to build up a composite picture. In many cases, the measures reinforced each other to give a unified favourable or unfavourable result, but quite often different perspectives and dimensions revealed more complex outcomes. Whereas Rowe *et al* obtained only the social work viewpoint, we asked the three participants and sometimes their opinions were at odds with each other. The following general points emerged from our analysis of the detailed responses.

In nearly three quarters of cases, parents and social workers were in agreement on whether the placement was helpful or not. When their views were divergent, however, it was nearly always parents who held a more negative opinion. There was a very close correspondence amongst all three parties on whether completed placements had lasted as long as planned or not. There was much less agreement about duration in relation to need. The clearest difference of opinion was between parents and social workers with over 80% of social workers feeling the placement had lasted as long as it was needed, but only a third of parents. It was noted in Chapter 3 that many parents had high hopes that intensive help in care was the right solution, whereas social workers were more circumspect about what care could offer and placed a high value on returning the young person to the community as soon as possible. Social workers therefore could believe that a placement had lasted as long as it was needed, even if some of the problematic behaviour persisted, whereas parents had hoped for more fundamental and lasting change.

Placements which lasted until the end of the year were usually rated as successful in meeting their original aims and benefiting the young person, but this was true for only a minority of the placements which had ended. Both social workers and parents thought a higher proportion of longer than shorter placements had helped with the original difficulties. Placements which were deemed to have ended prematurely in terms of the original plan or the young person's needs were nevertheless still often seen as having brought benefits.

Nearly all the placements in residential schools were considered to have succeeded on every criterion and according to each of the three types of respondent. Yet at the beginning these had often been seen as the placement of last resort by social workers and feared by young people. In several instances social workers spoke of young people having 'blossomed' in ways which were quite unexpected.

Most residential unit placements were seen as satisfactory but few were depicted as very helpful. In a good many cases, social workers were pleased with the outcomes for a young person who had stayed in a residential unit, but the young person and even more often the parents thought the ending was premature.

On most criteria foster placements included a higher proportion of both very successful and very unsuccessful results. Amongst completed placements, foster care placements were least likely to last as long as planned, but continuing placements were often rated very positively.

Usually early endings to foster care were seen as damaging or missed opportunities for personal development. Initial expectations for foster placements were often high and diverse, so the disappointment was all the greater when hopes were not achieved. The ending of a residential placement was less frequently seen as having such a fundamental impact, perhaps because the emotional investment was usually less.

When there was complete agreement between the social workers and young people that the placement had been clearly positive or definitely negative, these were as follows:

- *Most beneficial placements (6):*
  3 residential schools;
  3 foster homes;
  3 continuing; 3 ended.

- *Most negative placements (8):*
  5 residential units;
  3 foster homes;
  All 8 had ended.

The agency results showed a consistent rank ordering. For instance the proportion of placements rated by social workers as very helpful ranged from 25% in Agency A to 50% in Agency E and 68% in Agency C. This may be related to the low usage of residential schools in Agency A. However, most foster placements were in Agencies A and C and the proportion considered to have helped a lot was very different, 33% and 75% respectively. On the other hand, more young people in Agency A rated their placement as helpful than did their workers.

Our information suggested that feeling good about oneself at the start was likely to lead to a more favourable outcome, but provided no evidence that the experience of a good placement had raised self-esteem. A larger proportion of young people who started with a high Coopersmith rating benefited a lot from the placements. However those whose placement benefits were rated positively and/or whose placement aims had been fully met were no more likely than others to have a higher Coopersmith score at the follow-up stage.

We found no significant connection between the Rutter scores and the level of benefit from the placement. Nevertheless, those who had scores which indicated substantial difficulties yet still had positive placements are worthy of close consideration. Three people with low self esteem and a high Rutter score had very positive placements. Two of them had moved out of the family home at the age of 15 after long standing family difficulties failed to be resolved. Both had mothers with significant psychological difficulties and were later helped to establish themselves in supported accommodation. This illustrates how placement in care can be positive even for older adolescents with major problems.

Residential Care

As we have seen, the responses to 'outcome' questions posed in relation to all placements revealed that residential schools nearly always evoked favourable replies, whereas the picture for residential units was more mixed. In addition, detailed information was obtained about the experiences of each placement which will now be reported.

Initial Reactions to Residential Care

The young people's initial attitudes towards residential placements were mixed. Given the option of describing themselves as pleased to be living there, accepting of the situation or unhappy, two thirds chose the middle option, indicating that their attitude was one of passive acceptance. A quarter were pleased to be there and approximately 10% were unhappy.

Four out of every five said that they were getting on well with the key worker and most young people identified other aspects of the placement which they liked. These included having friends and companions, the units' leisure facilities and the nature of the accommodation. A high proportion of those in residential schools valued the fact that they felt more comfortable and able to learn there, in contrast to their previous educational experiences. One boy was enthusiastic because 'they've got a workshop in the school like they didn't have at my old school and you can strip engines and that'. On the other hand, almost half had encountered some difficulties with fellow residents. Another common complaint was that there were too many rules.

Most parents whose children were in residential care were positive at the start of the study. They commented on the friendliness of staff and their ability to help establish communication with the young person:

> 'They made you feel at ease. I found them very understanding.
> Very nice people.'
> 'The key worker acted like an arbiter between me and him.'

'The staff (in the school) brought me and my daughter closer together.'

Parents generally valued units where they felt that staff were in control. When they made negative comments, this usually concerned staff being seen as too lax:

'He never learns discipline there, he escapes punishment. Care has to be more firm.'
'He keeps the same company and does what he likes. We told the staff they didn't know their jobs.'

Parents believed that keeping control was in the best interests of their children and were pleased when residential care helped young people settle down or be reintroduced to formal education.

In order to develop a clearer understanding of the strengths and weaknesses of particular types of care, social workers were asked several questions about the quality of care provided in the placements. Firstly they were asked to rate the appropriateness of the level of affection, security, discipline and encouragement which each placement offered. In relation to residential schools, social workers considered that all but one placement had provided these aspects of care appropriately. The majority of other residential units were also judged to have a suitable level of care but over 20% of units were thought to lack enough control, whilst in 10% control was thought to be too rigid.

Social workers' views were also obtained on whether the care staff had been skilled enough to provide the type of care which the young person needed. Two thirds of staff in schools compared with 40% in other units were considered skilled enough to provide fully the kind of care the young person required. Several social workers pointed out, however, that staff skill was not the only factor which determined whether teenagers' needs were met. Most young people required individual attention but the time available to provide this depended largely on staffing levels. In units where there was normally only one person on duty there was little scope for more than basic care.

The fact that children's units were generally the least favoured placements was reflected in the fact that social workers would have preferred a third of their residents to have been placed in another type of care. The alternatives they thought preferable included – foster care; a more specialised setting for young people with particular emotional difficulties; a bridge placement to independent living.

When the teenagers were asked whether they would have preferred another placement, half those in residential units and three quarters of those in schools stated clearly that they did not want to be anywhere else. Some were unaware of what other options there might be. Perhaps as a result, when a preference for somewhere else was expressed, it was a placement nearer home rather than a different type of establishment which was asked for.

Changes in Attitudes to Placements

At each interview young people were asked about their general attitudes to placements they were living in. In relation to the initial placements more were favourably disposed by the follow-up stage:

Table 7:1 Young people's attitude to the initial placement at the initial and follow-up stage

	Initial Stage	Follow-Up Stage
Pleased	24%	43%
Accept	65%	41%
Not pleased	11%	16%

However when we compared changes in the attitudes of individual young people we found that approximately half of them had changed their attitude and that movement had been in both directions. More of the positive shifts in attitude were shown by young people in residential schools.

End of Year Appraisals of Residential Care

Social workers were satisfied or very satisfied with the outcome in four fifths of the residential placements and considered that over 90% had been able to achieve the aims set for them fully or in part. They were dissatisfied with the outcome in a third of placements in residential units, but there was no dissatisfaction with any residential school. Whereas social workers believed four out of five completed residential placements had lasted as long as they were needed, young people considered that this applied to just over half the placements and parents put only one third in this category. On the other hand three quarters of parents, two thirds of young people and half the social workers thought that the placements had lasted as long as they were planned. Thus parents often thought that the duration of placements was as intended but insufficient, whereas more social workers said the ending was different from expected but adequate.

Asked to state the benefits from residential care, social workers primarily cited progress in the areas of personal development, schooling, reduced offending and improved social skills. The processes identified as contributing to these improvements may be summarised as:

- support, attention from staff;
- help to develop/mature;
- opportunity to learn social skills and new ways of relating to others;
- receiving education (when the teenager had previously been a non-attender);
- opportunity to take stock, consider future plans and/or breaking unhelpful patterns;
- providing a safe place.

Social workers' detailed comments indicated both the achievements and what had helped towards them:

> 'She gained a lot of inner security, was able to regress and gain trust in adults.'
> 'She learned as much as she could about how to live independently and was free to come and go with support.'
> 'The placement offered a lot of support, practical and emotional and help to look at problems.'
> 'Broke pattern of behaviour between young person and his mother and gave him other ways of dealing with problems.'
> 'Education was provided, pattern of offending was broken. Allowed L. space to change pattern of behaviour.'
> 'Time to discuss plans for the future. Work on plans with a bit of space.'

Young people's views of how the placements had been helpful were consistent with the social workers' accounts, though understandably they used different language. They often described themselves as having 'calmed down' or changed their behaviour.

> 'I don't get into trouble now.'
> 'I've kept out of trouble, off the glue.'
> 'When I came here I was mental, would do anything. I'm not that bad now, not stealing or truanting.'

In common with social workers, young people commented on how they had learned to co-exist with others and to make relationships:

> 'I was a loner but I learned how to make friends, you have to.'
> 'I've learned to accept people for what they are.'
> 'It broadened my outlook. I lived with people I would not normally have got to know.'

Teenagers in residential schools were often pleased that they were making educational progress:

> 'My school work's better.'
> 'I've learned to spell.'
> 'I'm a bit better at my maths.'

Young people whose social workers thought they had matured usually agreed that they had been helped to 'grow up' but their explanation of what was helpful in this process was somewhat different from the social workers' view. Whereas social workers more often mentioned support, a number of young people commented on being 'pushed' or forced to do things which, left to their own devices, they would have avoided. At the end of the day they recognised that being forced to go to school, do some household chores or find a job had been good for them. A young man who had spent a few months in care at a critical point in his life defined the benefit for him in the following terms:

> 'The main thing that helped me mature was getting a job,
> being with adults all day. The home pushed me in to getting
> a job, made me get it, so it helped in that way.'

Exerting pressure of this kind was no doubt only effective in the context of a supportive relationship and in circumstances where the young person was able to cope with the set task. However it was striking that several young people spontaneously acknowledged the value of having been spurred into action.

In common with social workers, some young people recognised that the placement had helped by providing 'space' to work out relationships or future plans. Several felt that the placement had merely provided somewhere for them to stay while they sorted out the problems, sometimes with their parents. The residential staff were not given much credit for having helped. The following quotes illustrate this viewpoint:

> 'I suppose it gave me time to think about what I wanted,
> fostering or whatever, but that could have happened
> anywhere.'
> 'Being here only helped because we are not together now
> and I had to accept I could not go home. I had to talk to
> my mum about that but we did it ourselves. It doesn't
> work when other people try to interfere.'

Berridge and Cleaver (1987) also comment on the value of residential care as a place where young people can take stock and have space to make choices. Several seemed to need to be apart from each other to avoid conflict:

'It's been good to have a break. We're not suited to live together. We can get on fine, but if we're in the same house too long, then things don't work out.'

The majority of the most positive comments were about residential schools and these showed that residential schools achieved more than educational progress. Social workers believed that young people had been able to learn self control and to start considering other people. It was hoped that these new patterns of behaviour would equip them to cope better in the future. The care and stability offered by schools was seen as enabling these changes to take place.

The increased benefits from residential schools were also apparent from the responses social workers and young people gave when asked whether the placements had helped with specific problems. In the eyes of both social workers and teenagers, residential schools had been more effective than residential homes in helping with virtually every problem, apart from help to get a job. They were seen as particularly effective in changing behaviour and improving school performance, the factors which also accounted for their popularity with parents:

Table 7:2 Specific benefits from residential placement according to social workers and young people

	% Residential School		% Residential Unit	
	SW	YP	SW	YP
Improved school performance	89	74	40	41
Improved behaviour	79	74	37	48
Changed attitudes, point of view	53	63	30	41
Aided maturity, independence	63	68	26	17
Provided activities	68	63	23	34
Helped get a job	0	16	28	21

It is noteworthy that half of the young people said the placements had helped reduce tension with parents by giving them a break from each other, but only 1 in 6 thought there had been help with family tensions through talking things over.

Disadvantages of Residential Care

Only one in ten young people could identify no benefits from the placements in residential care. However, when asked if the placement had in any way made their life worse, a third believed that it had. The most common drawback was simply being away from home and young people felt this keenly even when they recognised substantial gains from being in care. There were also comments about the stigmatising effects of care and young people cited examples of discrimination on the part of the police, employers, schools and the general public.

Living with other young people whom they found annoying or aggressive also made life worse for a number of our sample. Asked specifically whether they had been bullied or ill-treated, one in six young people said they had. Social workers estimated that fewer than one in ten had been bullied but were unsure in a further 10%. This uncertainty reflected the difficulty in determining when mutual rough treatment among young people became abusive.

Residential Care, Self-Esteem and Adjustment

A frequently cited drawback of residential care is its potential for stigmatising young people and consequently having a negative impact on their self-esteem. Thus, in addition to helping young people deal with the difficulties which led to their admission to care, residential placements have to help teenagers cope with the implications of entering a care system which is viewed negatively by the public and social workers alike. The impact of a residential placement on the young person's self-esteem will therefore reflect not only whether living in the unit provided positive experiences and validation of the teenager as a person but also the extent to which the stigmatising aspects of care were reduced or productively managed.

Among those teenagers who had spent some or part of the year in a residential school a higher proportion had raised their self-esteem in the course of the year than among the rest of the sample. Social workers' assessments indicated an improvement in self-esteem for half the total sample, for 40% of those in residential units but for 88% of those in residential schools. The Coopersmith ratings showed a similar pattern, though less strongly. Almost a third of those in residential school moved into a higher category at the end of the year compared with a fifth of young people in children's homes. It would appear that the experience of making progress in school work and controlling behaviour had compensated for being placed in the most stigmatised form of care. In fact, several residential schools in the study placed great emphasis on demonstrating their acceptance of young people and finding imaginative ways of making them feel good about themselves.

We were interested to know whether the more effective performance of schools was related to the type or level of difficulties the young people brought to the placements. A comparison of those in residential schools with their peers in other units did not indicate any significant differences in severity of problems as measured by parents or teenagers themselves. However, on the initial Rutter ratings, social workers placed 70% of the residential school population but only 48% of those in other units in the most difficult category. Moreover, offending or truancy were issues for virtually all the young people in residential schools but for only a third of those in other units. Thus, if anything, the schools were doing better with a more difficult population.

On the other hand, the young people who went to the schools began with higher levels of self-esteem than those in other units:

Res. Schools		Res. Units	
High	15%	High	–
Medium	70%	Medium	60%
Low	15%	Low	40%

Of the school residents, 15% had initial Coopersmith scores which placed them in the group with highest self-esteem and 15% were in the lowest category. In contrast there were no high scores from young people in other units while 40% obtained scores in the lowest band. As noted earlier, young people who started the year with high self-esteem were more likely to have a positive placement so this would have contributed to the more positive results for residential schools. There was also evidence that those in the schools usually had more family support, illustrated by the fact that by the end of the year many were entitled to considerable home leave.

Since placements in residential schools were longer than others, there was little scope within the time scale of this study to gauge whether new patterns of behaviour would be maintained after leaving the school. However most cases were managed in such a way that the dichotomy between the school and the home was minimised. Teenagers normally retained close links with their families and communities while they were resident in the schools. Virtually all returned home at weekends and some schools were geographically close enough to allow the young person to spend some evenings at home each week. Even when the school was located some distance away, older teenagers were able to travel home by public transport. Another contributing factor in the successful school placements was the involvement of the social worker in sustaining links with the family and continuing to work on family problems while the young person was away from home.

Young People's Views on Particular Aspects of Residential Care

Relationships with Staff: When asked what they liked about the residential unit, young people made it very clear that they most valued the relationships with staff and other residents. The following comments were typical:

> 'Staff were like a family. I got really close to a couple of them.'
> 'Liked my key worker. There was always someone to talk to.'
> 'The staff listen and help. I've got good mates.'
> 'I liked the other lads and lassies.'
> 'I made lots of friends and "aunties". I liked how you called the staff "auntie".'

Two thirds of the young people referred to carers when describing what they liked about their placements. Even where placements had been rated by young people as being of little help, they often spoke warmly of the friendliness and helpfulness of the key worker or staff in general.

All but three young people in residential care had a key worker and three quarters said that they and their key worker got on well with each other. Less than 10% felt that the relationship with the key workers was poor. Four out of every five teenagers said that they were able to speak quite freely to their key worker, though this did not necessarily mean a willingness to confide or talk over personal matters.

Since key workers were often changed (some had had three or four changes in the year), it was fortunate that most young people were on good terms with at least one member of staff other than the key worker. Approximately three quarters of the teenagers were also able to identify another member of staff with whom they felt relaxed and could talk easily.

Three quarters said they had no preference about whether their key worker was a man or a woman but many added the qualification that they would only discuss matters concerning their sexuality with someone of their own gender. This was also the reason given by those who did prefer a key worker of a particular gender (mostly young women).

We asked the young people to tell us what made the key workers approachable. A vital quality was the willingness to take time to listen. Favourable comments included:

> 'She took a lot of time with me.'
> 'She was a good listener.'
> 'Friendly and gives you time.'
> 'He gets me to talk about here, about what winds me up.'

A recurring phrase was 'he/she sits and listens'. In contrast, young people disliked staff who failed to give them a fair hearing or never had time to speak:

'The last key worker – he didn't listen to you but the new key worker – yes, he sits and talks, asks you what's up and listens to you.'

From the young people's descriptions of their relationships with staff it seemed that there were two main types of carer who were popular. Several young people liked staff who were young, who were 'a good laugh' and who shared some of the interests and life style of teenagers. However these young staff members were not always seen as people who would help with problems. Older people, seen more as substitute parents, were valued in difficult times. A comparison made by R. illustrates this contrast:

'The first key worker was a good listener. She helped me to see a lighter side of life. The other key worker was young. We got on well, we liked the same music, exchanged records etc. but she seemed too much like a friend to discuss serious or personal things.'

Another young man, L. explained that he had got on very well with his key worker but could never have confided in him because:

'He was too like us. He's mad, would jump out on us and everything. If you talked to him about anything serious, you would expect him to laugh.'

Instead L. confided in another worker whom he described as:

'Just so caring. She was an older woman. She used to bring me sweets and talk to me for ages. When you were feeling down, she always seemed to know. She would talk to you.'

It may be surprising that a group who often saw adult involvement as interference should put such a high value on the companionship of staff. It is also a good example of how staff with different qualities can be recruited to fulfil varying roles.

While most comments about care staff were positive, a few young people did say that staff had not made time for them nor seemed to care about what happened to them. It is worth noting, though perhaps co-incidental, that these negative comments were all made about workers in centres which offered a more focused style of intervention and were more generously staffed than ordinary children's homes. One in five young people who had been in a residential unit spontaneously said they particularly liked always having someone there to talk to. Though the opportunity to talk over troubles was appreciated, teenagers also enjoyed the variety and fun of everyday chat. Some young people keenly missed this when they left, particularly if they moved to live on their own.

Relationships with the Other Young Residents: These were often as important as those with staff. Sometimes fellow-residents were very supportive, especially in helping new-comers to settle in. Several young people acknowledged that friends were preferred as confidants to staff and that advice would be taken from them before approaching staff on a difficult issue. However, living with others produces its own stresses and, not unexpectedly, a majority of young people (60%) said that they got on well with some of their fellow residents but not others.

A few complained about repeatedly having their belongings stolen and one in six had experienced some form of bullying. While some teenagers had developed some understanding of other's difficulties, it could also be distressing or annoying to live with teenagers who were 'mad, on drugs and attempting suicide'. Any unit striving for normalisation could only cope with a limited number of very disturbed teenagers or crises without becoming destabilised itself.

Rules: By far the most disliked aspect of care was having to conform to rules. Restrictions on the number of cigarettes allowed per day, arrangements for allocating pocket money and set times for returning in the evenings were cited as annoying, but most young people seemed to appreciate the reasons for having the rules. What angered them was unfairness, for example when everyone was punished for misdemeanours committed by a few or when staff were inconsistent. As P. remarked:

> 'You're treated like an adult one minute and a five year old
> the next.'

She suggested that if there were separate units for older teenagers staff would learn to relate to them appropriately.

Physical Environment or Care: Pleasant surroundings were appreciated. A few young people liked the fact that the building was modern and well maintained. Others had been pleasantly surprised on admission to find modern, attractive furniture and decor and this had raised their spirits considerably. The main complaint about the physical environment was lack of privacy and several young people complained that they could not lock their bedroom doors (cf. Gardner, 1989). Though each person who mentioned this also said that there were plans to put locks on bedroom doors, there was anger that this action had taken so long. One young woman was exasperated because it took so long to arrange anything practical:

> 'Simple things, even getting an appointment for the
> dentist, seemed to take ages. I had no dental treatment all
> the time I was there, though I kept asking.'

The lack of privacy extended to telephones where often it was not possible to have a private conversation with a parent or friend. A number of young people commented favourably on the food. Some simply said they liked the meals but others enjoyed having food made for them and contrasted this with the situation at home where they usually fended for themselves. Naturally there were also some who disliked the food they were given.

Complaints

One in five young people felt that they had been unfairly treated while in residential care. There were a few instances where staff were thought to have used sanctions in an unfair way or to have taken a personal dislike to a particular young person. Other examples of unfair treatment included informally making plans for a young woman's future in her absence and being subject to too many restrictions. Two young people spoke of incidents when they had been assaulted by staff and both had formally complained about it.

Almost two thirds of residents in children's homes had been given information about how to make a complaint but in residential schools the proportion was only a third. The advice was usually to report the matter to a member of staff or the social worker. The practice of giving information about how to pursue a complaint outwith the unit was largely confined to two agencies. Three quarters of the young people in Agency A had been given information on how to make a complaint and 60% of those in Agency E, but only 14% in Agency C.

In Agency A young people were routinely given written information on admission to care. This included a prepaid post-card addressed to the district manager which could be used to initiate a complaint and most young people were aware of how it could be used. Agency E largely relied on posters rather than distributing information to each individual. Notices alerting teenagers to the existence of departmental and independent help were in most units and one young woman had called Childline when unable to resolve a disagreement with staff.

Running Away

There has been concern in recent times about the dangers young people in care can be exposed to when they leave the home without permission. This was a particularly sensitive issue in one agency due to the fact that, while the study was in progress, a young person had been killed in a car crash after running away with a group of other teenagers.

Almost half the young people in residential care said that they had left the placement at least once without permission. Usually they sought refuge with friends. The 'absconders' divided into two roughly equal groups of occasional and habitual absconders. The first group had run away no more than four times and had usually been away for only a few hours or at most one day. The second group were more worrying. They had run away more than four times and for some there had been periods when it was a daily occurrence. Absences were also longer, sometimes extending to a week or more.

When asked about why they ran away, occasional absconders spoke of impulsive reactions to one-off events, whilst the reasons given by habitual absconders reflected deep-seated problems. Those who had run away once or twice had often done so in response to a particular incident or situation. One boy was being bullied by other residents and another objected to his home leave being cancelled. Though the number of habitual absconders in our sample was small, it was striking that many of them felt let down by both their family and the care system. N's family had cut off all contact and he had had no education for several months. He described how he had started running away when there were problems and he was bored but admitted that it had become fun:

> 'I go to parties, steal cars. I like it now. I don't really want to stop.'

An intensive programme based on individual tuition and activities had been devised to help this young man break the pattern of absconding. A worrying aspect of his behaviour was that he had made several attempts to take his own life.

S. was facing up to the fact that his parents were never going to offer him a home. He described how he ran away when his alternative hopes for supported accommodation were not fulfilled:

> 'If they [Social Services] had been getting me a place to stay
> outside it might have been better but nothing was happening.
> I didn't want to stay there [in care] for ever. I had mucked
> up my job. I just didn't want to be there.'

S. spent much of the subsequent year in custody.

Running away was therefore often a response in situations where the teenagers felt powerless or hopeless in relation to an immediate crisis or longer-term prospects. B. said 'When I was feeling depressed, I'd just run away'. Though young people were obviously more likely to abscond if they were living in a unit where this was usual behaviour, some of them had developed the habit of running away while living at home. All the young people in our study who became serious absconders had been let down by their families *and* by the care system, so it would be too simplistic to see the problem as merely a management problem for residential staff. Yet absconding is often one of the main justifications for placement in secure units (Kelly, 1992; Harris and Timms, 1993), where the custodial setting may exacerbate rather than help the young person's despair.

Contact with Family and Friends

Almost half the young people would have preferred to see more of their friends and some simply went out without permission in order to do so. Distance and the fact that young people in care were expected to return home by times which they and their peers considered too early were the main barriers to contact. It was not uncommon for young people to acknowledge that they could never see enough of their friends but others were glad to have the opportunity to break away.

Contact with parents and siblings presented less of a problem and only a quarter of the young people were not satisfied with the level of contact. In most cases young people acknowledged that this response indicated a general wish to spend more time outwith the unit. Where there was a specific wish for more family contact, the barriers to contact were generally to be found in family tensions and conflicts rather than restrictions imposed by being in residential care.

Parents' Reflections on Residential Care

Parents' views about what constituted a good residential unit did not alter in the course of the year. At follow-up, they made it clear that they liked well organised units where the young people were under control:

'They kept good tabs on him. Didn't let him away with too much.'
'S. did not run away. Staff were good. Plenty of staff.'
'It was well organised and you felt there was plenty of supervision.'
'I think it saved K. from being out on the streets now.
The discipline they have there is strong enough.'

Equally they had valued friendly staff who gave support to both the young people and themselves when needed:

'The staff were friendly and they would help if we had
problems at home . . . there is a fair amount of discipline.'
'Key worker was easy to talk to. They always kept me in touch
with what was happening.'

Most parents whose children were in residential schools were pleased that suitable education was being provided:

'I liked everything about it – small classes and teachers and staff
were nice and concerned. He obviously benefited,
especially educationally.'
'It gave him schooling and kept him away from bad company.'

Several parents were grateful that they now had to cope with less anxiety because others shared the responsibility and they knew where the young person was. Although many were pleased to have some relief from their children and the worry they had caused them, most parents were pleased that regular contact could continue and that weekends were usually spent at home. T's mother put it this way:

> 'T. is away but not separated from us. You get a break during the week but she is home at weekends. If we have problems at home we can phone the school and they take it up with her when she goes back.'

Just as parents praised well organised units where staff were friendly, they were critical when there was a lack of control and staff seemed to leave the young people to their own devices. Some described a state of apparent anarchy:

> 'The kids get up on the roof if they don't like what's happening.'
> 'It's too lax. They [the residents] can do almost anything they like then the staff bring in the Police.'

One mother commented that there had been too many staff changes which gave the young people no sense of security. A few parents had felt unsupported when they reported serious misbehaviour at home to the unit and then the young person had not been challenged about it. Several parents complained about not being kept informed when young people had absconded or were in some kind of trouble. They only found out when the Police called at their home. A few commented on the fact that young people were given too much money which led them to expect a standard of dress which their parents could neither extend to the rest of the family nor keep up when the young person returned home.

Fortunately parents had found that the majority of placements were staffed by friendly people who were in control. Residential staff appeared to be as popular with parents as with the young people. No parent said that they had a poor relationship with residential staff and over 80% said they got on well or very well. Parents had got on equally well with staff in all types of residential placement.

Over half the parents had found that the placement helped the young person as much as or more than they had expected. There was particular praise for residential schools: 85% had met or exceeded the parents' expectations which applied to only 42% of other residential placements. In general residential schools were praised for their organisation and the complaints about lack of control primarily applied to other units.

The best residential schools provided effective support to whole families. Staff kept parents informed and were available when crises arose. The close involvement of the social worker was very important in maintaining links and helping ensure that parents and young people made progress in tandem. On the other hand there were problems for one young woman who had no social work support and who returned to unchanged family attitudes every weekend while she herself had become much more insightful and mature. Several families had been counselled to find more productive ways of approaching long standing problems.

Flexi-care arrangements in some residential schools suited some families well. Mrs G. was glad that her son's school had enabled him to concentrate on subjects he liked and also cherished 'the space it gives me – the couple of days he's in there ' when she had a break from sorting out fights between K. and his brothers and sisters.

Social Workers' Wishes for Additional Resources

With respect to 60% of residential placements, social workers reported that additional resources would have made the placement more effective. Sometimes they referred specifically to the need for more generous staffing levels, but the most commonly identified gap was in educational provision. In each agency social workers spoke of a lack of provision for children who needed special education because of emotional or behavioural difficulties. Although it was a problem everywhere, lack of educational provision for children in care was most often cited as problematic in Agency A, where the breakdown of certain placements was attributed to a failure to provide suitable education.

In some cases it was anticipated that young people who had made good progress in residential schools would find it difficult to return to mainstream schooling because there was no 'sheltered' setting within mainstream provision. That could delay their full return to the community at the same time blocking a place for others needing this intensive resource.

Lack of supported accommodation could also limit the effectiveness of placements. When a suitable semi-independent resource was not readily available, young people remained too long in children's units or became impatient and moved out to live with friends or into some other kind of unsupported situation. Thus there was a personal disadvantage for the young person as well as an inefficient use of residential care for teenagers who were ready to cope with less supervision and support.

In Agency C a number of social workers believed that therapeutic, individual help was lacking. In some instances the social worker wanted more time for workers currently involved to provide this but at other times a psychologist or other specialist service was thought to be needed, for example to help with an addiction. On the other hand, as we saw earlier, young people usually indicated that they preferred people they knew to specialists who often seemed remote. Sometimes the wish to refer young people for specialist help was reflecting the social workers' uncertainty about their skills.

Foster care

Preferences for Residential or Foster Care

All the young people living away from home at the start of the study were questioned on the merits of residential and foster care. In fact, they proved to be fairly equally divided on this issue. Asked in which kind of placement they would rather be, 24 young people expressed a preference for foster care and 23 for residential care, with 6 having no clear or strong preference. Some had very strong views. One spoke of running away if placed in a foster home, for instance. Although their preferences were generally clear cut, very few teenagers (10%) said they had been offered a choice of placements by their social workers.

The main reasons for preferring residential care were – already having a family or concern about hurting their own family; greater perceived independence or freedom in residential care; liking the company of peers; and seeing families as stressful. The family loyalty factor was illustrated by T. He had wondered about asking for a foster placement, but changed his mind fearing that his grandmother (with whom he stayed each weekend) would be jealous. Even more strongly, F. asserted that he would not want to consider a new family as 'I see nothing wrong with the family I've got'.

The principal grounds for favouring foster care were the individualised or personalised care, more relaxed atmosphere and the normality of family life. One young man who was glad to be in a foster home had seen the only alternative as a tough children's unit 'and it isn't a very nice place'. Another said 'people steal your clothes and you don't get much attention like here in a foster home'.

Overall Appraisals of Foster Placements

At the beginning of the study, social workers rated 75% of the foster placements as being good in terms of physical qualities and 90% were seen as good emotionally (compared with only 40% of residential units). More of the teenagers in foster care were said to be getting on well with their carers. The teenagers' own comments in the main supported this positive initial impression. Most of those in foster care said they got on well or very well with their foster mothers and foster fathers. Parents whose children were in foster care were also generally pleased even when they had doubts about it to start with. Several parents who were initially mistrustful of a substitute family had come to recognise benefits.

In the interviews at the end of the year, the picture was more mixed, with mainly negative feedback about foster placements which had ended, but positive accounts of those which were continuing. In all, nineteen young people answered detailed questions at the follow-up stage about their current or recent foster placements. With some exceptions they gave a reasonably positive account. Half said they were pleased with their foster homes (9), and a further four indicated that they simply accepted them. Just over half said they would not have wanted to stay anywhere else, but a minority would have preferred a different placement.

More later than initial foster placements were thought by social workers to have met their aims and to have helped a lot. This may reflect the fact that often the young people who went to a foster home later in the year were better known to the service, having transferred from another placement in care. It also suggests that social workers need not give up following the breakdown of an initial foster placement.

Foster Carers' Skills

When social workers were asked to comment on the adequacy of foster carers' skills to meet the needs of the particular young person under consideration, their ratings were almost equally divided between the ones thought to have the appropriate skills 'fully' and those only 'partly'. Amongst the skills and qualities recognised were – being good with adolescents; being tolerant but firm; an understanding personality; having appropriate expectations about contributions to housework. The perceived deficiencies were – lack of experience with adolescents; inflexibility; being unable to withstand manipulation. What seemed to be crucial was to achieve the level of firmness which social workers and parents usually wanted, without alienating the young person by being too rigid. In a few cases, social workers indicated that the demands of the young person were so great that almost any family might have failed.

Benefits of Foster Care

Amongst the specific gains from foster care identified by *social workers* in relation to particular cases were:

- realising she no longer needed to be responsible for her younger sister and brother;
- experience of an orderly, supportive household;
- improved budgeting and self-care;
- shed some of the burden of the past and gained self-confidence;
- learnt a lot about living with people and firm boundaries;
- first time she's had a consistent adult and she likes that;
- they set firm boundaries and she knew where she was.

Several stressed the importance of stability and definite boundaries. One worker believed that the availability of the right foster home at the right time had been crucial in assisting a repeat offender to settle and keep out of trouble.

This teenager spoke very positively of her single foster carer as relaxed, flexible and understanding.

The main things *young people* liked about being in a foster family were – individual care/attention and being part of a 'normal' family. According to one, it was good to be 'living with a proper family now'. They enjoyed doing things together as a family and mentioned their liking for individuals in the foster family. This was particularly valued when the adolescent felt accepted:

> 'They trust me.'
> 'They treat me like their own children.'
> 'I get on with her as a friend, not a foster mother.'

Several mentioned the more relaxed and trusting atmosphere compared with their previous experiences.

Family activities and outings were also enjoyed:

> 'We go to the theatre workshop and do drama.
> I would never have believed I would have done that.
> The whole family is great.'

This could lay the foundations for personal guidance:

> 'I enjoyed their company and I listened to them and
> took their advice. They kind of helped me to mature more.'

Fostering could be seen as offering welcome liberty and two emphasised this aspect. J. said 'I don't need to ask to do things. As long as I'm back by a reasonable time, it's OK'. H. also liked the freedom he was given – 'I can go out every night with friends'. This was accompanied by feeling 'cared for properly'.

Whilst likes and dislikes about the placements understandably centred on the household relationships, when it came to identifying benefits the young people most often portrayed these in terms of changes outside the home. This indicated that the families were not just comfortable places to be, but were effective in altering behaviour in other contexts in ways likely to improve the teenagers' life chances. Five spoke of improvements at school and five referred to keeping out of trouble. For instance, one young man thought that the high expectations and regular routines of his foster home had helped him to apply himself better at school and hence get a place in college. Others mentioned having matured and gained security.

Amongst the more specific gains reported were:

- feeling more settled and having made new friends;
- help with schoolwork;
- feeling cared for;

- learning to trust people;
- learned to consider other people's feelings.

In the follow up interviews, young people provided information in response to a list of closed questions about 15 foster placements where they had been living at the time of the first interview. Over half indicated that they had been helped with regard to – improvements at school; improved behaviour; greater maturity; seeing things differently. Overall, ten of the fifteen thought they had been helped by the placement with the difficulties which led to them being in care (six substantially). When things had got better, this was generally a result of assisting the young person directly to improve their own behaviour, sense of self or motivation. For instance, G. thought she had been helped a lot, as she had stopped taking drugs, improved her school attendance and was no longer in trouble with the police. B. felt she had fewer hassles now and had become less violent. K. described how her foster home had 'made care feel a good experience', whilst J. emphasised her greater self-confidence and the fact that she returned to school after an absence of several months.

Parents also often spoke positively about their children being in a family and were not necessarily jealous. What they usually valued was the family atmosphere and the opportunity for the young person to break away from bad company. It was important for them to feel their children were respected and well cared for. One spoke of 'a decent family' who helped R. a lot. A different parent described a foster mother as 'kind and interested in W.'. One father had been initially suspicious, but came to see the foster home as caring and helpful. Several spoke approvingly of progress made:

> 'The whole idea was to get him into a family environment . . .
> I think he's been lucky. There have been wee hiccups now
> and again but they've talked that out so he's quite happy now.'
> 'He's making progress because his school work is improving.
> K. (foster mother) used to have a lot of problems with him but
> he goes to school now and she keeps a check on him, which is
> what he needs.'

Difficulties and Dislikes about the Foster Placements

Several parents expressed discomfort about fostering since it seemed to symbolise dismissal of themselves as the rightful family:

> 'At first I felt like somebody else doing my job. I think
> maybe deep down I was frightened they were going to do
> better than I had or I thought I had.'
> 'I didn't see why he should be put with foster parents when
> he has a home.'

With respect to the current or recent foster placements, half of the teenagers reported difficulties about the placement, though several also made positive remarks. When foster care had not worked out, this tended to colour the whole memory of the placement, so that five young people said that looking back there was nothing they liked about the foster home. At one extreme, a girl had been sexually abused by the male foster carer. She also resented the female foster carer for emotional blackmail when trying to persuade her to keep quiet about what had happened. Another girl had been abused by a family friend who had taken her in on a private fostering basis. A young man described his remand foster placement as 'worse than jail', because he was bored, far from home and disliked the carer.

Otherwise, resentment usually focused on rules and restrictions by the foster carers, which contrasted with the freedom which others in foster care said they enjoyed. Contrary to the image of foster care as being 'normal' and unrestrictive compared with residential care (Hawkins and Breiling, 1989), one of the main problems was that some young people found rules irksome, even intolerable. Either they had previously been used to greater freedom which they wanted to continue or else they had expected more independence now they were away from home. Problems often centred on the expected time for coming in at night and the need to ask permission to go places. The teenagers felt these rules were inappropriate for their age. Of course such conflicts over autonomy and authority are a common feature of adolescent-parent relationships (Collins and Laursen, 1992). Quite often the young people openly challenged the rules, which led to animated disputes. These did not always lead to a disruption. One young person said there had been arguments about the time for coming in, but they had sorted that out.

Parents, too, identified tension about the teenagers' autonomy as one of the main difficulties with some foster placements, although they themselves often supported the restrictions. One observed that her daughter had 'run away' from the foster home to be with her boyfriend, steal and take drugs. Another said her son had resented rules she herself approved of, such as having to come in by times he regarded as too early. In a third case, the parent liked the family atmosphere, but observed that 'he didn't like anyone telling him what to do'.

Although some placements suffered from unclear plans, resentment could also arise if contracts became too prescriptive or too one-sided. One young man complained that foster care felt more like 'care' than being in a home, because of the emphasis on the contract, meetings and so many rules. Another complaint about contracts came from a parent. She expressed the view that her step-child had been subject to a contract which placed expectations on the young person but was silent on what the carer should offer. She in fact argued that creating this atmosphere was dangerous since young people did not know what to expect from carers and so were not empowered to complain if carers behaved inappropriately.

This point had wider significance. Two young women in the sample had been subject to inappropriate sexual behaviour by male carers, one in an approved foster home and the other in an officially sanctioned placement with family friends. There is increasing awareness both of the risk of sexual abuse and of the vulnerability of carers to false allegations. The use of contracts is a potentially important means of making the dangers explicit and clarifying basic measures which should be taken to provide some protection to all concerned.

A few young people were critical because they had been given little pocket money, which was particularly annoying when they were working and had to hand over most of their earnings. The amount of money given to them was determined by social services regulations, but could nevertheless sour relationships with foster carers who actually handled the money. In at least two foster placements, financial issues had played a part in the placement ending, when the teenagers had not been allowed to retain as much of their earnings or allowance as they thought reasonable. Hostility also arose in a few instances when foster carers tried to tackle behaviour problems, like heavy drinking or drug use.

Sometimes there was a mismatch in expectations about family life, some of which may have been rooted in earlier attachment patterns as illuminated by Downes (1992). One young man declared 'I can't express myself . . . I don't feel part of the family'. Teenagers who wanted or were used to operating quite autonomously found the pressure to join in and become a family member difficult to accept or handle. T.'s carers complained that he was using their place like a bed and breakfast. They found his failure to join in with the rest of the family hard to accept, but he felt little warmth from the female foster carer and so concentrated on his friends and activities outside the home. Three teenagers also mentioned difficulties with the foster siblings (eg sharing a room, competing for attention, getting less pocket money).

Even when there had been problems or even premature ending of the particular placement, this did not always mean that the adolescent was disillusioned with foster care as such. Four of the seven people who expressed a preference for a different placement still wanted to be in a family setting. They had not generalised to all fostering situations their dissatisfaction with the particular placement (itself following some kind of difficulty in the original family). For example, one young man whose placement had disrupted said his foster home was the best of the 3 placements he had and he certainly would not want to go to residential care again. Another said he wanted a different kind of foster home, with more flexible carers and closer to his home area. At least two said that with the benefit of hindsight they would like to return to a former foster home, because they now appreciated that they had not been as unreasonably restrictive as they had felt at the time.

Relationships with the Foster Carers and Other Children in the Family

Of the young people in foster care, half stated that they got on well with the female foster carer and could confide in her. One fewer found their male foster carer easy to talk to. The reasons given for finding foster carers approachable or not were:

- *Easy to talk to* – friendly; interested; it feels safe; relaxed; sense of humour; treats you as an adult; shared activities.
- *Difficult to talk to* – leads to arguments; not understand; too strict; too busy; not interested.

Evidently, the teenagers got on well with people who they felt respected and accepted them for who they were. They complained when they thought their behaviour was being checked by rules and unsympathetic telling-offs. K. was particularly positive about her female foster carer, who 'says all the things a social worker says, but then you can have a good laugh'. By contrast, D.'s foster father 'contradicted everything I said. He would say "Well, that's not right" and go on about what I should be doing'. Two teenagers who were unhappy with their placements stated that the problems had centred on the female carer's coldness and excessive expectations of conformity, whereas they found the male carers much more sympathetic and approachable. A third related well to her female foster carer, but found the husband's authoritarian style oppressive.

Foster siblings may make up for poor relationships with the carers or offset good relations. At the start of the study, only 3 young people in foster care were on their own. Usually, there were one or two other children living in the foster home, but occasionally more and in one case there were six others. Three were not getting on well with the foster carers' own children and three more got on well with some but not others, leaving 10 who said they got on well with all of them. T. attributed the difficulties he experienced over 'stupid' rules to the fact that his foster carers had no experience of looking after teenagers, since their only son was half his age. This also meant the two boys had little in common and did not get on well.

To conclude the key factors affecting success of foster placements appeared to be (a) young people's feelings of being cared for and respected and (b) congruent expectations about the level of autonomy to which the teenagers was entitled. In the placements which worked well, young people felt that the carers were sympathetic and genuinely concerned. Advice and guidance was given in a manner which they found acceptable. This supports the view of Downes (1992) that the emotional qualities of the carers are crucial, as is their ability to respond to the differing attachment or detachment needs and experiences of adolescents. At the same time, clarification *prior to placement* that expectations are compatible also seems essential.

After-Care Services for Young Adults Living 'Independently'

Over the last ten years major efforts have been put into improving support to older teenagers leaving care, in part due to earlier research findings about the massive problems they face (Stein and Carey, 1986; Garnett, 1992). Sadly, our study showed that many of the same difficulties still persist. Experience continues to belie hopes and expectations. This is not surprising when we recall that few people with good material and social supports attempt to manage on their own at 16–17 years, the age at which the vulnerable youngsters in our sample were trying to do so.

Social workers attributed nearly all young people's moves to independent living as being the latter's 'preferred' choice, apart from two who were seen as having no alternative. Many young people in care do have a precocious wish to enjoy adult freedoms, but their preferences may also have been influenced by the absence of suitable niches for young adults within the care system, on top of their conflicts with or alienation from parents.

Overall Progress

Asked at the follow-up stage to say how well they were coping, about a quarter of the young people living independently said they were coping well, though only one of these made no reference to any problems. This young person was living with friends and 'paying' his own way through casual work. The rest of those interviewed were about equally split between those who indicated that they were not coping and those who were 'just managing'.

Social workers conveyed a somewhat more positive picture suggesting that a quarter of the young people were managing well, one third as not well and the rest (42%) as 'quite well'. There were a number of situations where social workers said that the teenagers were coping well or very well but the young people themselves said they were struggling.

Only a minority of these young people saw themselves as having been well prepared. Parents broadly concurred with this view with only a couple of them seeing the young person as having had adequate preparation. Social workers again more often thought preparation had been satisfactory, although some certainly wanted to see more preparation taking place.

Social workers assessed significantly more young people as managing well when they had had some preparation. Likewise, those young people who said that they were not prepared 'enough' were somewhat more likely to say themselves that they were either not coping or just managing. All of those who had good preparation said that they were at least 'just coping'. When it came to those young people who were prepared in specialist units, the numbers were too small to draw firm conclusions but the suggestion was that these had the edge on the rest. Yet one of them, apart from feeling disappointed at the absence of follow-up support from the unit, also commented on the inadequacy of the preparation. She observed how after she left the unit she had 'no clue about cooking or anything' and that it was her social worker later who helped her to budget and put money aside for food, bus fares and other things. She claimed to have cooked only one meal whilst in the unit. Even the washing machine at the unit was different and much easier to handle:

> 'You can throw anything in and everything turns out.
> When I moved in here the first four or five washings
> I done were dyed, everything was just ruined.'

Although social workers often underestimated the difficulties young adults were facing, there was broad agreement about the main problematic areas, which often combined practical, social and emotional difficulties. Access to suitable *housing* is obviously a fundamental prerequisite. A minority had difficulty getting housed at all. One young person said the absence of housing forced her to go back to her mother's, but once there they fell out again and there was nowhere to go. Local authority housing, in spite of its limitations, offered greater stability to young people than other forms of housing. With one exception all of those in these tenancies were still there at the time of the follow-up, even though there were doubts about how much longer some of them would be able to continue.

For those who were assisted by the local authority or a housing association, a major problem was the poor quality of the neighbourhood. Some young people felt besieged by threats and wanted to move elsewhere. Both they and parents complained of: 'too much vandalism', 'harassment' and being 'burgled more than once'. Some parents deplored the fact that 16–17 year olds were housed in areas where they stood little chance of avoiding trouble either with drugs or offending. One young person felt so fed up and depressed that she added:

> 'Because of everything that's been happening now I just
> can't be bothered with the house and can't be bothered with
> anything, can't be bothered going looking for a job. I just
> don't want to do anything.'

Another criticism was the distance between the accommodation secured for the young person and their previous support network. A number of them felt cut-off from relations and friends and had to spend a lot of their limited income on bus fares to visit them. As an example, one young person was accommodated at the opposite end of town from her original home area and, not having registered with a new G.P., she did not know what to do when she was suddenly taken ill. Luckily, the neighbours rallied round and made arrangements for her to see a local doctor.

As almost all the young people were unemployed or on YTS schemes, *money problems* were very real and the young people had to fall back on the social security system. Many were too young to qualify for Income Support, since people under 18 have to satisfy certain prescribed conditions which can take time to establish (Bannister *et al*, 1993). The youngsters in our sample had only a very hazy idea about how the benefits system worked and, according to some, information about this had not featured in their preparation. Although they were in apparently similar circumstances, some were in receipt of significantly different amounts of benefits depending on the area in which they happened to be living. For example, one of them claimed to receive £48 per fortnight whilst another in a different district was getting £63 (both had the rent paid on their behalf). Sometimes a Benefits Office would agree to use special hardship category funds, whilst another tried to place the responsibility on the social services. Local policies on financial aid varied within the same Social Services (Work) Department too. One district ensured that the young person had at least some income to tide them over when in difficulties, whilst in another they said that the young person was now over 16 and no longer their responsibility. The absence of clear policies by either the DSS or local authorities about this age group was proving confusing to many young people and left them vulnerable and exposed.

The resulting poverty led to major problems, including in some instances the threat of eviction and fuel disconnections. One young person commented:

'The DSS will not give me any money, I've had no money
for 3 weeks . . . My partner gets £59 a fortnight but that doesn't
last. I phoned yesterday, told them we had no food.'

A graphic Catch 22 description was given by a young person who said:

'Couldn't stay with anyone for too long because I had no
money. Couldn't get a job because I had no address.'

In some instances, young people resorted to crime in order to obtain money. One had turned to shoplifting and another sold medical prescriptions.

Money difficulties were usually attributed by the teenagers to inadequate income and only occasionally to poor budgeting or to their own behaviour such as drinking. Social workers, though, made more reference to the absence of budgeting skills. It was very rare for a parent to give money to a young person, as most of them were on benefits themselves. More usually, social workers produced a few pounds to help out.

Employment and Unemployment: As far as could be ascertained, no young person living independently and featuring in this sample had a stable job at the time of the interview, though one person was on a YTS scheme and at least one other was studying. Three others had already finished YTS schemes. Another three young people had 'lost' or given up jobs, two of them finding them boring and one had left after some prank against her in the work place. One gave up his job as a 'mechanic' because he felt he was being taken advantage of by being paid only £29 per week. A couple of young people occasionally secured casual jobs lasting for a few days each time, but this was unpredictable. As with housing, the job situation was worse than they had expected a year ago.

The few who gave up jobs at a period of recession could be described as 'irresponsible', yet in a different economic climate, job changes by young people could be seen as part of growing up experimentation, until they found the job that suited them. Many of these young people, as others in the whole sample, were beginning to resign themselves to a future without a job. A minority made connections with the absence of skills or of educational qualifications, some still hoping that they might go on to a college for further study. A few others were contemplating the Forces as a way out. In the past, the start of work usually signified for young people entry to the adult world and work itself contributed to a definition of their identity and sense of life. In the absence of work, engagement in anti-social activities can become an alternative way of trying to establish a sense of identity, as well as source of income.

After money problems and debts, *loneliness and boredom* were the most frequently quoted problems about living independently, affecting at least a third of the young people concerned. One claimed that her dog was her only company. Others said:

> 'You feel as if nobody wants to know you, nobody coming up to visit you.'
> 'Some days I'm all right, I can sit and I enjoy it, but there's other times when I sometimes don't feel like I can cope, when I sit and cry about it. That's the only way I can cope.'

As a result there were strong pressures on the sample group to be sucked into a peer culture of drugs, offending and vandalism. Even when critical of it, some recognised that this offered the only company they had to fall back on. Some young people were drawn back to parents or relatives. This was usually only for occasional visits, either because they could not afford to travel more often or out of fear that a spark would reignite previous conflicts. As one of them stated 'It's only contact, not going back'. Another spent the day at her mother's place whilst the latter was at work and left before the mother returned home. One young woman found great solace in regular visits to her grandmother.

Loneliness is not unusual in adolescence and can be see as the price paid for independence from family (Blos, 1970). However, most families remain supportive when a person leaves home, yet our sample included many who were estranged from relatives and had little contact with friends and previous carers. Thus their solitude and unhappiness were all the more intense. Several were sustained only by the solicitude of one person – perhaps a relative, a partner or the social worker. Hence the issue of *support* was usually vital.

One of the young people said appreciatively:

> 'He's done that much for me, I just can't put points on it you know – he's helped me physically and mentally and just he's helped me a lot . . . he respects me for what I am and he wants to get to know you. If I didn't have the help that I had my head would be really f . . . ed up. I wouldn't have been able to get through what I've been through.'

Another person was very grateful for her social worker's continued support at a time when she was feeling low and lonely:

> 'I see her about once every fortnight. She came round the other day and we went out for a meal. If I need anything she's always there. I don't know what more she can do . . . When I had no money and there was no milk or nothing in the house and I phoned her, she brought extra money round and that was really nice of her . . . She's never let me down.'

In contrast, she felt let down by the lack of contact from the care staff of a specialist unit who had helped her to prepare for independent living. Youngsters generally indicated that residential staff they had lived with either had no time to offer continued help or had moved on. A young person who tried to re-establish some contact with her former residential unit expressed her disappointment:

> 'I phoned a couple of times but like it's a new boss and everything it's all changed . . . it's like a stopover . . . there's not really anybody up there that I know any more.'

Still on the same theme, one young person remarked rather bitterly that whilst she was in the home the staff made all sorts of promises of help after she left, 'but they never got round to doing it. And once you're out that's it, they just forget about you'. She claimed to have visited a couple of times but did not feel welcomed.

Possibly in answer to such criticisms, one sample agency plans that its new residential units will not only make it easier for residential staff to keep young people longer, but also to welcome them back if needed and give them support after they leave. In addition it plans to offer young people the opportunity to try things out in the community and return if they fail.

Although young people were more likely to get help from their fieldworker than residential carers, some had received little or no help from either source:

'The social worker left and was not replaced – it was left up to me to get in touch.'
'There was some help at the start, but since I came here I've seen no-one.'

D.'s main support was her former foster carer with whom she talked over how to manage bills or fill in forms.

Although some young people had left their previous home determined to manage unaided, nearly all soon realised that they needed help. They wanted assistance to get better housing and a more secure income, but also interest in themselves and more skill development. Several said they wished for someone to call on them or for 'more informal contact to see how I was getting on'. Only two of the young people did not want any further help, because they believed they could sort things out themselves.

Whilst a number of young people had been keen to be out of care and free of social workers, they were now surprised and disappointed not to have had any contact from them. A few of those in Scotland also felt that the system there was deliberately bringing their supervision to an end at the age of 16 so that 'they' would be absolved of any responsibility for them. They felt the department was washing its hands of them. One said:

'Just when you turn 16 you feel they are just sort of trying to get pushed out the door as quickly as possible, which I don't think is right . . . I wanted a section kept because I know that if I had kept my section on me I would have more support . . . I was quite annoyed because they just said to me that they think I'm a mature young person and I wouldn't need their supervision.'

A young man in an English agency had similar anxieties but at least they came two years later. He resented the 'pressure of knowing that when I'm 18 I've got to leave'. However a young woman in a different English authority was glad that the Children Act 1989 made her feel entitled to social work support until the age of 21. She was certain she would need her social worker's support for another couple of years.

Young people who had left care interpreted the open invitation to 'get in touch with your social worker if you need help' as a face saving device. Others were equally inhibited about taking the initiative to ask for help:

'She said if I was not managing I was to tell her, but I would have liked her to come round.'
'She could have helped without me asking.'

One young man felt he couldn't go back because he had let his social worker down by offending again. Stalker (1990) makes a similar point about parents of children with learning difficulties who said they found it difficult taking the initiative to ask carers for more respite care.

Generally parents of teenagers living on their own agreed with the teenager's evaluations of the social work support they received. One satisfied mother said that 'the social work support was excellent and still is' adding that the social worker was her daughter's main support. In contrast a different parent remarked:

> 'Not satisfied at all. Once the order stopped 10 months ago
> they abandoned her. L. feels rejected by them.'

Some social workers were unaware of the need for support or else described a level of contact which was not confirmed by the teenagers themselves. For example, there were situations where the social worker said that there were frequent visits during the first 2–3 weeks and grants made available, while the young person said that he/she had no help since living independently. In one instance, the social worker referred to 'occasional visits' to the young person, but the young person said the last visit was 10 months ago.

Almost half the social workers involved with these young people would have liked to have given more support to them in areas such as preparation with a pregnancy, more frequent visits, making available counselling opportunities, offering groups or just seeing the young person more often. A variety of reasons were offered for not doing so. These ranged from the young persons' apparent resistance to departmental policy to simply lack of time. In one case, the department withdrew its support when it discovered that the young woman concerned was living with her boyfriend.

At the start of the study, young people who thought they might eventually move to independent living were asked to say who they would turn to for *help in an emergency*. Of 41 planning to move to independence before long, 46 per cent said they would turn to their parents and a few to relatives, almost one fifth to the social services, 12% to friends and 9 per cent to foster carers. Just 9 per cent did not know who they would turn to.

A year later, those now living independently were again asked who they would turn to in an emergency. More spoke of getting in touch with a parent or relative (two thirds) and a quarter with a social worker/residential worker or former foster carer, but now as many as a quarter said they didn't know or to no-one. Friends were not mentioned but one young person mentioned a friend's parent. Emergencies were apparently viewed as situations when you turn to older people for help rather than to friends.

When asked to say what *help had been given by their families* since they moved to living independently, both the teenagers and their parents were in agreement that about half had given some help and half none at all. Family aid mostly took the form of meals and companionship. A few parents also helped with

---

household items or offered very small sums of money on special occasions. A minority of young people were assisted by other relatives. For example an aunt took a microwave oven to one young person and another youngster stayed with her aunt for the week-end when she wanted to. Some social workers were unaware of such help. Asked what more help they would have liked from their families, young people put the emphasis on supportive visits, company, encouragement and material aid, eg 'see them more and get some money from them'.

About a third of the young people claimed to have had no *help from friends* during this period, but others described having had practical and emotional support. This consisted of being lent money, being put up when homeless, advice about benefits but especially companionship. What they wanted from friends was mostly visits and emotional support. Only two young people were totally isolated from any contact with family or friends.

Conclusions

The majority of teenagers in the study were positive about their care placements and were seen to have benefited from them. Indeed, sometimes parents or social workers expressed regret that similar intervention had not started sooner. A young person's best interests may sometimes conflict with agency policies aimed at avoiding substitute care whenever possible.

Residential schools were highly regarded by all three parties for providing a caring atmosphere and effective help not only for schooling, but also for family conflicts and offending. It should be borne in mind that these were mainly teenagers admitted from their family homes rather than those referred after a series of failures within the care system. Even so the schools were dealing with a more difficult clientele than fostering or residential units yet were holding and helping them better. Essential ingredients seemed to be personalised care, interested staff, interesting activities and opportunities to achieve.

Some teenagers responded very positively in both foster homes and children's homes, but each of these forms of care had worrying levels of placement turnover. The picture of residential units in the study was consistent with the view conveyed in reports of recent enquiries. Staff were often hard-pressed but nonetheless managed to provide many teenagers with a positive experience and much needed help. Many young people would be helped more effectively if staff had more time, and each unit had a clear role within a network of services for teenagers. By contrast, carers' time and commitment had contributed to success in several foster placements. However others ended in disappointment, because of abuse or a mismatch of expectations. Some foster carers wanted to impose rules or have a degree of intimacy which conflicted with the young people's desires to lead a more separate social life on their own terms.

The sample also included a number of young people who were trying to manage on their own. Preparation for this was often inadequate and their current circumstances were generally bleak. The emotional, social and practical problems they faced are part of a wider social phenomenon (Killeen, 1993), but usually exacerbated by poor family relationships. Help and support from social services was variable, rarely sufficient and sometimes non-existent. Living independently would be challenging for any youngster at that age, but it is much more so for those with major problems and discontinuities in relationships. The question has to be posed of whether a longer period of care and phased independence would be better. That this is not offered may have as much to do with cost considerations as young people's best interests.

8 Decision-making and Participation

We now turn to issues dealing with consultation, joint planning, choice and participation. Given the increasing stress in policy and practice on participation of both young people and parents, we were interested to find out how well this manifested itself at individual case level. The duty to consult with children according to their level of understanding has been incorporated in legislation since 1975, but has been given added momentum and gained ground during the 1980's (Harding, 1991). Consultation, participation and joint planning are also key features of the Children Act 1989 and the Guidance regulations that followed it (Thoburn and Lewis, 1992). The ratification of the UN Convention on the Rights of the Child reinforced this trend. The Convention includes rights to participation, alongside rights to survival, proper development, protection and provision (Asquith and Hill, 1994). All these developments resulted in the creation of 'children's rights officer' posts within a number of local authorities. During the course of our study, one of the agencies published a Children's Family Charter applicable to both Social Work and Education Departments as well as the Health Board, whilst another recently established a Children's Rights Officer. A third agency preferred not to have a single person responsible for children's rights, but sponsored strong local groups of young people in care and involved them in the development of revised policies and procedures.

The extent to which young people and their parents are or can be consulted is influenced by a number of factors. For example the legal or administrative system dealing with the young person will impinge on the extent to which participation in decisions is possible or permitted. We were interested in comparing the English Juvenile Justice and the Scottish Children's Hearings systems in this respect. The latter incorporates periodic reviews by the Children's Panel which should encourage the child to express his/her views. Within each agency, policy and resource availability influence the scope for taking account of the views of young people or their parents and, in individual cases, the personal and professional stance of key participants have an impact. We were also aware that there were several types of decisions and that opportunities for participation might not be the same for each. A young person may, for example, have little say in whether he or she is admitted to care but be consulted about the type of placement, about contact with family members and friends or about whether he or she wants to change schools or Homes.

A Decision-making and Access to Services

The Decision to Intervene and Choice of Placement

Social Workers' Views

At the first interviews social workers indicated that most of the current interventions had been initiated by family members, social services, the legal system or the young person. Each of these accounted for between one fifth and one quarter of the cases in our sample. The other significant agency prompting action was the education service (12%). Family members initiated 40% of admissions to care but only a quarter of new supervisions or interventions in the community. This is consistent with the fact that several parents spoke of how difficult it could be to obtain a social work service at an early stage. There were no significant differences between England and Scotland, but somewhat more referrals came from parents and educational services in England than in Scotland. The relationship between the source of referral and better outcomes in terms of success/change were in order of importance: parents, police/hearing and young people. The worst outcomes were those in which more than one agency was involved, possibly reflecting the serious stage the situation had reached.

The young people themselves were seen as initiating only 8 (16%) of admissions to care and very few services in the community. However over a third of decisions involving moves while in care had been prompted by the young person. These could include positive moves (eg when the young person requested foster care), return home or a move to a more restrictive placement in response to the young person's unruly behaviour.

All social workers were asked to assess the extent to which the young people's views had been taken into account in decisions about the most recent intervention. Their replies were as follows:

Table 8:1 Influence of young people on initial
decisions N=116

Fully or to a great extent	49	(42%)
Partly or to a limited extent	41	(35%)
Very little or not at all	18	(16%)
No response or not asked	8	(7%)

Limited attention to the young people's views usually stemmed from the circumstances of the case, for example if parents had opposing views, if the young person's views were seen as unrealistic or the decision rested with the court. Lack of suitable resources was also cited as limiting the extent to which young people could have a choice.

Perhaps surprisingly, a majority of the social workers said that the initial placement in care was their first choice, although this sometimes meant it was the best of the few available. Of those who identified that a different kind of placement would have been more appropriate, two thirds considered that a foster placement would have been preferable to residential care.

Young People's Views

Young people considered that social workers had been more active than their parents in precipitating admissions to care and saw the legal system as most prominent in supervision cases:

Admission to Care		Supervision	
Social worker	44%	Panel/court	69%
Parents	31%	Social worker	13%
Panel/court	25%		
Young person	24%		

About half of the decisions were seen as joint decisions with two or more parties contributing.

Even in cases where young people were being admitted to care against their wishes, they usually accepted that care was the inevitable consequence of their actions. Though a few said that care could have been avoided if the court or Children's Hearing had given them another chance, most felt that it had really been up to them to change their ways or make use of the 'last chances' they had been given. Typical comments included:

> 'Well really the only reason I came here was because of my behaviour in class so the only person that could really stop it was me.'
> 'If I had gone to school within two weeks I wouldn't have had to come here.'

These represented a passive contribution to the entry to care. Almost a quarter of the young people accepted a more active responsibility for the decision to come into care. Fewer than 10% felt that they alone had made the decision about care and only a few had directly asked to be taken into care but several had acted in such a way as to ensure that care was the end result. One male teenager explained:

'I decided myself when I ran away from home . . . Mum had to talk to the social worker and the social worker talked with me and I was all for going into care. I wanted to go into care.'

Another girl had similarly:

'Wanted a way out, kept running away, that was a way out to me.'

In each of these and in similar cases the parent had made the request for care but the young person was clear that he or she had made it inevitable. This ability of teenagers to use a range of strategies to influence decisions and shape what happened was a significant factor and contrasts with the comparative passivity of most younger children involved with social services.

We asked young people about opportunities they had had to influence or express an opinion about the decision to intervene. Over half (56%) of those in care and 42% of those on supervision recalled prior discussion. Less discussion was possible when teenagers entered care in an emergency. Most emergency admissions involved on-going cases rather then new referrals and the general practice of duty teams was to leave any discussion to the case social worker. Two thirds admitted on a voluntary basis but only one third in statutory care recalled prior discussion. Interestingly three quarters of those who described themselves at the interview as decidedly happy or unhappy about being in care said that the decision had been discussed with them, whereas only a third of the majority (64%) who said they just 'accepted' care recalled any discussion about coming into care.

A third of the young people in care said they were given a choice about the type of placement, though several of them found this question quite strange and patiently explained to the interviewers that 'You don't get a choice'. Half of the young people in foster care had been given a choice but fewer than a quarter of those in residential schools. This partly reflects the fact that placing teenagers in residential care is more routine, whereas foster care is less often available and requires special consideration or consent.

Those young people who said they had some choice about placements were more likely to identify benefits from being in care at the follow-up interview. The differences were more marked among young people who had had a choice about the placement they were in at the end of the year. It seems the probability of success is lowered when young people are not listened to.

Parents' Views

Around 85% of the parents interviewed said that the social worker had involved them in discussions about the circumstances which led to the start of intervention. One quarter were very pleased that the situation had been amply discussed on several occasions. A small minority, however, were bitter that a decision had simply been announced to them. This mostly applied when younger teenagers were placed on statutory supervision

About half the parents had some reservations about placement. Some wanted a more strict or secure setting and one mother could not understand why a foster placement was made when her son already had a family. Conversely a few would have preferred fostering to residential care. While there were parents who thought that admission to care had been unnecessary, others regretted that their son or daughter had not been removed from home. One father argued strongly that his daughter should have been admitted to care because she was at high risk and he himself was being intimidated by her and her friends. He resented that the agency left the responsibility with him and took no action to alleviate the situation.

Decisions about Care Placements During the Year

At the follow-up interview a year later, social workers and young people were asked about placement/resource related decisions in the course of the year. Depending on the young person's circumstances, there might have been a decision to end the initial placement, or to move into one or more new placements, either on admission to care or when changing placement. In several instances there had been a decision to end contact. It seemed that usually adolescents were consulted about *changes* of placement. This accorded with a survey of about 500 young people in care which revealed that over 80% were asked beforehand about moves (Fletcher, 1993).

Decisions to End the Initial Placements

Young people and social workers presented a broadly similar view of who had *suggested* the initial placement should end. Both agreed that approximately half the proposals had not been made by a single person but emerged from discussions among the key parties: young people, social workers and foster or residential carers.

When it came to *deciding formally* that the placement should end, social workers saw themselves as contributing to the decision-making process in three quarters of the cases (Table 8:2). Young people were involved in 58% but parents were party to only a third of the decisions. These proportions were similar for residential and foster care cases. Carers were named as taking part in the decision to end the placement in half of all placements. Again the decision to end was seen as a collaborative process in three quarters of cases.

Table 8:2 Main parties named as contributing to the final decision that the placement should end: social workers' views (N=45)

Social Worker	34	(75%)
Young Person	26	(58%)
Foster/Residential Carer	24	(53%)
Parents	14	(31%)
Court/Panel	13	(28%)

Most social workers and young people said that at the time they had been in favour of the decision that the initial placement should end. The greatest doubt was about the ending of foster placements. Social workers were in favour of only 64% of foster compared with 90% of residential placement endings. However there was no indication that foster carers had forced young people out. It was usually the teenager who wanted to leave when social workers would have preferred them to stay. Over 70% of young people in both residential and foster care said that they had been in favour of leaving the placement. Social workers seemed to be well informed on how the young people had viewed this decision. In 35 cases for which we obtained the opinions of both, three quarters of the social workers' assessments of the young person's attitude were correct. In only two cases did the young person directly contradict the social worker's view.

Young people and social workers held different views about 50% of foster placements ending but only 16% of residential placements. This may in part reflect different expectations about foster care with social workers hoping for long term gains and young people taking a more immediate and pragmatic approach.

When asked whether they believed, in retrospect, that ending the placement had been the right thing to do, only three social workers expressed any doubts. Four social workers who had opposed the placement ending at the time, considered with hindsight that the decision had in fact been correct. However, more young people later regretted this decision. At the time of the second interview, over a quarter of those interviewed believed that leaving the placement had not been the right decision for them. Approximately half had agreed with the decision at the time and half had opposed it. For example, one young man said he now realised that the apparent rigidity of his previous foster home was less than in his subsequent home and now he appreciated the caring attitude of the first carers.

Decisions about Placements which Started During the Year

The characteristics of decision making in relation to placements made during the year were similar to those which had governed the initial placements:

- young people were often influential in determining that placements should end but seldom initiated an admission to care or move to another placement;
- social work staff were highly involved in decisions to admit young people to care and transfer to new placements but they had less control over the decision to leave;
- with hindsight, more than half the young people regretted their decision to leave care placements.

When the decision involved access to resources young people and their parents were generally consulted and kept informed, but social work staff remained very much in control of the process. Young people were aware of this and several spontaneously distinguished between being told what options were available and actually influencing decisions. Social workers, parents and courts/Children's Hearings all had more say than the young person. Even as joint participants, the influence of young people and parents was much less than that of social work staff.

At the end of the year only half the social workers said they had agreed with the decision to end the most recent placement. In most instances ending the placement also meant discharge from care and those who disagreed were worried about how the young people would cope. Most had no effective support in the community. Some were using drugs and risked being seriously exploited. Unfortunately the social workers' concerns were often borne out by the young people's current circumstances at the follow-up interview. Over half the young people doubted whether leaving care had been right and one young woman bitterly regretted that decision. Few of them any longer had a social worker.

Virtually all social workers had made an accurate assessment of the young person's wishes on leaving the placement and had correctly anticipated that they would find it difficult to cope. However social workers acknowledged that there had been no legal grounds to hold the young people against their will. What seemed to be lacking was a means whereby young people could be encouraged to remain in care for longer or be enabled to seek help if things did not work out. Engaging teenagers in such a way that they are helped to make informed choices about what is in their best interest requires skill and enough flexibility in resources to offer scope for negotiation and real choice. We found that these ingredients were seldom all present.

Decisions to End Social Work Contact

Decisions to end contact were taken quite differently in the English and Scottish agencies. Since most Scottish young people were subject to statutory supervision requirements, the decision to terminate contact was taken at a review Children's Hearing. This gave young people and their parents an opportunity to express their views and ensured that the decision was approved by the Children's Hearing. In contrast most young people in England received a service on a voluntary basis or were supervised on a time-limited order set by the court. The result was that far more Scottish than English young people and parents said that they had participated in the decision to end contact and they were much clearer about when and why the contact had ended. However the Scottish system did not necessarily ensure that contact continued as long as it was needed. There were some complaints from both parents and young people that Hearings usually terminated orders when young people reached 16, irrespective of the young people's circumstances, and that this resulted in a reduction in service from social workers. Several parents indicated that they found legal orders reassuring. One couple had persuaded the panel to continue a supervision requirement to help control their son, even though both he and his social worker had asked for the order to end.

The majority of parents and young people were in agreement with contact ending, but this was for opposite reasons in different cases. Some felt satisfaction that all was well, but others believed that contact had been useless anyway so there was no point in continuing. A minority of both parents and teenagers wished that support had carried on. One parent and son who were living apart both regretted that the social worker no longer acted as a go-between, whilst others thought there could have been benefit from continuing opportunities to talk things over or receive practical help.

B Participation and Representation

Having examined the characteristics of key decisions which shaped the young people's care careers, we now turn our attention to the processes through which the views of young people and their parents were obtained.

The Young People's Perspective

Participation is a complex process. It should be on-going, neither excluding nor confined to crucial meetings. To be effective more than just the presence of young people at key meetings is required. It is not sufficient to ask 'Was the young person there?', but also a number of associated questions such as: were the meetings accompanied by on-going dialogue about the central issues? Was the young person given adequate information to make sense of what was going on at the meeting? Did the young person's views have any impact on the decisions made? We explored these issues both in our group consultations and in the interviews of the main study.

a *Group Discussions*

Our discussions with groups of young people outside the main sample gave us valuable insights into the strong feelings many young people held on decision making and the extent to which teenagers' views should be taken into account. To stimulate discussion, we invited the groups to consider situations where a young person was being asked to live somewhere against their wishes, such as go into care, moving home or staying where they were when they were unhappy. Opinion varied markedly about the extent to which they thought their views would count for anything. The majority in all the groups affirmed that they would be given a say in key decisions. The problem they felt was that this was often a formal right only, since meetings with several people made it hard to express themselves. Several noted that it was particularly difficult to say what they thought with strangers at a Hearing. Some stated that social workers or panel members would ignore their wishes or simply seek to persuade them of what they thought best: 'You can have your say, but then they talk behind your back too'. A few social workers were considered to be responsive, but in the main young people thought that it would be other people who would stick up for them – particularly parents, but also key workers, teachers, IT workers.

The groups were asked to suggest ways in which young people could get their views across better. Some urged that young people should be persistent in stating their views, but the most common suggestion was to talk to a trusted adult, who could then act as an advocate. This might be a teacher, key worker, relative or a social worker. Usually parents and other relatives were perceived to be on the young person's side and likely to have more influence than they could themselves. Several said that friends could speak up for them. Both friends and teachers were seen by some as people who would know the more positive side of young people, whereas social workers, courts and panel members only know the bad side. In only one group was external assistance mentioned, namely NAYPIC, whose help would be invoked if prior attempts to take the matter 'to the top' had failed.

The young people participating in the group discussions made the following suggestions for ensuring their views carried weight:

- shout
- repeat what you want
- put your views in writing
- spray them on a wall
- go to people further up the hierarchy
- involve NAYPIC
- walk out
- run away

The groups concluded with discussion of the changes the youngsters would like to see. For instance, several groups wanted courts and panels to be less intimidating and to give young people more opportunities to express themselves. This applied to the supposedly more informal Scottish panels as well as English courts. Specific ideas included – have the decisions made only by people who know you; have fewer people involved; let you speak more and take more account of your views; do not bring up private details amongst strangers; have a fairer tariff of disposals.

In relation to residential care, there was a wish for young people's views to influence rules, normally in the direction of less strictness eg later bed-times (several groups said this), being allowed to smoke. A prominent wish expressed by several was to be able to see friends more easily. There were also requests for more respect by staff and greater privacy (see also Buchanan et al, 1993). Nearly all the groups emphasised a desire for greater respect. Asked what changes they would like to see in adults in general, most argued that adults should treat young people with more respect and not like children. Several wanted more freedom and fewer restrictions by adults. The final question on the individual self-completion forms handed out in the groups asked about the one thing they wanted to make life better for young people. The most frequent reply was for more recognition and understanding of their viewpoints.

b   The Main Interviews with Young People

Participation at Court, Hearings or Reviews

Opportunities for young people to make their views known were clearly affected by the context in which decisions about their future care were being made. Of particular interest was the issue of teenagers' participation in formal legal settings. Young people being dealt with in the English juvenile courts (as they were still called at that time) had no expectation that their views would be asked for or taken into account directly. They relied on their best interests being served by the advocacy of professionals, through 'having a good solicitor' or 'getting a good report from the social worker'. Decisions were seen as part of a tariff system and making a contribution to decisions consisted in trying to ensure the least punitive disposal. This view of decision making was shared by their social workers who were clear that 'assessment' involved making sure that the lowest acceptable tariff disposal was recommended. It was seen as self evident that all steps should be taken to avert custody and young people were encouraged to agree to involvement in alternative measures.

In Scotland the Children's Hearings system is supposed to operate more on the basis of participatory discussion leading to consensual decision-making based on the welfare of the child, although panel members determine the final disposal (Martin and Murray, 1982; Lockyer, 1994). Nevertheless, the initial responses from many young people about their ability to participate in and express their views at Hearings were not very positive. This echoes the findings of another recent Scottish study (Freeman *et al*, 1994). In our initial interviews a third of those who had attended a hearing said that they had been able to put their point of view and that this was listened to but the remainder either found that they were too nervous to say anything, that they did speak but were ignored or that they were given no opportunity to speak. Some stated that 'the Panel did all the talking' while others believed that their parents' views were given far more attention than theirs and they got all the blame. One boy explained this very clearly:

> 'Well they said they were trying to help but from where I was
> sitting it just looked like everything was getting pushed on me,
> that I had been going out sniffing and motor bikes and that,
> but anything that my mum and dad had done to make me
> do it, that wasn't brought up. It was just what I was doing and
> they never asked for a reason why I was doing it.'

There seemed to be several separate difficulties which hindered the young people's participation. A number of them talked about the unfamiliarity of the situation which made them feel apprehensive and uncomfortable. Typical comments were:

> 'I was a bit scared because it was the first time I had been to one.'
> 'It's just talking. I didn't say anything.'
> 'All the people asking you questions I just didn't like questions
> at all. It's strangers you know. I just didn't like it.'
> 'You feel funny at a Panel but once you have been a few times
> you get used to it.'

There seemed to be a general impression of passive involvement, not dissimilar to that reported in relation to the English juvenile courts by one teenager who said:

> 'They asked questions and I answered.'

Some young people believed that if they plucked up the courage to speak at panels they had more influence on what happened. Others felt that the decisions were made on the basis of reports before the Panel began and that the young person's views were only taken into account if they happened to coincide with what the panel members wanted to do. One boy with substantial experience of the hearing system said:

> 'I think personally that they make their decision before you go in,
> but I mean that's not necessarily the way it's done. It might not be,
> but that is what I think. Some of them (try to understand) but
> some just want it over and done with and they take the social
> workers' and the places' recommendations all the time.'

However, another young person described how some Hearings can work effectively in helping to resolve problems:

> 'They would take my point of view and then just take (step-father's) point of view . . . to see what was wrong, what was happening and was it working out.'

In the follow-up interviews we examined with each young person an example of an important meeting they had attended during the year. More than three quarters said they had been to a meeting where a decision affecting them had been made. In the main, these were either judicial occasions (attendance at panel or court hearings) or regular child care reviews.

The judicial decisions were mainly about the beginning or ending of placement or a legal order, whilst the review meetings were mostly concerned with care or educational plans. A substantial majority of young people said they agreed with the eventual decision (75%). Most of the rest disagreed, but a few were unsure or felt they had no choice. Under half of those who disagreed had conveyed this opinion to the meeting. Most young people felt they had been able to get their opinion across, although not always adequately, in their view. At least one fifth said they had not been able to do so at all. These judgements are similar to the survey organised by Who Cares? which also found that about 60% of young people felt that they were listened to at reviews or case conferences (Fletcher, 1993). As might be expected, none of the few who chose court hearings as an example thought they had got their views across even a little, whereas two thirds believed they had done so as much as they wanted at panel meetings. This was more positive feedback than we received at the start of the study in response to a different question about previous experience of panels in general. It confirms the earlier findings of Martin et al (1981) that communication by young people at hearings is effective for most, though not all, young people. Even fewer expressed dissatisfaction about participation in relation to reviews. A Scottish study of child care reviews also found that about three quarters of the young people were satisfied with the process (Kendrick and Mapstone, 1991). In our sample, the proportion of those who had not got their views across did not vary significantly with age or gender, nor between those who were supervised and those in care. Agency E was the only authority where fewer than half (43%) felt they had put their ideas across satisfactorily. The figure in Agency C was 70%.

Just over half of the teenagers in our study said they had met with someone beforehand to prepare for the meeting they were using as an example, which meant that nearly half had not. This preparatory talk had usually been with the field social worker (56%) or a residential worker (33%). A few had spoken with a lawyer or solicitor and only one person mentioned a parent. Although some young people had received preparatory help before each type of meeting quoted as an example, the proportion was highest for courts and lowest for panels, with reviews in between. It was more likely for young people in England to have been prepared than in Scotland.

Asked how they got their views across, some simply responded that they 'just told them'. Many did describe the process in rather more detail. They often referred to the helpfulness of having rehearsed beforehand what to say, usually with the aid of a key worker, foster carer or social worker. Sometimes the carer or worker had also brought up things in the meeting which the young person wanted discussed. One young person felt that her foster carer stood up for her at child care reviews and prevented the others from imposing decisions on her, but another thought the reviews were just an occasion for the foster carers to complain about him. A number of young people were content for someone else to convey their wishes on their behalf. Repeated attendance at panels for reviews made communication easier:

> 'If they know who you are and they start to like you, they would be a bit easier on you.'
> 'They knew me – we developed a relationship.'

Another youngster who had attended many panels asserted that they usually did what he wanted. However, one boy saw panels as being too formal – 'like a court'. Several thought it was necessary to be very assertive or even use threats. They felt this approach had been effective for them. B. advised that 'You have to tell them you'll run away if they send you somewhere you don't want to go'. N. claimed to shout at the panel – 'You have to stand up for yourself'. K. had walked out of a review, claiming to have got the decision changed later.

When asked what might have helped them to present their views more effectively, young people clearly wanted improvements in preparation, more choice over the size and composition of the meeting and a relaxed, responsive style. A careful consultation with young people in care carried out by the Dolphin Project revealed that most wanted a quiet discussion with their social worker or key worker before their reviews (Buchanan *et al*, 1993).

Several young people noted disapprovingly that people were present at reviews who they did not know and who they did not want to hear about their private concerns. These included teachers, senior social workers and minute-takers. When young people were asked if it would be helpful to have anyone else to speak on their behalf, many did not think so. Either they felt well able to speak for themselves or else thought that existing support or advocacy from social workers or carers was adequate. The minority who mentioned someone to act as an advocate referred to a wide range of people, that is a social worker; a good friend; a parent; a person with experience of care; an IT worker; a professional; a lawyer. Clearly there was no consensus and it would be desirable to let young people make individualised choices rather than have a standard person imposed on them. As one teenager put it, the main thing is to have someone you trust and who takes the time to understand your point of view.

We also asked if they could think of situations when other people's views should count for more than what the young people themselves want. This is quite a complicated notion and some were uncertain how to respond. Some definitely felt that the young person's view should always hold sway – after all it was their lives being discussed. It was also pointed out that decisions made without the young person agreeing would only give rise to conflict and rebellion. Several proposed that young people should be allowed to do what they wanted first, but if it failed then the suggestions of other people should be tried. However, a few did state circumstances when other considerations should take precedence over the young person's own wishes. They referred to the young person being immature, wanting to be 'bad', 'violent', 'racist' etc. or needing punishment for wrong-doing. It was usually emphasised that adults' discretion to decide what was best in the face of opposition from a teenager should be exceptional. Occasionally, with the benefit of hindsight, teenagers recognised that decisions they had opposed themselves at the time had worked out for the best. Two admitted that they had not wanted to be placed away from home but had in fact benefited.

The Parents' Perspective

At the initial interviews six out of ten parents thought they had been able to get their views across successfully at key meetings, but one quarter had been dissatisfied in this respect. In a few cases, the social workers were completely unaware of the parents' feelings of exclusion as they stated that the parents had been adequately consulted.

Positive comments included:

> 'Our views were always sought and respected.'
> 'Panel members listened.'
> 'The panel tried to put us at ease.'

On the other hand, a few parents felt both courts and panels either blamed or condescended to them. Several commented that the professionals and officials had no more idea what to do with a 'difficult' teenager than they did, which could be a source of comfort or frustration.

Approximately 60% of the parents said they would not have wished to have more influence on what was decided. Those who would have liked more say were mainly parents of younger teenagers placed on supervision. Although in a distinct minority, dissatisfied parents felt very strongly about not being consulted enough:

'We had no respect in the eyes of the social services.'
'You don't have much influence as a parent.'

Similar views were expressed a year later. In all, about half the parents interviewed felt that the social workers had taken their views into account when key decisions were made during the year. Some praised the social workers for giving them very careful attention. One mother had been asked to write down her views before meetings to ensure they were considered while another was always consulted by the social worker before a review. However other parents said their opinions had either not been sought or had been ignored. This led to frustration at being left out and resentment that their knowledge of their own child was disregarded. Understandably, those who felt excluded tended to be more vociferous:

'The social worker tried to say P. did not suffer from asthma.
I know she did. Who is she to contradict what I know about
my daughter?'

Another said 'They are making all the decisions about H. and have hardly met him'.

Parents who said that they were able to get their views across at the start of the care/supervision episode, were about equally divided a year later over how beneficial the measures had been. However, among those who were *not* confident that they had managed to get their views across, less than a fifth considered that the young person had benefited from intervention. Further analysis showed that consultation and participation were not decisive factors in themselves but were an important part of a total package; availability of resources, quality of supervision and family work were other important ingredients in effective intervention. In other words, doing one thing right was not enough.

As noted earlier, many of our first interviews took place around the time when the Children Act 1989 was introduced in England and Wales after which 'care plans' had to be agreed for those placed away from home. At the follow-up stage we asked parents to say whether there had been a written contract or plan. Four out of five said there was none, but 14 per cent had been involved in drawing up a contract and in the remaining cases the parents were uncertain. The number who had a written contract were too small for statistical analysis, but it was clear that this applied to more parents in English than Scottish authorities. However most parents in Scotland had attended a Children's Hearing at which there had been discussion about nature of the planned social work contact.

Only two thirds of the parents who had signed an agreement said they had received a copy and half had been involved in drawing them up. The others had been written by the social worker. One parent observed that the contract indicated what herself and the young person were expected to do, but not the social worker. Where there was a contract/plan there was a greater likelihood that parents would say they got the help they wanted from the social worker. Even though this may have made no difference to eventual outcomes in relation to the young people, its existence helped some parents feel more involved or informed.

Those parents without a written contract were asked if they would have liked one. Most replied that it was not necessary because they were well informed anyway or it did not seem relevant. A few simply replied that what they wanted was action (eg about schooling or accommodation). However a fifth of the parents would definitely have liked a contract in order to feel included, to be more informed about the social work plan or to be assured of more social work contact.

Social Workers' Views on Participation

Involvement of Young People

At the initial interviews two thirds of social workers gave unqualified support to the idea that young people's views and wishes should be sought and acted upon. This was seen as important both in terms of principle and to gain young people's co-operation. The remaining third of social workers agreed that young people should be consulted and their wishes respected if possible but thought that there were many situations in which social workers or other adults would have a clearer idea of what was on the young person's best interest.

In the follow-up interviews, two thirds of social workers thought the influence of the young people's wishes on decisions during the previous year had been about right. One described the young person's wishes and his own assessment as going 'hand in hand'. Another stated that 'R. was fully involved in discussions about her future, her wishes and needs being taken account in all plans'. Workers referred to:

- *principle*   eg 'Client's choice was always priority';
- *practicality*   eg 'It would have been impossible
                      not to take account of her views'.

Several noted the need for young people to experience mistakes and learn from them, as when a young woman came to realise that supported accommodation was preferable to living alone in a high rise flat. In the minority of cases when the social worker thought the young person's influence had not been appropriate, interestingly more believed there had been too much influence rather than too little. Amongst the situations where the young person's influence was thought to have been excessive and, by implication, negative included the teenagers' resistance to attempts to change behaviour or premature return home from placement. In the social workers' views insufficient impact on decisions by the teenager corresponded with what were perceived to be unhelpful influences by social services or parents. Examples quoted included:

- departmental review processes counteracting young people being given informed choices;
- not enough resources available;
- the system being parent/panel/agency focused as opposed to child focused;
- children who were too dominated by parents to say what they thought.

In addition, several pointed out that teenagers' opinions could be changeable or unclear. A diverse group of other constraints were mentioned which affected the extent to which young people's views had been taken into account. Naturally when courts or panels were involved, they had the power to override whatever the young person or even the social worker might want. Sometimes, risk to the young person had outweighed their wishes (eg drug-taking, sleeping rough). Several spoke of the inflexible application of departmental procedures. For instance, K. wanted to stay with her foster carers on a long term basis, but was not allowed to because they were approved for 'temporary placements only'. J., aged 17, was told he could not stay with friends' families without police checks, although he had done so before coming into care. In response to fixed choice questions about factors which had outweighed the young person's wishes, the following answers were given (N=101):

availability of resources	35%
police/court/panel	22%
views of parents	21%
views of carers	14%
views of teachers	10%
social workers' judgement	9%
departmental policy	9%
management decisions	8%

Insufficient resources could significantly limit access to money or certain placement options.

Involvement of Parents

Most social workers indicated that parents' views had been 'partly' taken into account. Several social workers said that parents had 'had their say' or had been 'listened to', indicating that they had had an opportunity to express their point of view but not necessarily to influence events. Another frequent comment was that parents had not objected to the plan, in which case social workers assumed they had acted in accordance with their views. When social workers were asked the extent to which parents views *should* be taken into account, most social workers indicated that, where there was any dispute, the views of the young person should have priority, especially if they were older or were no longer living at home. Occasionally social workers would say that parents' views should be considered in order to gain their co-operation. Sometimes it was thought that parents' views could be discounted or overridden because the young person was operating independently or needed protection.

Because of the separate legal systems, parental involvement was different in England and Scotland. In English authorities, parents had less influence on court decisions but since more supervisions or admissions to care were on a voluntary basis, parents were more involved in inaugurating the service. Conversely they could disrupt plans by withdrawing their support. Plans for some young people in care were unclear because parents refused to attend meetings while other teenagers had been removed from care in haste at their parents' request, often to be readmitted or to leave home shortly afterwards. In contrast the Children's Hearing system required Scottish parents to attend Hearings, which both provided an opportunity to participate in key decisions and underlined parents' responsibilities to their children. Parents' requests for young people to leave care had to be considered and approved by the panel.

It seemed that social workers in England had to work harder both to engage parents and to prevent unnecessary disruption from ill-considered actions.

Decisions about Access

It is now widely accepted that considerable efforts are needed to help younger children who are removed from home to retain links with their family and community. We found that retaining contact with family and friends was quite different for teenagers. Usually young people spent time at home rather than being visited by their parents. Seeing friends was often as important as contact with their parents, if not more so. Under a third of young people were aware of the existence of an access agreement though just over half said that they had been asked about the type of contact they wanted. There were clear agency differences with three quarters of the young people in Agency A, half of those in C and one third of those in E saying they had been asked about the type of contact they wanted.

The absence of an agreement did not mean the teenager's wishes had been ignored. In fact when young people said that their views had been considered they often meant that they had been given scope to arrange access with their parents whenever they wished. This suited most of them well, since there was a general reluctance for contact to be regulated. As one girl explained:

'No I don't have a set agreement. That's one thing I didn't
want . . . It's arranged between the two of us and the staff are
informed so that they know when I see my mum.'

Such scope was more often accorded to young people aged fifteen and older. Access had been formally agreed for only one third of this age group. Several teenagers refused to visit their families in spite of their social workers' encouragement to renew contact, whilst a few young people who were hoping to renew contact with a lost parent did not look to social workers to help facilitate this. Where family tensions had led to admission to care, contact with parents was obviously an important part of rebuilding relationships, but it seemed that most teenagers believed that they and their parents had to tackle it at their own pace:

'We just didn't want to see each other really. She (SW) tried to
persuade us but the two of us weren't keen.'

Some social workers had, however, managed to 'persuade' reluctant young people or parents to retain contact. Access was more often regulated in residential schools than units. Though practice varied between schools, most encouraged a pattern of home leave at weekends (and only at week-ends) unless family circumstances or other factors mitigated against this. Only three of the young people in residential schools said that they had been asked about the kind of contact they wanted but two thirds had a formal agreement.

Some young people made it clear that returning to their communities at weekends was very important to them. The granting or withholding of home leave was explicitly used as a means of controlling the young person and the hope was that improved behaviour would have become habitual by the time the young person returned to the community:

'I've got to be in at a certain time at nights. I've got to be in for
my tea and no drinking or anything.'

One problem with this use of access was that it could lead to difficulties being concealed from residential staff since to have admitted to problems would have stopped access for the next weekend (cf. Kelly, 1992). It could also lead to a cycle of absconding if home leave was refused. Fourteen young people identified problems with access to their family or friends. Most of them said they would like more contact, but a few found the demands of parents or other relatives difficult during access. Social workers were apparently aware that access arrangements did not suit the young people in only half of these cases.

On the whole young people were keen to retain control over contact and to keep it as flexible as possible. There seems to be no clear policy about how persistently access should be pursued with this age group. Contact is encouraged, but if young people or parents refuse, the response depends on the individual social worker. Some social workers readily left the matter to the young person, even when they chose to have no contact for as long as a year, while others placed considerable emphasis on re-establishing links as soon as possible.

Summary

Most young people had been consulted about decisions, but many still felt they had had little influence. For those in care, dissatisfaction at the end of the year was associated with lack of choice about the placement. Real choice could only be offered if a range of resources were available.

Some young people had become quite skilled in presenting their views at meetings during the year but some still reported feeling intimidated by formality, large numbers and the presence of people they did not know. Preparation for meetings and the availability of someone to help convey the teenagers' wishes were viewed positively. Often this could be the social worker or carer, but others prefered to rely on parents or friends. There was little enthusiasm for independent advocates who were not already known to the young person. Social workers were clearly important in facilitating the young people's involvement in decision-making as they were the source of information about choices and available options.

Parents' influence on decisions declined in the course of the year and more parents than young people felt excluded from decisions. However the majority were satisfied with the level of involvement. The Scottish Children's Hearing system facilitated more parental participation but also underlined their responsibilities. This was important since parents who felt excluded at the start of the year acknowledged little benefit from the intervention and unco-operative parents could disrupt plans for voluntary care or supervision.

Most social workers believed that young people's wishes should take priority over the parents' views. In practice, lack of resources, decisions by the Court/Hearing and parents' wishes were thought to have often outweighed the young people's wishes. Whilst a few young people believed that their wishes should hold sway regardless of the consequences, most were wanting more respect and involvement, not the right to determine absolutely what happens.

9 Progress During the Year

Introduction

In this chapter we consider the extent to which the initial circumstances of the whole sample had altered over the year. Since the services were intended to improve the young people's well-being, behaviour, relationships or environment, this will provide evidence about the degree of success of the interventions which we explore further in Chapter 10. However it cannot be assumed that changes during the year were simply the results of the care or supervision episode (Rossi, 1992). Many other factors could have contributed to these changes including pre-care experiences, maturation, subsiding of a family crisis ('natural recuperation'), life-events and other environmental changes (Weiss and Jacobs, 1989).

First we present the evidence about observed changes or stability in the teenagers' health, behaviour, self-esteem, educational progress and relationships over the course of the year. This is followed by an analysis of the more subjective impressions of the participants – how did they view the year overall? To what extent were their initial expectations met? How confident or optimistic were they about the future?

A Progress and Changes in the Teenagers and Their Relationships

In this section both the end positions and changes on different dimensions are described. For each measure, cross-tabulations were performed with key variables like age, gender, agency, living situation and type of intervention, but these are only reported when there were noteworthy associations.

Health and Related Issues at Follow-Up

The majority of teenagers were thought by each of the 3 participants to be in good health at the follow-up, although more young people held the view that their health was 'fair or average' than did the adults involved with them. Almost half the young people said they had had some 'particular health problems' during the year and social workers noted one fifth as having had 'serious physical or mental health problems or been involved in an accident during the last year'.

Most of the young people stated that their health had not changed during the year, but 11% thought it had improved and 14% said it had got worse or varied.

A comparison of the teenagers' self-ratings on both occasions revealed changes which were sometimes inconsistent with their own perceptions. For instance, at the follow-up stage 12 young people described their health more positively than they had done the previous year but only 2 of these were amongst the 10 who said their health had improved.

Girls were significantly more likely than boys to say that their health had varied or got worse during the year while boys more often reported an improvement. Social workers agreed that more girls than boys had only 'fair' health (38% compared with 11%). There were also variations between agencies in the proportions of young people reporting changes, with those in Agency C the most likely to say that their health had stayed the same. Social workers more often reported serious health problems for young people during the year when they worked in Agencies A or D.

Interestingly, parents of adolescents on supervision and not in care during the year more often rated their health as 'fair' than parents of young people with a care experience. Though hardly surprising, this suggests that the differing assessments of their health between parents and young people may have been related to the amount of daily contact and familiarity parents had with their children. It also emphasises the importance of social workers and carers ensuring that the health needs of young people living away from home are not overlooked and that teenagers in care are given advice and encouragement about using the health services.

A very varied range of conditions were mentioned, when participants were invited to give more details about the health problems experienced over the year. The number of problems, as well as their severity, varied from person to person. Collectively they related to 65 young people (56% of the total sample) but in many instances they were only reported by one of the participants. Woodruffe and Glickman (1993) found that the most commonly reported chronic illnesses for children aged 0–15 were respiratory (8%), eczema (2%) and ear complaints (2%).

In our follow-up, the most frequently mentioned problems related to broken bones or injuries (18 cases). Several of these took place when playing sport, while some others were the result of attacks or muggings. One young man admitted that his arm had been broken while doing a burglary. The second most frequent group of problems (12 cases) were infections of various kinds: tonsillitis, flu, frequent colds, boils, chicken pox etc. Sometimes these infections were linked with frequent headaches, tiredness or poor diet. Eating problems were mentioned 10 times. These ranged from being under or overweight to serious anorexia nervosa. A similar number referred to asthma or eczema, but these were often reported to be under control through medication and had not really been a 'particular problem' during the year although at least one person had been hospitalised as a result. Another group of 9 adolescents had been having difficulties with hearing, eyesight or their teeth. Eight young people had had stomach, bowel or kidney problems, whilst gynaecological issues were mentioned 5 times. Four teenagers were reported to have taken overdoses during the year and depression or more general mental instability was mentioned 6 times. There were references to 4 cases of serious drug or solvent abuse.

Treatment for these problems obviously varied greatly and sometimes depended on the co-operation of the young person. In a few cases parents expressed serious worries about the consequences of not taking medication or the probability of further deterioration. About half of the parents who reported problems thought they would or might possibly have a lasting effect on the young person. Social workers did not minimise the gravity of some young people's situations, but rarely indicated that the care or supervision programme was affected by any of these conditions.

One or two young women already had a child or were pregnant when first interviewed. Two babies were born during the year and three others were expected. One young woman had had a miscarriage and another decided, after much heart-searching, to have a termination. As far as social workers were aware, none of the teenagers had tested HIV positive during the year but concern was expressed about the risk of sharing needles in one case where the young person was abusing drugs. Nearly two in five teenagers said they had been given advice about how to avoid AIDS/HIV, either at school or from a variety of other sources, in the last year. All but four of them were young people who said during their first interview that they were already aware of the dangers of unsafe sex. Social workers had discussed issues of contraception and close personal relationships with about a third of these young people and also with quite a number of others during the year. Some parents had done so too and these issues had at least been aired with well over half the sample.

Social workers admitted during the follow-up interviews to being concerned about just over one-third of the young people's current abilities to handle sexual relationships. Parents of one in four said they had worries about their son or daughter's sexual behaviour. Social workers and parents were only talking about the same teenager in 6 cases and together they expressed concerns or worries in this respect about 53 young people (46% of the total sample). There were no significant gender or age differences associated with the social workers' concerns, but parents were more often worried about daughters than sons. Parents and social workers both mentioned anxieties about unprotected sex and the risks of pregnancy and AIDS. Social workers linked some of their concerns to other events or relationships where there had been problems eg 'she was raped in the past, puts up with violence from boyfriend', 'has not matured, has so little experience of positive relationships at all', 'under pressure she'd react as she does with her dad', 'derogatory attitude to women'. In some cases social workers had referred young people for specialist counselling or to groups, but mostly they tried to tackle the issues themselves through discussion. They admitted that these attempts were sometimes resisted by the young people through embarrassment and that the topics required a sensitive approach.

Adjustment at Follow-Up

At the follow-up stage we only asked parents to complete the Rutter scale, partly because the interview schedules for young people and social workers were already very demanding. The scale was completed for 74 young people and in 63 of these cases a rating had also been obtained in the first round. There were 3 cases where the follow-up scales were completed by carers instead of parents and in 2 other cases different members of the family were involved.

For the analysis of the results we used the same 3-way division of scores as in the first round (see Chapter 2). While a 'low' score of 0–8 points indicated no observed disturbance, a 'medium' score of 9–19 or a 'high' score of 20+ points were indicative of moderate or severe behaviour difficulties. At the end of the year, one third of the teenagers had a 'high' score, one half a 'medium' score and the rest were rated 'low'. There were no significant differences in the Rutter scores at follow-up of those who had been in care, on supervision or had experienced both types of intervention, but generally more favourable ratings were scored by young people who only experienced supervision and teenagers who were living at home with their parents at the end of the year.

The responses for the sample as a whole showed a substantial reduction in the proportion of very 'disturbed' young people, although most of the sample continued to score well above average:

Table 9:1 Rutter scores at the start and end of the study

	Initial Score %	Follow-Up Score %
High	63	36
Medium	33	49
Low	4	15
(N)	(78)	(74)

The reduction in 'high' scores was more noticeable in the older age groups than among 13–14 year olds. The improvement suggested by these results was confirmed when individual Rutter scores were compared for the 63 cases rated both times. There were 8 young people (13%) whose scores had improved to the extent that they now showed no disturbance, compared with just one whose score had deteriorated and become 'high'. Nevertheless, despite this sign that some improvement had occurred, more than one-third of the young people were given 'high' ratings on both occasions by their parents. Furthermore, over 80% of the teenagers who were rated both times still showed levels of disturbance which would merit further investigation if they had been tested at random. This emphasises the continuing difficulties faced by many participants, even when there had been improvement.

Table 9:2 Rutter scores compared (Parents' ratings at first round and follow-up)

	N	(%)
'low' scores both times	2	(3)
now 'low' (improved)	8	(13)
stayed or changed to 'medium'	30	(47)
now 'high' (deteriorated)	1	(2)
'high' both times	22	(35)
Total	63	(100)

With one exception, when parents' ratings showed improvement, social workers also thought the general behaviour of the teenager was better. The social workers' general views about alterations in the young people's behaviour over the year indicated an even broader pattern of improvement. In the 54 cases where social workers' views at follow-up could be compared with changes in the Rutter score, they considered 43% to have improved in contrast to 11% rated by parents.

When we looked back to see who had been identified by each of the three participants at referral as having emotional or behaviour problems we found that there were no significant associations between reports of these problems and whether the Rutter scores had improved or stayed the same at follow-up. In other words, whatever the severity level of problems at the outset, there was a similar chance of improvement in behaviour or none, as measured by the Rutter scales.

Self-Esteem

Teenagers who were not attending school completed the shorter 'adult' version of the Coopersmith Self-Esteem Inventory at follow-up and all the total scores have been marked according to this shorter scale. A total of 92 completed the Inventory at the end of the year, including 75 who had also done so during the first round. As noted in Chapter 2, the Coopersmith scores go in the opposite direction to the Rutter scale so that a 'high' Coopersmith score indicates a positive sense of self-esteem.

Among those responding at the follow-up 28% had 'high' self-esteem scores, 37% 'medium' scores and 35% 'low' scores. A significantly higher proportion of boys had 'high' scores (37%) compared with girls (10%) and, conversely, more girls (53%) had 'low' scores compared with boys (26%) but the proportions with 'medium' scores were the same.

High or low self-esteem at follow-up was not significantly related to the young people's experience of care, supervision or both. However, those who were still in care at the time had rather lower self-esteem than other young people. Although there were no significant differences according to where people were living at the follow-up, those in residential care and also those on their own seemed rather more prone to low self-esteem, whilst young people living at home with their parents tended to have better levels of self-esteem than the rest.

A comparison of the self-ratings made on both occasions showed that most had not changed substantially. Twelve of the 75 (16%) had improved self-esteem at follow-up and now had a 'high' score. However, nearly as many (10) had deteriorated and now had a 'low' score indicating poor self-esteem. None of the girls in this analysis of changes had high self-esteem both times, while one third had 'low' self-esteem at both referral and follow-up compared with one in ten of the boys.

Table 9:3 Coopersmith scores compared (Young People's self ratings at first round and follow-up)

	N	(%)
'high' scores both times	11	(15)
now 'high' (improved)	12	(16)
stayed or changed to 'medium'	28	(37)
now 'low' (deteriorated)	10	(13)
'low' both times	14	(19)
Total	75	(100)

The social workers' ratings of self-esteem at the end of the year also showed higher proportions in the upper range than at the beginning, although they did not always agree with young people over the cases where this had happened. Social workers tended to place more young people in the 'medium' bracket and they also considered that more teenagers continued to have low self-esteem.

Social workers who gave a rating at follow-up were asked whether they themselves considered that the young people's level of self-esteem had changed significantly over the last year. In 10 cases they were unable to say, usually because they were new social workers or else the case was now closed. Nearly half of the rest of the young people were thought to have improved during the year and the self-esteem of the others was mostly considered to have 'gone up and down' or else 'stayed much the same'. Nobody was thought to have undergone a major drop in self-esteem. When these responses were compared with the social workers' ratings of self-esteem at the first interview the results were in the expected direction, which suggests that the workers were reflecting quite accurately their own or their predecessors' professional assessment of the young people's state during the year. Young people whose self-esteem was rated 'high' or 'medium' at follow-up were much more likely to have improved than those now rated 'low'. All 4 of those considered to have deteriorated had 'low' scores.

Changes in self-esteem as perceived by social workers did vary according to where the young people were living at follow-up. Those in a residential school were especially likely to have improved. Other studies have also pointed to the relationship between educational success and the development of a positive 'self-image' (Jackson, 1989; Aldgate, 1990; Aldgate et al, 1993). Young people living with their parents were more often thought to have stayed 'much the same' than teenagers in other situations, but they had higher levels to start with.

Finally, when we compared changes in self-esteem measured by the Coopersmith scores with changes in the Rutter scores for the 50 young people who had ratings on both measures, the results were broadly in line with what might be expected. Teenagers whose parents considered their behaviour had improved also mostly had self-esteem which had improved or else had been high at both interviews while a girl whose behaviour had deteriorated had low self-esteem both times. However, rather more young people whose Coopersmith scores had improved now had 'medium' Rutter scores. This suggests that just as some social workers gave generous appraisals of improvements in behaviour even though the Rutter scores were still poor, so some young people appeared to have been encouraged by moderate changes in their behaviour. Such gains in the sense of self-worth are valuable in themselves and may lead to other improvements in a young person's life.

Education and Work

Many of the young people in the study were in the transition period between school and work, so little time was available in which to remedy past difficulties or plan for the future. About one-third of the sample reached the official school leaving age during the course of the year. Only a few of these had contemplated staying on longer when first seen. Social workers said they had been involved in helping over 80% of the young people with at least one aspect of schooling, careers, college, training or the search for jobs during the year. This ranged from offering general support or making appointments to very intensive efforts like negotiating re-entry to mainstream school after exclusion, arranging admission to residential school or ensuring on a daily basis that a young person attended a training scheme.

Although young people and parents were both asked about who was still at school and who had left, it was not easy to piece the full picture together because several young people were in the process of leaving at the actual time of our interviews. In some cases this was earlier than the official date but was generally accepted, while others were receiving alternative measures of assistance with their education such as a home tutor. One 16 year-old had started a vocational course at college a term early with the agreement of his former school and two others were attending sixth form colleges. As far as we could tell, somewhere between 62 and 73 young people had either definitely left school or were in the process of doing so at the time of our follow-up. The proportion of young people aged 16 or over who said they were still at school (16%) was close to the national average of 19% (Church, 1990). They were among 38 teenagers who answered questions about their current experience of school.

In general, the young people's attitudes to school were positive rather than negative as 58% said they liked it and only 5% 'really hated' school, but one-third did not like it much or 'put up with it'. When we compared their current attitudes towards school with their previous ratings at referral almost half of the 35 who answered both times had changed their opinions, that is 6 to a more positive view and 11 to a more critical stance. It was probably not surprising to find that higher proportions of those with positive attitudes at referral were still at school and only 16% of those who 'really hated' it last time remained in school at the follow-up. Two out of five of those who were still pupils said they had moved school during the last year. Most of these considered that their new school was better than their old one, because of smaller classes or more constructive attitudes. One of those who had disliked the move had found it difficult to adjust as the new school was 'not friendly'.

Compared with those who had left school, slightly more pupils had improved self-esteem over the year. The same was not true for those with Rutter scores at both times as nearly half those still at school had 'high' scores each time (indicating more disturbance) compared with one in five of those who had left school.

Parents of 31 of the teenagers still at school were interviewed and said they thought 58% were doing 'as well as he/she could' at school, while 35% were not doing as well and they were unsure about 6%. When asked to express their more general satisfaction with the young people's education during the last year, a similar proportion of parents said they were 'satisfied', 11% were partly satisfied and a quarter were 'not satisfied'. Problems with attendance and also adolescents' negative attitudes towards school were the main reasons for parental dissatisfaction. Parents were more satisfied with the teenagers' efforts and progress if they were at residential schools than in mainstream schools. Parents of teenagers who had left school during the year usually gave less positive appraisals of both their personal efforts and their education in general. In some cases it seemed that their replies were influenced by the young people's progress since leaving school. Their disappointment was sometimes due to a realisation of the effect of poor achievement in the past on current prospects and parents were less likely to be satisfied if the young person had not managed to obtain any qualifications.

A total of 15 young people said they had obtained some qualifications, usually GCSE or Scottish Standard Grades, and another 14 were planning to take exams, making 30% of those interviewed at follow-up. This is slightly lower than average (DES, 1992). Admission to care and placement either in residential schools or units with education on the premises was associated with a commitment to obtain qualifications and this, in turn, contributed to greater parental satisfaction with education. Nearly half those who had already obtained a qualification had stayed on at school beyond 16.

Just 15 young people were currently in paid employment (2 part-time), ie less than a quarter of those who had left school. Only three of them had obtained qualifications. In all about 60% of the sample were either attending school regularly, on training courses or working. Those supervised at home were significantly more likely than those who had been in care to be unemployed.

Social workers were also asked to assess the young people's progress at school or since starting training or work. Their opinions did not differ significantly from those of parents. They also seemed fairly well in tune too with the teenagers' attitudes to school. An important consideration was the extent to which the teenagers who had been identified by either parents or social workers as having school problems at referral had improved during the year. Rather more of the parents who had originally said there were school problems remained dissatisfied with their children's efforts and achievements. Similarly social workers assessed only 13% of those with initial problems as making good progress, compared with 40% of those where no school problems were noted at referral. On the other hand fewer than half (42%) of those with initial problems were said to be making 'poor' progress at follow-up. It is encouraging to note that social workers saw improvement in a considerable number of teenagers with poor initial schooling assessments. Nevertheless, social workers rated one third of the teenagers as doing poorly in education, training or work. None of these were in residential schools, as distinct from residential homes.

We established that at least half of our total sample of teenagers had been in receipt of residential or other forms of specialist education either in the last year or earlier. This highlights the centrality of schooling difficulties amongst teenagers in touch with social workers (Heath *et al*, 1994). One-third had attended residential schools, mostly as boarders, or had received education on the premises of a residential establishment. One in ten had attended special schools, sometimes as boarders, and alternative measures such as home tutors had been provided for a further 7%. There were others in the sample who had been given assistance within their mainstream schools.

Details about residential schools as care placements have been given already (Chapter 7). Young people who had been in these schools or had received other forms of specialised educational assistance during the year were asked what they found better or worse about them. Almost all of their comments were positive. Amongst the *educational* benefits reported were accepting atmospheres and regimes, easier work and teachers who were more ready to explain things. Three teenagers summed up these features in the following ways:

> 'People don't laugh if you don't know things. You don't feel stupid if you don't understand. Teachers explain, the work is not too hard.'
> 'Classes are smaller. Everyone is in the same boat, they all have some kind of problems so you don't feel awkward.'
> 'It's not hard work at all. There's only five people in the class. The teachers go over things all the time and help.'

They also stressed that fellow pupils did not ridicule them because they were performing at similar levels.

Parents also spoke of the benefits of smaller classes, more individual attention and the teachers' ability to handle difficult teenagers. A couple of pupils made adverse comments about the distance of their schools from their homes and another criticised the teachers at his special school for being aggressive and not interested in him. A few parents thought that the subject range was too narrow or there was not enough discipline. One parent mentioned the stigma of being in a special school as 'everyone thinks he's stupid'. Another wryly commented that her son had 'learnt a great deal, not always the right things – can make things and look after himself but has learnt about drugs'. About half the young people said they had a special or 'key' teacher to whom they could turn if they had problems to discuss or needed extra tuition. These 'key' teachers were often the ones to attend meetings or reviews about the young person and in some cases they were more like 'key workers'.

Family and Network Changes

Changes in Teenager-Family Relationships

At the follow-up point, just over half the young people said they were getting on well with their parents. About one tenth described their relationship with their mother as poor and one fifth were not getting on well with their fathers. This represented a small decrease compared with the proportion who said they did not get on well at the beginning of the year. Many teenagers themselves felt that relationships had improved, but amongst the minority who had experienced a deterioration, this was again more likely to be with fathers than mothers:

Table 9:4 Relationships with parents at follow-up

	Well	50:50	Not Well	N
Mothers	54%	33%	13%	**83**
Fathers	52%	26%	22%	**62**
	Better	No Change	Worse	N
Mothers	59%	34%	7%	**83**
Fathers	41%	45%	14%	**62**

The parents too confirmed that relationships had improved in just over half the cases and deteriorated in only a few. Some of these changes were thought not to result from external help, but usually parents said that improvements were mainly or partly due to the measures of care or supervision. Overall a third of young people thought that social work intervention had brought about positive changes in family relationships.

The picture with regard to step-parents was more negative and, interestingly, the gender patterns were reversed. Most of the teenagers with step-mothers described the relationship as poor, though a few said it had got worse. Relationships with step-fathers were more likely to be described as 50:50, although one third were poor. A higher proportion of relationships with step-fathers than step-mothers were reported to have improved:

Mothers	59%
Step-fathers	42%
Fathers	41%
Step-mothers	15%

Fewer relationships with siblings or other relatives were thought to have changed compared with parental relationships and in only a handful of instances was the change seen as resulting partly from the social work intervention.

Information about Family Background

It is now widely accepted that it is important for adopted or foster children to be given reliable information about their birth families and help to understand the reasons why they did not continue to care for the child. Similarly it is recognised that when parents divorce it is often in the interests of the child to retain contact with the non-custodial parent and that arranging this can require sensitive negotiation between the adults involved. In this study, only a minority of those identified as having a need for communication about their family history or identity in fact received such help during the course of the year.

At the follow-up stage, just over a third of the young people who had previously indicated a need for more information about their family background, reported that they had acquired some. Some others had found out about an aspect of their family, though they had not identified a gap in their knowledge a year before. Only 16% of the young people identified by social workers as needing more family information had found out anything new.

Issues about fathers predominated in the information which had been uncovered. On reading his birth certificate, one young man had found out that he was registered in a different name from the one he used, although his ideas about his father's identity were confirmed. Two young men who had been eager to contact their estranged father had changed their mind on finding out that the fathers were 'no good'. A young woman who had also been keen to find out something about her father was disappointed when her mother explained she was unable to say who he was. Others felt they had improved their understanding of why their parents had divorced or had set up second families without them. A few teenagers had been told about step-siblings or grandparents of whose existence they had previously been unaware.

These revelations appear to have been largely unconnected to the social work intervention. When asked who had helped them to obtain or make sense of this information, no-one said that a social worker or other professional had done so. The teenagers had found out either by themselves or through relatives. One young man had found details in a social work report without the knowledge of his social worker or carer.

Parents showed unease on this subject. Few parents interviewed at the follow-up stage had discussed an aspect of the family background with their son or daughter during the course of the year, including less than a quarter of the ones who had stated at the first interview that their son or daughter needed more information.

Many more social workers said that they had had discussions with young people about their family background (55 cases). Yet only one quarter of the teenagers themselves admitted to new information, so presumably the conversations had mainly been concerned with increasing understanding or clarifying existing knowledge. It was also the case that there had been no such discussions with half the young people whom social workers had identified as in need of information at the initial interview.

Family Support

At the follow-up stage young people were asked whether they had confided in a family member or asked a family member for help. Although over half had originally stated that they would be able to ask for help only a third said that they had in fact done so in the course of the year. The 'help' sometimes involved practical assistance, for example lending money or helping get a house, or it might be more personal. A number of young people had talked with a family member about problems in their relationships with peers or difficulties at school. Of those who provided help two thirds were parent(s) and the rest other relatives or siblings.

Although older teenagers had expressed more reluctance to ask for help at the initial stage, more 16 year olds had received help from family than those in the other age groups. Almost half the 16 year olds had been helped by a family member, compared with under a third of the others. The initial lower expectations of help expressed by teenagers from reconstituted families were borne out. Only a quarter of them had received assistance from a family member, compared with a third of young people from single parent households and just under half of those who lived with both natural parents.

Social Networks

We turn now to the teenagers' overall social networks, which included their families of course, but extended to friends, professionals and others. At the end of the year, almost half the young people (46%) said they had lost contact with at least one of the key people identified in the first interview. The proportion was the same among young people who had spent part of the year in care and those who had remained in the community. It was most common for teenagers to have lost contact with friends (30) but 16 were no longer in touch with a parent and some of these young people had also lost touch with step-relatives or a parent's partner.

Approximately a third of young people who had lost a contact thought that this could be attributed, at least in part, to the social work intervention. The most frequent scenario was that coming into care had involved moving to another area from where it was difficult to keep in touch with friends. There were a few complaints that rules set by foster parents or residential units discouraged contact. Loss of contact with parents or relatives was generally not attributed to social work intervention. In some instances the young person and parent had been drifting apart for several years and in others there was a clear rejection during the course of the year. One young man was not sure why his parents had failed to visit him during almost a year in custody but did not look for the social worker to pursue this. Another teenager acknowledged that the social worker had tried everything to get his father to meetings but had not been successful. In contrast one young woman felt that she and her mother might well have lost touch but for the fact that they ignored restrictive access conditions and continued to see each other. There was also a complaint about lack of social work intervention to help one young woman retain some contact with members of her extended family after a plan that she should move to live with them was abandoned.

As some contacts had ended, so had new friendships been formed or old relationships renewed. Almost three quarters of the young people had added at least one significant person to their social network in the course of the year. By far the majority of new relationships were with friends (76%), but there were also some renewed contacts with parents, siblings and other relatives.

Though admission to care could disrupt friendships, it also provided opportunities to meet new companions. A third of those teenagers who said they had made a new contact attributed this, at least in part, to being in care or having a social worker. This applied to 45% of those in care and only 18% of young people on supervision. Residential care necessarily involved meeting other young people and some teenagers had formed friendships they valued. Several renewed old relationships. One young woman was pleased to have re-established contact with a brother since returning to a foster home in her home area and another young man had more contact with his father after moving out of his mother's care.

Peer Support

As with relatives, the receipt of help from peers had not fully matched expectations. Less than 40% of the teenagers recalled actually receiving help from friends in the course of the year. Help from peers was more available for older teenagers and more girls had been helped by friends than boys. While only a quarter of young people in the 13–14 year old age group had received help, almost half the seventeen year olds had been able to call on a friend for assistance. Similarly just over a third of young men but almost half the young women had relied on friends.

Compared with family members, more friends had helped by listening or talking over problems, though practical help such as lending money or providing temporary accommodation had also been appreciated. It was important that some friends had remained loyal when the young person was in difficulties. Friends could be a mixed blessing and 60% of the young people acknowledged that their friends had got them into trouble at some time. The help friends gave was not always legitimate and included help in hiding from the Police and telling lies on the young person's behalf.

B Perceptions of the Year and of the Future

Views of the Past Year

We began our follow up interviews with young people by asking them to tell us in their own words what had happened over the year. They were then invited to say whether they saw their situation as better, the same, worse or mixed. Two in three said their situation had improved and only 12% thought they were worse off. At the end of the interview, they indicated their satisfaction with the way things had turned out. About one quarter were very satisfied and most of the rest quite satisfied, although again 1 in 8 were not. A few were satisfied despite perceiving their overall situation as having deteriorated. Similarly a small number registered dissatisfaction even though they recognised that their position had improved. Thus, most of the teenagers felt that they were better off at the end of the year than at the start. This is a positive finding, even though it is necessary to examine other evidence to ascertain the part played by the intervention in that general improvement.

Table 9:5 Teenager's view of current situation compared with last year, by living situation at end of year N=97

Where Living At Year End	% Situation Better	N
Foster home	80%	10
Parental home	79%	42
Residential home	66%	12
Other	64%	11
Resid. school	60%	10
Independent	33%	12

The places where the young people were living at the end of the year and their feelings about them were likely to have made an important contribution to their assessments of their situations. More of the young people who were living with a family, either their own or in a foster home, considered their situation was now better than those who were living in residential settings. Only one third of those currently living independently thought things were better than before.

Teenagers who had been helped by groups were not more likely to give a positive overall evaluation of the year than those who had not been helped, suggesting that other factors impinged more on their lives. The proportion of those who were very satisfied ranged from over one third in Agency C to only one eighth in Agency A, which also accounted for half of all those who were dissatisfied.

There was an association between views of the past year on the one hand and self-esteem and personal difficulties on the other hand. Teenagers with low self-esteem or a high Rutter score at the follow up point were much less likely than others to think their situation had improved or feel very satisfied about the last year. Within the small group whose situation was in their own eyes worse, six out of ten were involved in offending according to their social workers (four in a major way) and five in drug-taking (one in a major way).

There was only a weak connection between young people's overview of the year and their feedback on the social work intervention itself. Although the majority of those who saw their lives as better at the end of the year than at the start also believed they had been helped a lot by the social worker, nearly one third stated that they had not been helped at all. This fits with the assertions of some that changes came about through their own efforts or other external factors. Even more strikingly, half of the young people who said their situation had deteriorated over the year nevertheless stated that the social worker had helped them a lot. Clearly the direct action of the social worker can sometimes appear marginal in its impact within the wider context of young people's lives.

Four fifths of the young people who were very satisfied with how things had turned out for them in the year also got on very well with their social workers, but so did half of those who were dissatisfied with developments over the year. Over half of the small number (11) who thought their situation had deteriorated nonetheless had a very good relationship with their social worker.

In turn, nearly all the social workers were able to tell us of at least one positive development in the last year for the teenagers. The most common ones concerned better family relationships (17) and improvements in schooling (15). Also important were, in order – settling well in a good placement and finding security; returning home from care; keeping out of trouble; doing well at work; learning to survive independently; achieving greater maturity; and growing more self-confident. Although these mostly concerned amelioration in the problems which were prominent at the start, they also included references to personal growth and gaining insights.

Similarly over three quarters of parents thought that their son or daughter had changed over the last year and with a few exceptions they spoke of improvements rather than deterioration. Nearly half said that they noticed greater maturity. Significant progress had also been observed with respect to temper control, better family relationships, greater attention to self-presentation (manners and appearance) and reduced offending, drug-taking and drinking. One parent said things were '100% better', with more politeness, improved appearance and an end to truancy. Another was pleased with a big improvement at school, more mature outlook, seeking help for medical problems and no longer looking 'like a slob'. Sometimes the improvements were qualified, because the changes were small, subject to lapses or accompanied by continuing problems in other areas.

Were Expectations Met?

Although the majority of teenagers were reasonably pleased with how the year turned out and were thought by parents and social workers to have made gains, these positive developments were not always closely related to the original problems or to the areas targeted for intervention. Therefore, it was important to check how far initial expectations were fulfilled and this gave a rather less rosy picture. As we shall see, fewer than half of the initial hopes for the year were fulfilled, even partially. This appeared to reflect not only the inherent difficulty of solving certain problems, but also the frequent failure to identify and agree jointly on the objectives of intervention or the corresponding actions which needed to be carried out by each person involved. We also observed in Chapter 3 that parents and young people were mostly concerned with immediate changes, whereas more of the social workers set longer-terms goals in relation to the young person's personal needs and development.

However we should also be mindful that expectations were often fluid, that the views of the different parties were sometimes very different and that an expectation could be met in one area of the young person's life but not in another. The following case example illustrates these complexities. At the start of the intervention there were a cluster of problems including family conflict, school non-attendance and offending. These were given different emphases by each party, with the parents stressing schooling, the young person his own behaviour and relationship with parents. The social worker described all of these, but linked them to personal development within an overall context of wishing to avoid reception into care:

Parents
Expectations: To resolve school problems.
Achievements a year later: Home tutoring arranged. Behaviour outside the home improved since not going to mainstream school.

Young Person
Expectations: Change behaviour at home and stop stealing and fighting outside.
Achievements a year later: Still trying to get a job. Not getting into trouble. Better with parents.

Social Worker

Expectations: Maintain young person in the community. Work on self-esteem – tied to school. Improve family relationships. *Achievements a year later*: Building-up self-confidence, self-respect. Mediated between young person and father.

For the analysis of the accounts by the whole sample, an expectation was regarded as having been met even if this was only 'partly' or 'slightly':

Table 9:6 Proportions of expectations met

	Number of Expectations	% Met
Social workers	203	29%
Young people	124	48%
Parents	98	41%

Social workers had on average stated larger numbers of expectations at the beginning and, perhaps in consequence, a smaller proportion of these had been met. By contrast, many young people had a single dominant goal either to stay put or return home and many of them managed to achieve this. They did not look beyond their pressing needs.

Expectations were more frequently met in relation to certain key areas of concern than others. For example, when parents or young people had wanted change in relation to offending or drugs, this was forthcoming in 60% of the cases according to both parents and teenagers, whereas hopes for a successful move to independence were reported to have come to fruition in fewer than one quarter:

Table 9:7 Percentages of expectations met according to problem area

Areas Targeted	Social Workers	Teenagers	Parents
Family functioning	26%	47%	43%
Personal development	40%	33%	–
Offending, drugs	33%	58%	60%
Schooling	23%	46%	44%
Independence	24%	26%	14%
Living situation	33%	62%	–

The accounts by each party of how their expectations turned out in relation to the main problem areas will now be discussed in turn, with attention to both the reported successes and the disappointments.

The Social Workers' Perspective

Social workers naturally saw themselves as playing an important part in achieving their goals. This applied particularly in supervision cases when the worker often provided the main or sole input. For teenagers in care, expectations were to be met by a combination of efforts between themselves and foster carers or residential staff. However, in most social workers' eyes, fulfilment of expectations depended chiefly on the young person being motivated, open and communicative and the parents being co-operative and responsive.

Social workers, much more often than parents or young people, identified attention to the teenager's *personal needs and development* as their most successful area for meeting stated expectations (40%). They referred to these in the following ways:

> 'Learned self-control.'
> 'Was able to take responsibility for her own life.'
> 'Able to share her fears about being alone and chance to reflect
> on her time in care – positive image building.'
> 'It facilitated her confidence and self-awareness.'

In the case of D., the social worker had stated at the first interview, that a key expectation was 'to help raise low self-esteem'. At the follow-up interview he reported that D. had 'developed as a person and was very happy in the foster home'. These personal gains were attributed to experiences such as – 'having a consistent adult to relate to', 'an orderly, physically supportive environment' and 'being well settled in the foster home'.

Relatively few *educational expectations* were fulfilled (one quarter). When significant change was recognised by the social workers this was usually associated with placement away from home, particularly in residential schools but also in some foster and residential homes. In several cases the combination of the young person living at home whilst attending as a day pupil at a nearby residential school was considered to have improved significantly the young person's school attendance record.

The social workers' expectations for improvements in *family relationships*, which included creating and maintaining a social base there for the young person, were in their estimation met in about a quarter of the cases. These were mostly supervision cases, since social workers were more likely to plan joint work with parents and a teenager when the latter was at home. Also a move out of the family often indicated that family work had not succeeded. Typical positive comments included:

> 'Family work has been most effective. Father not drinking,
> parents co-operating.'
> 'Enabled the family to work through the difficulties
> and remain together.'

Support to young people to become more *independent* was the only area in which as many social workers thought their expectations had been fulfilled as young people (although still only a quarter). Some were satisfied because they were unaware of the difficulties which were reported to us by the teenagers. Social workers mainly took credit themselves for success in this area, through helping young people to obtain housing, work or financial help and by giving general support:

> 'Gave him structure and some skills for independence and support.'
> 'Got her away from home and provided support.'

It was noted in Chapter 3 that social workers set fewer expectations than anticipated in the area of helping to reduce *anti-social behaviours.* Where clear targets had been set, the social workers' expectations to reduce or stop offending/drug taking were met in one third of the cases. Given that failure in this area is more overt and can have dramatic consequences, cases where re-offending/drug use had stopped or diminished were reported with considerable satisfaction:

> 'The activities provided diverted him from crime.'
> 'Supervision put the brake on offending; not so extensive as before.'

Sometimes residential units and schools were said to have broken the pattern of offending, but lapses were noted on return to the community. It was not often that a youngster was able to meet all the expectations set by the social worker. Here is an example of mixed outcomes, where improvement in one area was accompanied by little apparent progress in others:

> 'There has been no more offending over the year, but return to
> school has not been achieved, neither has the effort to get K. to
> "drop the curtain and be himself".'

In just over one quarter of the cases, social workers reported that none of their expectations had been met. The main reasons advanced for the absence of change were lack of motivation on the part of the young person and the family's unresponsiveness. Some spoke of no change in the teenager's attitude or behaviour. Others referred to temporary containment in care (eg 'the unit simply kept him from offending whilst there'; 'He simply saw himself as doing time'). Social workers rarely alluded to inadequacies in their own expertise or in the provision of more specialist services, which might otherwise have helped overcome resistance.

The Young People's Perspective

The young people who had at least one expectation met attributed this to their own efforts, to their social workers' help, the stability provided by a residential or foster home arrangement or occasionally to the improved situation at home. Though the reasons they offered for improvements overlapped with those stated by social workers, a major difference was that young people thought more of the positive results had been brought about by their own efforts. They reported concrete achievements like – 'stopped buzzing glue'; 'no drugs'; 'got my GCSE, now doing 'A' levels'; 'managed to keep out of care'; 'got a job'. Young people not only put less emphasis on personal needs but equally reported few such expectations as having been met. One or two did refer to interpersonal or intrapersonal issues eg 'slightly better relations with Dad'; 'more patient'; 'more mature'.

Among young people, the highest level of expectations met concerned their basic *living situation*, when a desire to stay put, not to move into care or to return home had been fulfilled. About half also recognised positive change in relation to offending, family functioning and schooling, but only a few whose aspirations had centred on independent living felt they had been fulfilled. Of 45 young people who said at the initial interview that *offending and drug taking* were one of the major reasons why measures were initiated, 19 had set expectations to stop or reduce this behaviour. By the follow-up stage, over half of these (11) reported improvements. In contrast, of the 26 who had not stated a resolve to stop or reduce offending and drug taking, only one fifth (5) reported improvements. The figures are too small to allow for any wider conclusions to be drawn, but they give support to the contention that clear acknowledgement of offending behaviour and commitment to change are more likely to result in success than when the problem is denied or side-stepped.

Young people reported improvements in *family relationships* with their father or mother but less so with a step-parent. The changes could be minor, but still made life 'a bit more tolerable'. Sometimes improvements took place after the young person had moved out and relationships became less intense. A significant number of young people were pleased with themselves for improved *school* attendance, passing exams or going on to college. One said 'Now that I am with foster parents I attend school regularly'.

Reflecting on the year that had passed since the first interview, some young people could identify a mix of things that worked out as they wished and things that didn't:

'Stayed out of trouble with police but haven't got a job and the flat didn't work out.'
'Back home but not at mainstream school.'
'Getting on slightly better with dad but school no better.'

For 40 (or 43%) of the young people interviewed, none of their expectations had worked out as they hoped. Their explanations for this took various forms. Just as some took the credit for things going well, now a fair number took the blame for things going wrong, admitting to being lazy, easily led or unrealistic. Wider social factors were mentioned in relation to housing, jobs and the pushing of drugs. A few whose foster care arrangement broke down, blamed their foster carers for making unreasonable demands on them which led to the breakdown of the placement. Several expressed their frustration at lack of change by their parents:

'Me and my step-father will never get on.'
'Dad is still picking arguments and putting me out.'
'The only thing that is better is that I am away from my mum.'

For some, exclusion from school represented a point after which everything went downhill. Failure to continue with schooling and perhaps obtain some qualifications was a source of dissatisfaction, too (eg 'been in trouble, left school, no exams').

The Parents' Perspective

Like the young people, parents judged whether expectations had been met largely in terms of observable benefits, mainly behaviour. According to parents, most improvements had taken place in the area of reduced offending and drug taking, followed by educational progress and somewhat better family relationships. They identified a number of factors that contributed to improvements, but the main ones were the young person's resolve, residential provision (mainly schooling) and the social worker's efforts, in that order. They made comments such as:

'T. has grown up a lot.'
'No offending in the year and better at home.'
'All the problems have abated considerably.'
'Most benefit at school; less in trouble outside the home.'

The idea that outcomes are not always either wholly good or bad, but often a mixture of benefits and losses is further illustrated by parents who were more cautious in their comments or pointed to mixed results. For example one parent said: 'K. is doing quite well. Things have improved all round. Still ups and downs but nothing to what it was before'. Another said 'He is still engaged in some offending but not as bad as before'. In one case shop lifting had stopped, but the parents and young person were still not speaking to each other.

Two fifths of the parents said that none of their expectations were met. This was mostly blamed on the young people. Hardly any parents accepted responsibility themselves for lack of progress, although a few did point to their partners as playing a role in maintaining the problems. Some believed that lack of change was due to the unresponsiveness of the social services. A few noted that improvements in behaviour while away from home had not been sustained on return home (eg 'She is back to her old tricks'). In some families, concerns had shifted once the teenager left school. New worries included sexual behaviour, drug-taking and offending.

Levels of Congruence Between the Three Parties

We observed in Chapter 3 that there was little congruence between the three parties in the setting of expectations (13%). As a result it is not surprising that this was also true of their outcomes. In only about one third of the cases where information was available from all three parties did everyone agree that expectations had been met fully or partly for at least one of the comparable problematic areas of family relationships, offending/drugs or schooling. There was more agreement between parents and young people about positive outcomes than between either of them and social workers.

A brief example illustrated a situation where there was broad agreement about positive change in line with expectations. At the start of the study the mother described W. as breaking up things within the home, insulting her and occasionally attacking her physically. She claimed to be on tranquillisers and threatened to walk out of the home, leaving W. alone. He, on the other hand, felt that his mother was 'nagging' and generally provoking him. A year later each party described the situation as follows:

> *W:* 'I have ironed out the difficulties with my mother. I feel more mature and more responsible, more grown-up.'

> *Social Worker:* 'He broke up the pattern of bad behaviour with His mother. He manages to control his temper better.'

> *Mother:* 'He has improved in his behaviour though still a bit disobedient.' (There was no more talk of leaving the house)

A second example of congruence is that of J. who was involved with drugs and had a number of offences involving break-ins. His relationship with his father was very poor at the outset and both parents were very worried that he would end up in jail. A year later the supervision order was revoked at the initiative of the social worker who said:

> *Social Worker:* 'J. has not offended again; relationship with his parents improved; he is being helped with career and jobs.'

> *J.* 'No problems since I last saw you a year ago, no drugs and no police trouble. Spend most of my time with my girl friend; I help her father with his furniture removal business.'

Mother: 'No more problems with the police or drugs. Improved relationship with his father. His father is trying to get him a job at his place of work.'

It was not possible to establish whether such concurrence always produced better results, as there had so often been little agreement at the start about the key issues to be worked on. However, in the small number of cases where the expectations of all three parties were broadly the same at the start of intervention, there was a higher likelihood that hopes would be fulfilled.

It was uncommon for no-one to think that anything had been achieved. In a number of cases when one party reported that nothing had turned out as they had wanted, one of the other two would say that a particular expectation was 'partly' or 'fully' met. In one instance the teenager had wished to stop 'buzzing' glue, to get back home and have no social worker. At the end of the year, he claimed that he was indeed not in any trouble and was no longer bothered about having a social worker. In contrast, the social worker had aimed to improve school attendance, family relationships and self-esteem. She believed none of this had happened and that the situation was worse.

In conclusion, trying to establish a relationship between initial expectations and positive outcomes in such complex and changing situations is fraught with difficulties. The discrepancies in the ways different parties perceived outcomes in relation to their expectations suggest an absence of regular communication to help reduce these gaps in perception.

What Helped

Given the variety of circumstances and expectations, it is not surprising that diverse explanations were given when matters had largely worked out as intended. The young person's own efforts were most often cited, ahead of help from professionals and changes of home or school environment.

One third of both parents and young people attributed improvements to the young person's personal efforts. The highest percentage came from Agency C, where social workers had placed considerable emphasis in their expectations on the personal development of the young people. The contribution of residential care, especially residential schools, received the next most frequent response from both parents and young people. One in seven young people and parents accounted for positive achievements in terms of actions by social workers. In all, one or more aspects of the social services intervention was thought to have benefited directly about half of the young people as regards expectations fulfilled.

Table 9:8 Factors which contributed to expectations being met or problems coming to an end.

	Young People		Parents	
	N	%	N	%
Self (Young Person)	24	32	16	31
Residential Care	14	18	15	29
Social Worker	11	14	7	13
Foster Care	8	11	2	4
Improved Family Situation	7	9	5	10
Change of School	2	3	4	8
Other (eg Getting a Job)	8	10	3	6
Don't Know	2	3	–	–
Responses	**76**	**100**	**52**	**100**

NB: This table presents responses. One person could have given more than one response. Those who denied that any expectations were met do not appear in the above table.

Perceptions of the Future

For most of the young people, the year of the study had brought improvements and satisfaction, but some had not done well and others still faced major difficulties. Hence it was important to learn how their prospects were viewed as well as their achievements.

Most young people reported feeling moderately confident about the future. At either extreme, about one in five admitted to lacking confidence that things would work out well for them or said they were very confident about the future. Understandably, confidence about the future was linked to confidence in oneself. Only one person with high self esteem on the Coopersmith scale said they had little or no confidence about the future, but nearly half of those with low self-esteem did so.

Several of those who were not confident went on to describe specific worries about the future and, in all, two thirds of the sample admitted to such anxieties. For the most part, these related to general practical difficulties such as unemployment and accommodation which were typical of young people from disadvantaged backgrounds, rather than personal troubles which had prompted social work intervention. Just a few teenagers admitted to anxiety about family or relationship issues, court action or social isolation. Some of those who did not acknowledge worries were perhaps being rather cavalier. For example, one youngster who was still regularly involved in stealing cars simply said that wasn't a worry because 'I'll grow out of it' (a view shared by many criminologists!).

The age group with the highest proportion who did not feel confident was the oldest: 17–18. Half of these older teenagers denied feeling confident and only two individuals were very confident. This may reflect the fact that many of them were care leavers without a family base. Half the young people living independently said they lacked confidence in the future and none were very confident. In fact, most of the teenagers who felt very confident about the future were living either with their parents or in residential care.

Confidence about the future bore little relation to perceptions of change over the preceding year. Amongst those who averred great confidence about the future were four who were dissatisfied with the past year and two who characterised their situation as worse than before, whilst the majority of those who were not confident had acknowledged improvements over the year.

Nearly half of the teenagers (44) thought the intervention of the social services had made no difference to their future prospects. Most of the rest viewed the intervention as likely to improve things (34). Just 6 stated clearly that it had made their future worse. Over half of the young people in Agency C said there had been a positive impact, which contrasted with one quarter in A and E. Higher percentages of young people who were still in voluntary care or on statutory supervision saw the intervention as helpful for the future (about 60%) than those in statutory care or no longer in contact with social workers (20%). The majority of those living in foster care at the end of the year believed intervention was likely to have made things better. When teenagers who had either attended a group or had a befriender were considered together, they also included more who believed the services had improved their prospects and who were satisfied with the past year.

Social workers and parents were asked what they considered to be the teenagers' strong points for managing life as an adult. In many cases two or three attributes were mentioned, most frequently ability, social skills and motivation. Social workers more often referred to intelligence, determination, humour and friendliness, while the main strengths recognised by parents were application (to school or work), friendliness and intelligence. Several workers referred to young people as 'streetwise', implying that they had qualities which might not be acceptable to many adults but would help them survive within a particular life-style or subculture. The majority of social workers thought that the intervention had enhanced the young person's capacity to cope, with half noting significant gains in this respect.

Nearly a third of parents, but very few social workers, could think of nothing positive to say. It was also noteworthy that social workers often admired determination, which parents saw more negatively as obstinacy. Although descriptions of the young person by social workers and parents were usually consistent with each other, they seemed at times to be talking about different people. For example, P.'s social worker thought there was nothing good to say about him, but his parents described him as kind and considerate. Conversely, T.'s mother felt very negative towards him, but the social worker noted his easy disposition, engaging smile, sharp mind and sense of humour.

When it came to weak points for managing as adults, the answers from both social workers and parents mainly centred on lack of control – of impulse, aggression, of negative peer influences – or low motivation towards conventional achievement at school or work. Immaturity, low self esteem and difficulties in relationships were also referred to quite often.

Half of the social workers said they felt fairly or very optimistic about the teenagers' future prospects, but the rest had significant doubts or concerns, with about one in nine confessing to being very pessimistic. Generally, there was little correspondence between young people's and social workers' attitudes to the future. When the young persons regarded their social workers negatively, the latter were significantly less likely to be optimistic about the future, but there are several ways of interpreting that finding!

When they felt optimistic, social workers based this on evidence such as the young person having responded well to placement, significant improvements in behaviour or good application at school or work. Qualified optimism or pessimism depended sometimes on the young person's own uncertain commitment or ability to sustain progress, but was just as likely to be contingent on external circumstances such as the availability of work or attitudes of family members.

When the living situation at the end of the year was examined, *optimism* on the part of social workers was most associated with residential schooling (80%) or living in the parental home (65%). This partly reflected the fact that teenagers with persistent difficulties were most likely to end up in custody, residential units or trying to manage on their own. When young people were no longer in touch and the case was closed, half the social workers were pessimistic. In these instances, the social workers had often withdrawn because they felt unable to influence an unsatisfactory situation. The very pessimistic workers were mainly those with responsibility for young people who had been accommodated or in care but who were now discharged in unpromising circumstances.

There was a link between social workers' view of the future and their estimation of young people's self-esteem. Favourable or unfavourable views of both tended to go together. It is hard to know how far negative views about the young person's prospects coloured social workers' perceptions of their self-esteem, but it is to be expected that people in the most difficult circumstances will appear to have a low opinion of themselves. Those with favourable outlooks had often done well educationally, supporting the view of Jackson (1989) that academic achievement can be an escape route for troubled youngsters:

> '(She) has conditional places at four Universities.
> Relationships with her family have improved.'
> 'Very well. She hopes to do well at school and go to
> college or university.'

Personal determination and a supportive environment were also regarded as important factors:

> 'I think K. will prove to be a very competent parent and will
> perhaps pursue missed educational opportunities at a later date.'
> 'I would hope that D. will remain with [her foster carers] and
> complete school successfully.'
> 'J. has ability and personality. If he applies himself, I do not
> foresee difficulties.'

Sometimes good prospects were conditional on either the young person sustaining a commitment (to school, training, work, relationships) or external circumstances (eg acceptance by the Army; availability of supported accommodation).

Social workers thought there were good prospects for over half the young people who had been involved in offending during the last year. However the poorest prognoses were associated with serious criminal records or major emotional and social vulnerabilities:

> 'F. will become more entrenched in criminal activity. This is
> his choice.'
> 'Enters adult prison system or seriously harms himself. G.
> does not want to achieve academically, can see no
> employment prospects – stated he wishes to live a life of
> crime.'
> 'Pregnant within two years and problems relating to care of
> child to follow. Vulnerable to violence from partner she
> chooses.'
> 'He will find it difficult to manage household chores etc. In
> my opinion, he will also be very vulnerable to peer pressure
> and being taken advantage of.'

The most extreme prediction referred to a teenager with a history of suicide attempts – 'I fear P. will no longer be with us'. A young heroin user had been sharing needles with a user with AIDS and was described as 'wasting away'.

In four out of the five cases where there had been sexual abuse, the social worker was pessimistic.

Social workers' worries about the future took 3 main forms:

- *Specific problems which had prompted intervention in the first place.* These included the risk or near certainty of re-offending; possible recurrence of family conflict; further drink or drug related difficulties; or (for females) concern about sexual activities or pregnancy.
- *The secondary consequences of separation and substitute care.* Can he cope independently? Can she resolve her feelings about her previous carer? Will she stay in the placement as long as she needs?
- *Doubts about the teenager's general ability to form satisfactory relationships or develop realistic goals.* Several workers expressed concern about the young person's capacity to form close, non-exploitive relationships or to cope with the demands of parenthood.

In contrast to the young people themselves, only occasionally did social workers refer to poor employment prospects, presumably because these seemed secondary to major personal difficulties.

Parents too were asked how well they expected the young person to cope in adult life. Just under half responded positively and confidently and the majority of the remainder gave qualified replies. One in six were definite that the young person would not do well. Asked if they were optimistic or pessimistic about their son's or daughter's future, parents were evenly split between those who veered towards optimism and those whose prognostications were more negative. About one in eight were very pessimistic, usually because of the young person's involvement in offending or drugs. The bleak employment situation, for young people in general or specifically for their own son or daughter, commonly contributed to parents' pessimism.

Two out of five teenagers said they would not approach the social services if they had difficulties in future and nearly half of the rest were non-committal. The usual explanation for this was that the department had been unhelpful. This often referred to the recent past, but a few people recalled with considerable bitterness a long history of unresponsiveness or instability in care. Several others simply preferred to do things for themselves or enlist help from family, friends or carers. Even so, one third of the sample said they would go back to the social services, mainly because they felt they had been helped in the past or had an especially good relationship with their particular social worker. This was true for a substantially higher proportion of females than males and for more teenagers in Agency C than elsewhere.

Social workers, when asked the same question, rather overestimated the extent to which young people were likely to turn to the social services if in difficulties in the future. About a half thought the young person would do so and most of the rest saw it as a possibility. In nearly half the cases where social workers believed that the young person would seek assistance, the young person had definitely said they would not. Of the 3 groups of respondents, parents were least likely to expect that the young person would seek help from social services in the future. Less than a quarter thought they would do so. In a third of the families the parents gave the opposite answer to their son or daughter, sometimes reflecting their own negative view of the social workers.

Conclusions

Given that the sample included a high proportion with major difficulties, it is gratifying to note that most felt their situation had improved over the year, with a significant proportion showing improvements in their behaviour, emotional adjustment and relationships with parents. Whilst some improvement was to be expected since the initial interviews referred to a time of crisis or major change, gains were mainly attributed to the efforts of the young person or to aspects of the social service intervention. On the other hand, only a minority of the initial expectations for intervention were met. In the next chapter we consider some of the factors which may have been associated with successful outcomes.

10 Overall Outcomes

It will be recalled from Chapter 1 that the study drew on the dimensions identified by Parker *et al* (1991) as most relevant for the measurement of placement or care career 'outcomes'. When applied before and after a care or service episode, such measures are really indicators of progress, which may be positive, neutral or negative. It is important to judge progress not only according to the position reached, but also in terms of the severity of initial difficulties and the subsequent degree of change. Thus, success might be ascribed to any of the following different paths:

- **from** favourable initial circumstances   **to** positive end position
- **from** any initial circumstances   **to** significant improvement
- **from** unfavourable initial circumstances **to** no deterioration

Furthermore results are often neither wholly good nor wholly bad so it is often a matter of balancing 'benefits' and 'losses' (Whitaker *et al*, 1985). In the present study progress was judged only one year after the onset of intervention and is therefore associated with the immediate after-math of measures of care and supervision. Longer term studies have shown that improvements may not be sustained, but also that there can be benefits which only become evident later. As we have seen in Chapter 9, the current study employed a range of measures of two broad types:

1 *Standardised developmental measures concerning the child/young person*:
   a an **end measure** of the position reached at the end of the year;
   b a **change measure** of differences between the position at the start and the end of the year.

2 Largely *qualitative and subjective measures* of participants' judgements:
   a a **satisfaction measure** with respect to overall developments in the year;
   b a **goal measure** assessing whether expectations for the year were fulfilled;
   c a **prognosis measure** concerning the young person's future prospects.

The second set of measures was important to take account of the varied circumstances of the sample. They enabled the follow-up position to be judged partly according to the initial problems and expectations related to each individual case. We anticipated that there would be discrepancies in the trends on various measures, because children can do well in some areas whilst lagging behind in others and the 3 main respondents could and did take different views of the same situation.

In Chapter 9 we presented evidence about observed changes or stability during the year in important areas of the teenagers' lives and an analysis of the more subjective impressions of the participants. Here these two kinds of data are blended into a summary measure to identify those cases which were largely successful, largely unsuccessful or mixed/in-between. This is then used to examine associations with key features of the sample and the interventions.

Overall Success?

One of the prime intentions of the research was to identify successful cases and to see whether these could be linked to particular forms or aspects of intervention. After the interviews were completed, we had our own ideas about which cases were successful based on impressions from up to 6 interviews per case. However, it was important to try and derive a less subjective measure from our specific data which might identify risk and protective factors and indicate service contributions to positive outcomes.

This was never going to be an easy task, since the study demonstrated that very different judgements could be reached about the relative success of a particular case, depending on which criterion was used or whose viewpoint was adopted. Even with respect to seemingly factual matters as measured in the Rutter scores, the three parties showed little agreement with each other. The nature of the data made complex analyses of variance inappropriate, so instead we devised a summary variable based on several dimensions for which we had information on most of the sample. This meant restricting ourselves to data from the social workers and the young people, plus the final Rutter score based on ratings by parents, where available. It was important to use measures from both social workers and young people in order to check against bias from either side. When only a few teenagers did well according to one variable, then two alternatives were used. We chose variables which corresponded best with the end, change, satisfaction and prognosis measures described at the beginning of the chapter:

1 *Position Scores at the End of the Year* (Psycho-social adjustment and self-esteem)
   If the case scored well on the Rutter scale OR self-esteem was high (according to both the Coopersmith scales and the social worker's estimate), then the case was regarded as a success on this dimension and scored 1 point.

2 *Position Scores at the End of the Year* (School and work)
If the young person was doing well at school according to the social
worker OR had left school and was at work/training/in further education, then the case was regarded as a success on this dimension and
scored 1 point.

3 *Positive Change in Behaviour over the Year*
If the young person showed improvement on the Rutter scale OR had
improved in behaviour according to the social worker, then the case
was regarded as a success on this dimension and scored 1 point.

4 *Positive Change in Self-esteem over the Year*
If the young person showed improvement on the Coopersmith scale or
had originally scored high so that improvement was difficult OR had improved a lot in self-esteem according to the social worker, then the case
was regarded as a success on this dimension and scored 1 point.

5 *Intervention Seen Positively*
If the young person stated that the intervention had been positive or that
the social worker had helped a lot AND the social worker thought that
the teenager had been helped a lot by the original placement, cur-
rent/most recent placement or supervision, then the case was regarded
as a success on this dimension and scored 1 point.

6 *Subjective Views of the Year*
If the young person was very satisfied with the year AND thought that
things were better at the end of the year compared with the beginning,
then the case was regarded as a success on this dimension and scored
1 point.

7 *Future Prospects*
If the social worker was optimistic about the future AND the young person was quite or very confident about the future, then the case was
regarded as a success on this dimension and scored 1 point.

In all there were 93 cases where both the social worker and young person had
been interviewed at follow-up, so that the case could be rated on each
dimension. In terms of *success*, these were classified as follows:

	Score	*Number*
Very successful	(5–7)	12
Moderately successful	(2–4)	38
Not successful	(0–1)	43

All of the 'very successful' cases ended the year with a low Rutter score and
ten of the twelve had high self-esteem on the Coopersmith scale. By and large
the ratings on this 'global' measure did identify the cases which we had also
concluded to be successful. However, there were a small number of cases

which were only 'moderately successful' on this criterion but it seemed to the interviewers that good progress had been made in unpromising circumstances. Sometimes the young person recognised a significant change, but not the social worker, and vice versa. In order to allow for this, a sub-score was calculated based on Variables 3 to 6 above which took account of *progress* but not end-position. This produced the following results:

	Score	Number
Extensive progress	(3–4)	19
Some progress	(1–2)	42
Little or no progress	(0)	32

Nine young people did well on both ratings and showed extensive progress as well as being very successful. Some of their experiences are described in more detail in a later section of this chapter looking at successful packages of services. Another ten had made extensive progress, even though they were counted as only 'moderately successful' because they had started from a low base or had long term difficulties which continued to cloud their future prospects.

The Connection between Initial Circumstances and 'Success' or 'Progress'

The relationship between these global measures of 'success' or 'progress' and factors present at the beginning of the study is important, because this helps to clarify how far the more successful cases were the easier ones to start with. It should be emphasised that any association is reported primarily for its descriptive interest and no assumptions should be made about the generalisability of the findings, let alone causation.

Examination of the Rutter scales showed that 'success' had occurred in similar proportions for individuals with low, medium and high scores at the start of the year. Thus good results had been obtained with some of the teenagers with the greatest difficulties and could not be readily attributed to easier cases. On the other hand, the Coopersmith measure did show a significant association between original high self-esteem and eventual success. In addition three quarters of cases who made extensive progress had begun with high self-esteem compared with only one third of low progress cases. Social workers' statements about self-esteem were in the same direction. A higher than average proportion of those with good school records at the start of the study went on to have a successful year. Thus a positive view of self and comparatively favourable educational progress seemed to be important assets or protective factors in negotiating the initial crisis or problem.

A higher proportion of the cases with 'extensive progress' were found in the group included in the study for admission to care than those placed on supervision or experiencing a change in care arrangements. Two thirds of the older teenagers who were referred to the study because they were moving out of care had had unsuccessful years. Overall, coming into care at the start of the year was more often associated with successful and broad improvement than living in the community or moving back into it.

The presenting problem associated with the largest proportion of successes was domestic conflict (as opposed to offending or school difficulties). When the social worker had reported that the young person had been involved in offending prior to referral the chances of high success were poor (3%, compared with 18% for the rest of the sample), although moderate success occurred quite often. Young people who admitted to involvement with drugs, solvents or alcohol in their first interviews had as good a record of success as others. However, continuing involvement in illegal activities during the course of the year showed a somewhat different pattern. As expected, the teenagers who had major involvement during the year in any anti-social behaviour, self-harm or abuse had lower rates of even moderate success (41%) than those who had not (61%). Nonetheless the majority of those who had been involved in offending in a major way had 'moderate success' (as regards our measure, not the rewards of their law-breaking!).

It was also interesting to see how far participants in the study had been able to foretell favourable outcomes at the outset. In general, there was only a weak association between the social workers' optimism in the first interviews about the year ahead and the teenager's eventual success or progress. Several young people about whom the social workers had initially expressed pessimism made substantial progress, whilst a number had done poorly despite high hopes for the intervention by the social worker at the start. The prognostications of carers at the start of the study proved to be no better guide than those of social workers, but very negative expectations by parents were largely borne out. When parents had been definitely pessimistic in the first interview, that was indeed followed by low level of ultimate success. This suggests that a very negative parental attitude is likely to presage lack of improvement, whether because they can make an accurate assessment or because they themselves are poorly motivated to change.

The Relationship between Overall Success and Intervention During the Year

The end of year picture showed that more of those currently in a care placement had good results compared with those living with parents or on their own, but the differences were small. Not surprisingly, stability of living situation seemed to be more influential than type of living situation. Two thirds of those who had stayed where they were throughout the year had successful outcomes, compared with half of the rest. However, a minority of those who made several moves during the year did well. It was the nature as much as the number of moves which was important.

It was not possible to derive a simple link between the specific type of care placement and outcomes, since many of the young people in care experienced more than one placement, usually in succession and occasionally in combination. The results in terms of the *original* living situation of the teenager showed that those who began the year in foster care included the highest proportion (one third) who went on to be 'very successful'. Moreover nearly half had made extensive progress, which was true for roughly one fifth of those in other kinds of placements.

At the end of the year, young people in foster care and residential schools had a relatively good share of success though living at home was more equivocal (Table 10:1). None of those currently living independently had had a very successful year. In spite of the reasonable evaluations of residential care and the generally good relations with key workers, nearly two thirds of teenagers in residential units had also had unsuccessful years. As Berridge (1985) noted, this can partly be explained by the fact that young people often end up here when other arrangements have failed.

Table 10:1 Placement at the end of the study compared with overall success (N=93)

	N	V. successful	Not successful
Foster care	9	33%	33%
Residential schools	10	20%	10%
With family	41	19%	46%
Residential units	13	8%	62%
Independent living	17	0%	59%
Custody	3	0%	100%

A good relationship with the social workers was connected with success. Presumably each reinforces the other. All but one of the teenagers who had very successful years said they found their social worker easy to talk to. Moreover, one quarter of the 60 young people who said their worker was easy to talk to had made extensive progress, which was true for only one of the 28 who did not find communication with their social worker easy. The quality of parents' relationships with social workers was not associated with success but if neither the parent nor the teenager got on very well with the social worker, then the rate of success was much reduced. Very successful cases did not involve more frequent contact with social workers than others, but less than monthly contact was associated with a poor progress record.

When the same social worker had dealt with more than one case, there could be quite different outcomes. For instance, three each had one case which was not successful and another which was very successful. Only half the proportion of closed cases as open cases had experienced extensive change. Whatever else it signalled, case closure within a year seemed more likely to indicate the absence of progress rather than the resolution of problems.

Social workers' own estimates of their success understandably tallied quite well with the global measures. For instance, when social workers said they had succeeded in help with offending, the teenager made some progress in over 90% of the cases. When the social workers said they had tried but failed to help with offending, there was little or no progress 90% of the time.

Successful Packages of Services

The diversity of the young people's initial circumstances and experience during the year made it difficult to draw generally applicable conclusions about which services or combinations of services had been most effective but it was important to gain further understanding of some of their essential features. We therefore examined in more detail the 9 cases where the outcomes were rated as 'very successful' *and* progress had also been 'extensive'. In this analysis we focused on the services provided and the support given to the young people. These were not the only components in these successful packages, as will become apparent from some of the case examples, but they reinforced themes which have run throughout this study.

We use the term 'package' to refer to the total provision during the year, though in few instances were the services planned as co-ordinated 'packages' from the start. Instead services were provided as they became available or were required in response to the young person's changing needs. More than one service might be provided at the same time (a combination) and/or in succession (a sequence). As the direct work of social workers applied in every case and was usually instrumental in obtaining the other services it has not been classified here as part of a 'combination' of services. All of the other services listed in Chapter 4 and evaluated in later chapters were experienced by at least one of the 9 young people (6 male, 3 female). Four of the teenagers came from Agency A, four from Agency C and one from Agency E.

a *The Services Provided.* There were examples of both stability and many changes among the packages which led to success as well as progress by the end of the year. In some cases the social work intervention had formally ceased or was waning in significance at the time of our follow-up but other teenagers continued to require active support. The nine packages comprised:

One service	= 3 cases
Sequence or combination	= 2 cases
Combination and sequence	= 4 cases

The 3 young people who had received just one service were in care placements which suited them and had lasted. Two of these were foster placements and the other person was in a residential school. The young people's acceptance of these placements and the ways in which they had settled and made progress in other aspects of their lives were important ingredients in their success.

Two more young people had spent part of the year in foster care but had now returned home. One of these moves represented a 'sequence' of services as the teenager was subsequently supervised at home, while the other was a 'combination' as the foster home was used during holidays from a residential school. The school placement had been the dominant influence in shaping a successful year as the young person had been enabled to take his GCSEs and motivated to work. Although his social worker considered that the foster home had supplemented this progress, the teenager himself and his parents were less positive about this part of the combination.

There were 4 young people who experienced both combinations and sequences of services during the year. They illustrated the need for a wide range of resources and for flexibility of access as situations changed. In one instance a planned foster placement did not work out and the young person had further unexpected moves in residential care during the year, while another teenager had two moves before reaching the residential placement which had been planned for her but previously unavailable because of a waiting list. She later moved to a foster home because she had made good progress and was ready for this transition. Both of these young people had received additional services during the year and were still in care at follow-up.

Home supervision was combined with attendance at groups for the other two young people and both of them needed spells in care as well. Admission to two different residential units provided respites for one teenager and her parents when things were particularly tense at home, while the other's stay in a remand foster home combined with outreach activities was enforced by the court prior to a spell in custody.

The three teenagers who were in residential care during the year experienced 8 different placements, making this the most frequently used service within these successful packages in numerical terms. However several of these placements were temporary stop-gaps due to crises or the unavailability of a preferred service. Foster care featured more widely as a service than residential care in these positive interventions as 7 of the 9 young people each had one foster placement. Thus foster care was part of the most effective interventions in almost four-fifths of the successful packages, even though it had been provided in only one-fifth of all packages. Nevertheless, 3 of the 7 foster placements ended unsatisfactorily and the provision of other services had made a greater contribution to the successful outcomes in the estimation of the young people and their social workers in these cases. As noted earlier, home supervision was part of the service for three young people, including one who went home from a long-term foster home. One of the two teenagers who had been in residential school was back home without any supervision and was managing quite well, while the extent of future social work involvement was a current issue for the other lad who was due to leave at the end of term.

It was striking that in several of the most successful cases the young person had made a decision, sometimes against adult advice, on important matters such as whether to change placements or to have contact with a parent. This supports the view that teenagers are able to make choices about what is in their best interest if they are given the information and opportunity to do so. It also underlines the importance of having access to different types of resources at different stages in the teenager's life. Unfortunately resource provision was seldom plentiful enough to allow for choice based on the young person's preferences or needs. This was particularly the case in relation to care placements. Consequently when they worked out particularly well, social workers often saw this as fortuitous rather the result of careful placing. Evidently young people could only be given a choice about placements if alternatives were in fact available.

b *The Support Given to the Young People.* Each of the services provided in these successful packages was delivered by individuals and a vital element was the ability of at least one person to give the young people the kind of support and encouragement which enabled them to deal with the problems which had led to social work intervention and generally to make progress in their lives. Sometimes the whole package was right in this respect and the teenager blossomed as a result. For others, one particular person, or several, provided the necessary help. Depending on the circumstances, this might be the social worker, a key worker or teacher, foster parents or the young person's own parents.

All the 9 young people who ended the year with success and progress had begun it with either very difficult relationships at home or else with no-one able to provide parental care. At follow-up five of these teenagers were living with one or both of their parents and the rest had some contact with at least one parent. During the year considerable inputs had been made into working to improve these relationships and renewed support from a parent had sometimes been the key to a successful outcome. One father returned to the area and set up a new home for his daughter. Another visited his son regularly in prison and helped him to understand both the folly of crime and its role in society. This led to much improved relationships on release and no further trouble with the police. Other parents also played a supportive part in the packages by co-operating with the programmes worked out for their son or daughter. Absence from home helped to reduce some of the tensions and created a better understanding, though one teenager claimed this was due to greater tolerance on her part:

> 'I've just learned more patience with my Mum and Dad.
> When they are saying things to me, now I understand it
> more than I would have months ago.'

Foster parents played the key role in providing the support which enabled the teenagers to flourish in three of the cases where the young people had not returned home. They also gave them an alternative base from which to negotiate the transition to adult life. In one case the attachment had become so strong that the young person planned to remain with the foster family indefinitely and attributed the change in his behaviour to his foster parents' care and their reasonable expectations. A second teenager gained so much from his foster family and all the opportunities they provided that his social worker had not needed to procure the additional group and outreach services which she had expected would be necessary to help him develop a greater personal and emotional maturity. The third young person settled well in a foster home after several residential placements. She was delighted with the peace of the carer's home and appreciated the trust and freedom she was given there. It was important to her that she was with a single carer, rather than a family. She said:

> 'I feel comfortable. It's really peaceful. I don't need to ask to do
> things. I just say I'm going out T. see you later and she says OK.
> As long as I'm back by a reasonable time it's OK . . . or I can go
> and listen to music in my room if I like.'

The other young person who had not returned home at the end of the year had had several moves but his self-esteem was high, partly because he now got on better with his mother after she had talked to him about what had happened in the past when her marriage broke down. Several people had given this teenager support during the year, including a key worker who maintained contact with him while he was in a secure unit. The young person felt that having a 6–7 month period of stability in one residential placement had enabled him to make progress and learn to take responsibility for himself. Attendance on a daily basis at the same residential school also provided continuity when he was forced to move from one residential unit because it was closing. Most of all, the young person appreciated his social worker's reliability and long-standing interest in him and thought that their discussions had helped him to mature.

Having a good social worker was an important factor in their success and progress for most of the 9 young people. An exception was a teenager placed in a residential school where the staff had played a more prominent role due to a gap of several months between social workers. Not only had the staff provided very good support to the young person himself, but also they had liaised closely with his parents and responded well when there had been crises at home. This won praise from the parents, who described the school as a 'happy place' and wished their son could have gone there earlier.

Generally, though, the social worker's continued input had been very influential in many of the most successful cases. The teenagers spoke particularly highly of social workers who were described as reliable, easy to talk to and conveyed a genuine interest in the young person. In several instances the social worker's ability to gain the teenager's confidence and/or help the family through a crisis had contributed significantly to the success of a residential or foster placement and had helped to restore better relationships at home. Social workers also enabled several of the young people to benefit educationally by obtaining special placements or through close liaison with their mainstream schools.

The value of skilled and persistent support such as this was acknowledged in glowing terms by one of the teenagers, who said that her social worker was:

> 'like a friend, not like a social worker. I'm really glad she has
> been my social worker . . . I don't know what it is, just the way
> she talks, she's brilliant.'

The social worker had been able to win this young person's trust and thus help her to understand some difficult issues and develop productive ways of dealing with them. Each new challenge brought the risk of failure but with the social worker's support C. was learning to keep disappointments in perspective and not be overwhelmed by them.

Thus a crucial element in creating successful packages, even when situations deteriorated or seemed disastrous, was the ability to hold onto and encourage the potential within these adolescents to overcome their difficulties. This resource needed to be harnessed just as much as more readily identifiable facilities such as residential units or groups. Each of the 9 young people had benefited from this encouragement as their self-esteem was high and there was other evidence of the extensive progress they had made.

Agency Differences

While this study was set up with the primary aim of comparing outcomes for individual teenagers, we were aware that other studies have shown wide disparities in child care outcomes amongst different agencies (eg Berridge and Cleaver, 1987). The problem is to identify which of the many factors involved are responsible, ranging from geographical size via relative prosperity to the nature and quality of services. The agency pattern in the present study (Table 10:2) showed that Agency A had its fair share of good successes according to our global measure, but few moderately successful cases so that it accounted for the highest proportion of not successful cases. In both Agencies C and E there was at least moderate success for over half the cases, with Agency E having the highest proportion (71%).

Table 10:2 Local authority successes

Agency	N	V. Successful	Moderate	Not Successful
A	31	16%	19%	65%
C	26	14%	43%	43%
E	27	11%	60%	30%
B & D	7	–	57%	43%

The agency differences can be seen in more detail by bringing together the indicators considered earlier in the book. The numbers for Agencies B and D are combined and must be treated with caution since the numbers are low, with sometimes nearly half the cases having missing information:

Table 10:3 Indicators of helpfulness, progress or success according to agency

	AGENCY			
	A	B&D	C	E
% very successful on combined measure	16	0	14	11
% very or moderately successful	35	57	57	71
% teenagers said the intervention likely to make their future better	32	45	62	27
% teenagers said situation at end of year better than at start	72	54	75	66
% teenagers very satisfied with year	13	36	36	26
% teenagers' expectations fulfilled	32	54	57	48
% teenagers said SW helped a lot	10	36	43	16
% parents who said the teenager benefited from seeing a SW	28	22	70	44
% SW optimistic about the future	38	58	48	65
% helped a lot by at least one placement or supervision (SW's view)	22	60	45	38
% SW's expectations fulfilled	30	46	47	39
% attending school/work at end	42	54	67	67

| | AGENCY | | | |
	A	B&D	C	E
% improved at school over the year (SW's view)*	50	*	54	81
% behaviour improved over the year (SW's view)	27	50	41	50
% teenagers with high self esteem at the end of the year	20	22	21	44

* Excludes those who had left school. B&D left out as numbers too small.

Table 10:3 illustrates how Agency C generally scored best, especially with regard to teenagers' own satisfaction, but Agency E did better when the social workers' viewpoints were taken into account. In assessing these results it is important to bear in mind sample differences amongst the local authorities (see also Chapter 2). It will be recalled that the Rutter scores and health patterns did not show significant agency variations. Also involvement in offending/addictions in a major way during the year was present to similar degrees in every agency. However each differed considerably from the rest in certain other respects. In the list which follows 'more' and 'fewer' refer to proportionate differences which take account of subsample size:

- *Agency A* – fewer girls; fewer involved with drugs; more referrals related to parents not coping; more outreach/befriending; more foster placements; more young people who moved 3 or more times in the year; more living with parents at end of the study.
- *Agency B* – fewer girls; more older boys; more referrals related to young person's behaviour; no residential school placements; very high proportion of offenders; fewer in care.
- *Agency C* – fewer with school problems at the start and more doing well at school; more foster placements; fewer supervision cases.
- *Agency D* – more older girls; more teenagers who had been sexually abused; no residential school placements; fewer supervision cases.
- *Agency E* – more younger girls; more referrals related to domestic conflict and school problems; more statutory cases; more group work; more residential school placements.

A much larger sample would be needed even to begin to disentangle which elements of the pre-referral situation and service response contributed to the differences in these outcomes.

Conclusions

In view of the diversity of the sample and of the service combinations provided, it is not surprising that this study revealed few straightforward answers to such questions as 'Who is most readily helped?' and 'Which services worked best?'. Successful cases included teenagers in very difficult circumstances, as well as some in a relatively favourable situation. Residential schools came out well on virtually all indicators, whereas few young adults trying to manage on their own had done well. However each service (such as foster care, residential units or counselling) was helpful for some teenagers but not others. Foster care had afforded some young people very satisfactory outcomes, but also had a number of breakdowns. What seemed to be important was the particular match of services to individual needs accompanied by skilled and reliable support.

11   Summary and Conclusions

This study took place against a background of considerable public concern about the troublesome and sometimes criminal behaviour of teenagers. There were calls for the imposition of stricter punishments and controls and the period also coincided with some major scandals about abuse in certain residential establishments which led to official enquiries. The aims of the study were to examine programmes of care and supervision for teenagers who become subject to social services intervention. It was important to single out this age group because of the scant attention paid to them previously, except in relation to specific issues like offending or leaving care.

Primary objectives of the research were to understand:

- the problems and expectations set;
- how one or more services would be made available over a period of time in response to the initial problems;
- how these services were evaluated by the key participants;
- what impact they had on the teenagers and their families.

The researchers investigated the range of child care policies, services and practice in five Social Services or Social Work Departments in order to understand how these impinged on the needs and problems of teenagers and their families. The study included arrangements for young people both at home and in substitute care. It was also important to consider the nature and extent of participation in decision-making by both teenagers and parents, in view of the increased attention to children's rights associated with ratification of the UN Convention by the United Kingdom and the emphasis on partnership with parents in the Children Act, 1989.

Most teenagers and their families negotiate adolescence in a way which is broadly satisfactory, by effecting a gradual transfer of autonomy, rights and responsibilities to the teenager within a context of continuing parental support and modified parental authority. For a minority of families, especially those affected by poverty or family breakdown (such as separation, single parenthood and reconstitution), this period proves more problematic and some of them come to the attention of social services as a result of concern about the well-being or behaviour of the young person. External resources and opportunities also impinge on the stresses and coping capacities of both parents and youngsters in these situations. While increasing numbers of young people are able to undertake extended education with prospects of a good job, a significant minority face a choice of unemployment or low-paid training once they leave school. It is often a combination of troublesome behaviour in the community, family tensions and bleak life chances which lead to referral to social workers, initiating the responses which were depicted and evaluated in the present study. The main task of social workers working with adolescents is often to achieve an equilibrium between adults' expectations and young people's behaviours, aspirations, autonomy and responsibility towards others. In the process they will be faced with resource issues and the need to find appropriate boundaries between care and control within a relationship of trust.

The study was planned on a longitudinal basis over one year in order to compare initial expectations with resource deployment and later achievements and in order to trace progress following intervention. A sample was identified of 116 teenagers aged 13–17 who were experiencing the start of a new form of social services intervention or a significant change in care or supervision arrangements. Participants in the study were recruited from three local authorities in England and two in Scotland. The inclusion of several agencies increases confidence in the generalisability of the findings compared with a focus on a single agency. At the beginning and end of the study, information about policies and services in each agency was gathered by means of discussions with senior staff at regional and district level, supplemented by perusal of relevant documentation.

The main part of the research consisted of initial and follow up interviews approximately one year apart with the young person, social worker and parents in each case, except when a potential respondent was unavailable or unwilling to be seen. In the first round of interviews, all three parties were asked about their expectations and perceptions in relation to both problems and services. On both occasions, the young person's current circumstances were explored in depth. Information was also gathered on dimensions like health, behaviour, and schooling to assess changes in young people and their progress over the year. The measures included standardised Rutter and Coopersmith scales, which assess psychosocial development and self-esteem respectively.

To supplement the interviews, certain details were extracted from case records. A short self-completion questionnaire was also given to the residential and foster carers looking after teenagers at the beginning of the study. In order to provide some check on the representativeness of the characteristics and views of the sample, wider statistical data were obtained in two of the agencies and group discussions were held with a further 62 young people after the first round of interviews.

Sample Characteristics

At the start of the study, about three fifths of the sample were living away from home, mostly in care (this phrase is taken to include those who were 'accommodated') though a few were already living 'independently'. The remainder of the sample were being supervised at home – on a court order (in England), under a supervision requirement by the hearing (in Scotland) or informally as a preventive measure. Whether a teenager stayed at home or not seemed to depend on factors other than degree of difficulty, such as the threshold of tolerance of parents or external agencies and the availability of other resources (like special schooling).

The young people were clearly a difficult population, with nine out of ten scoring above the normal cut-off point on the Rutter scale. Most had a history of poor schooling and many had low self-esteem. The teenagers living at home included just as high a proportion who were 'disturbed' or had low self-esteem as the ones in care. Only a minority of the sample were living in intact two parent households. Attitudinal and relationship difficulties were often compounded by financial and environmental stresses, though not invariably. Many parents had been struggling for years on low incomes in poor neighbourhoods, but some were in fairly good material circumstances.

Although a few young people were estranged from their parents, and some parents opted out of the lives of their children, the great majority of young people had important continuing relationships and felt close to one or both parents. Friends played a very important part in their lives, not only as companions but also as helpers. With important occasional exceptions, the extended family offered little long term support to young people. Few social workers were well informed about teenagers' social networks.

Problems, Needs and Expectations

Social workers had become involved with the teenagers and their families for three main reasons:

- disputes and conflicts between the teenager and parent(s) or step-parent;
- school-related problems, especially non-attendance;
- offending and/or involvement in drug, solvent or alcohol abuse.

Although there were some people in the sample with a quite specific problem or issue which resulted in intervention, the most typical pattern was for a cluster of family-school-behaviour problems to be present. In contrast to parents, social workers in their definition of the problems tended to underplay undesirable behaviours and the intensity of family conflict. Some young people were referred to the study because they were undergoing a major change or were moving to some kind of 'independent' accommodation. They were facing secondary problems arising from being in care, on top of their original difficulties.

Whilst a few teenagers in the study had been seriously abused, usually child protection issues did not feature or took a different form, compared with younger children. Many youngsters were exposed to social or health risks, which were partly caused and certainly made worse by the indifference or rejection of key adults in their lives. We also encountered some examples of the opposite situation where parents felt oppressed or even abused by their offspring, who combined physical strength with emotional immaturity. In the circumstances, and in the absence of specific policies and strategies, social workers were often unsure how to respond to requests for voluntary help, most likely because of other pressing matters, and the opportunity for early preventive intervention was consequently delayed to the disappointment of the parents. Compulsory measures were sometimes suggested to parents to ensure access to service provision.

Not unexpectedly, parents, social workers and the young people did not always see problems and needs in the same way and hence framed their desired solutions differently. For example, many parents saw the young person's behaviour as the key problem and wanted more effective controls imposed, which they felt no longer able to do themselves. In line with this perception, they also expected almost all change to come from the young person with hardly any from themselves. Although many young people did accept at least some responsibility for their problems, there were others who thought that inappropriate adult expectations and behaviours were at the heart of their problems. The main concern of some was to deal with the consequences of their acts (like court appearances) or with a need arising out of a preoccupation with their current problem. It was rare to link behaviour with some inner type of need. They framed their expectations largely in terms of immediate practical concerns and preoccupations, whilst parents put most emphasis on behavioural changes. In contrast, practitioners were more likely to formulate goals based on the perceived longer term personal and welfare needs of the young person, such as increased confidence, maturity and self-esteem.

There seemed to have been little systematic attempt to discuss openly the differences in definitions, perceptions of need or the setting of expectations. The latter were largely based on each party's agenda. The wide disparities found also suggested the absence of periodic reviews and feedback sessions to establish or maintain the direction of the intervention process. In other words, the implementation of principles such as partnership and participation, which ascribe validity and importance to the viewpoints of service users, were not pursued in any detail.

Available Support and the Range of Services Offered

At least one parent remained the main reference point and source of support for most of the teenagers in the sample, though this varied in commitment.

Friends too were key sources of support. It seemed that for many older teenagers, friends had to some extent replaced family members as the main support. Parents and friends were the people to whom most young people had turned to for help and were identified as the best 'helpers' in times of difficulty. However, in the course of the year fewer teenagers had actually received help from family or friends than had expected it would be available twelve months earlier. Any help was of limited duration rather than long-term.

Following intervention, social workers and their agencies brought into play a wide range of services. These reflected the diversity of family circumstances, the changing requirements of adolescents as they became older and the differing resources of the agencies concerned. The services most commonly arranged by social workers for the teenagers were:

- *Away from home* – residential units; residential schools; foster care; preparation for independence units and supported accommodation.
- *Home or away* – outreach or befriending by residential carers or volunteers; day places in residential schools; group work; psychological and psychiatric services; special education classes or unit; home tuition.

Alongside all of these was the *direct work of the social workers* themselves. In addition to their case management functions, they might try to assist through individual counselling, family work, mediation, practical aid and advocacy. The availability of services varied from one agency to another and also within agencies. In particular, foster care, group work and outreach were much easier to gain access to in some areas than others, even within the same authority. The same was also true about consistent individual and family work. Consequently allocation of services resulted as much from local provision and custom as from young people's needs or preferences. Yet better outcomes were usually related to the consistent deployment of a range of resources than to single forms of intervention.

Many of the placements in care were short-lived, a matter of weeks or months. This could be an appropriate period of respite, task-centred work or preparatory transition. However some moves resulted from delays until the first-choice placement was available or because the young person reached the upper age limit for an establishment. Others resulted from some kind of 'breakdown'. Although teenagers may be more able to adapt to changes than younger children, the placement turnover during the year left cause for concern, reinforcing the instability already experienced by many young people in their family lives.

Supervision at home took highly variable forms, according to the nature of the identified problems, the services available locally or the approach of the particular social worker. Usually work was directed mainly at the young person, but sometimes family work was carried out. Depending on the agency and the area, a range of measures were also used to supplement, complement or substitute for individual or family counselling. These included organised activities, group work, befriending and school attendance places.

Befriending was mainly offered to boys on supervision or young adults living on their own. Most groups were activity based, but some relied partly or mainly on discussion and verbal exercises. Although 'in care' groups were attended equally by both girls and boys, nearly all of those on supervision who were offered a group were boys. Group work was seldom used with older teenagers, except for specialist projects focusing on offending or addictions.

The study was primarily concerned with specialist provision over which Social Services/Work Departments had direct control. Nevertheless, it was evident that the difficulties faced by many of the young people were very much affected by more universal policies. Whilst some of the teenagers were undoubtedly not easy to manage, it remained true that the mainstream education system had often failed to maintain their motivation or adapt to their abilities and interests. At least half of the teenagers in the sample had been in receipt of specialist educational provision. The older teenagers, with rare exceptions, emerged from school with few worthwhile qualifications to face a generally unfavourable labour market. The availability of suitable housing in the community was of vital concern to many of those aged 16 or over and with no stable social base.

Consumers' Views of Social Work Intervention

The majority of the teenagers were positive about the social work intervention, but fewer thought it had a major impact on their lives. When young people were particularly pleased with what had happened, this could be attributed to:

- having a say in the type and choice of specific placement;
- some openness and congruence in the setting of expectations;
- planned individual and family work;
- resolution of conflict within reasonably supportive families;
- liking for the nature of schooling offered on a residential basis or by day attendance at a residential school;
- close, confiding relationship with the social worker or key worker;
- happy match between young person and residential or foster carers;
- shared goals and approach by social worker and family in relation to home supervision.

We encountered a minority of young people who were disenchanted with most adults and resented efforts to control their behaviour, but these were the exception. Even they usually had at least one adult they trusted and respected – a parent, teacher, group worker, key worker or social worker. Most young people related well to the professionals they came into contact with (except psychologists and psychiatrists). Generally social workers were well liked, but some were unaware of the critical attitudes held by young people or their parents. A liking of social workers did not necessarily go with positive change.

A clear picture emerged of the kind of adults that most of the teenagers related well to and were inclined to cooperate with. They:

- were informal in approach (eg were easy to talk to;
  took the young person out);
- respected young people, listened to what they said,
  tried to understand and did not lecture them;
- could recognise the difference between being frank and
  sometimes challenging from being 'pushy' and 'nagging';
- were available, punctual and reliable;
- kept confidences;
- did practical things to help;
- carried out their promises.

When the relationship was good and they respected their social worker, the teenagers welcomed straight talking and warnings about the consequences of their behaviour. Indeed a surprisingly high proportion in this group, claimed this had helped them to reduce or stop offending. On the other hand, some young people resented being 'nagged' and considered that it was largely up to themselves whether they carried on an anti-social life-style or decided to stop. However, some social workers were able to establish rapport and relationships with some of the very 'disturbed' teenagers as well as the less problematic ones, suggesting perseverance. This disproved the assumption that social workers can effect change only with the least problematic users. This was usually achieved through a combination of personal qualities, skills and a range of resources.

Preventive work with teenagers and their families in the form of support, counselling, respite where needed and activities aimed at diversion were variable and inconsistent and, where present, these were mainly reserved for those officially identified as 'a problem'. Some parents reported that they had found it difficult to get help from busy offices in the early stages before problems got out of hand. Facilities, such as family centres, are meant for younger children and there is a dearth of services oriented to working with families in ways which are appropriate to adolescents. The definition of the concept of 'in need' in part III of the Children Act, 1989 (S.17(10)(b)) with its emphasis on likely *significant impairment of health or development* could be interpreted as excluding most young people and their families from the receipt of preventive/supportive services.

In spite of the frustration expressed by many parents at the absence of consistent preventive services, by the follow-up period more than half said they got on well with the social workers and were broadly favourable about the service. Like their children, they valued the counselling and supportive role as well as practical assistance. However, significantly higher proportions of parents than teenagers complained that the intervention had been ineffective or different from what they wanted. A number were aggrieved that most of the attention had been given to the teenager. They would have liked more time devoted to themselves, either in their own right or to work on issues related to the young person. Some wanted more account taken of their views that their son or daughter should be treated firmly. This could conflict with the teenagers' wishes for more freedom and might be the opposite of a social work aim to help parents relax certain of their expectations.

Whilst it is sometimes helpful to see conflicting parties separately and appropriate to accord older teenagers individual help, it did seem that there were opportunities for family work which were not often grasped. Seeing the family together was sometimes part of an agreed programme of work, but all too often family meetings only occurred during a crisis, at a decision-making forum or by chance. Considering that many parents approached problem resolution with limited or fixed ideas, there were only a few examples of consistent work to mediate between them and young people and to help demonstrate a broader repertoire of possible responses.

Perceptions of Particular Services

Residential Homes/Units

Young people, their parents and social workers considered the majority of placements in residential units to have been beneficial and some had provided much needed care at a crucial point in the young person's life. However residential units were markedly less successful than residential schools in terms of placement stability and feedback from social workers and parents. Many establishments had only a small number of staff who had to cope with difficult and demanding young people. Lack of choice in resources often resulted in young people coming to the units not because it was the most appropriate placement but because there was nowhere else for them to go. This made it difficult to prepare for the placement or develop plans with a clear sense of purpose. There was some evidence to suggest that the more troublesome a young person was, the more likely that he or she would be moved around, which only made the situation worse. Even when they knew they were being difficult, young people did not like being moved, being 'abandoned' or visits spaced out. They also expected field and residential staff to stand by them when they were difficult, even when they openly said they wanted them out of their lives.

On the other hand, individual residential carers in all types of units were very highly praised by both young people and their parents. There were numerous references to the friendliness of staff who were appreciated for being 'down to earth' and informal. The value of placements was enhanced when residential and field work staff understood each other's roles well and worked in tandem to provide effective support to young people and, where appropriate, to their parents. Key workers appeared crucial for many young people and their availability and especially continuity was particularly valued. In spite of the positive responses elicited about key workers, it was our view that their potential had neither been fully recognised or exploited, particularly the importance of continuity. Similarly, positive relationships developed between parents and staff in residential units could have been built upon, by agreeing on a more flexible allocation of responsibilities between field and residential staff concerning family work.

Residential Schools

These proved to be the most popular and durable of the three main placement types for those who experienced them. Young people with a long history of discomfort about going to their local school found the environment much more acceptable. Key features were the small size of classes allowing for more individualised attention and programmes, 'fun' activities and reduced pressures to conform. If a similar setting had been available within a day school, there might have been no need at all for the child to be away from home. Indeed, some attended a residential school on a day basis.

Parents, too, were often delighted that their children were receiving education and not roaming the streets, even if they had some guilt or regrets about them being away from home. Most residents went home at weekends and contacts with family and friends were maintained. There were complaints in a few cases about the rigidity of home leave arrangements or distance from home, but generally access to home was not the major issue for young people in residential schools or units it has been for younger children. The latter are more reliant on being visited, whereas teenagers can travel themselves.

The population of residential schools comprised a high proportion of young people with significant behaviour difficulties so their more favourable outcomes than other residential units could not be attributed to them caring for a less problematic population. It should also be noted that most of the residential schools were in Scotland and in agencies where closer co-operation with Education Departments had been developed. However residential schools were not exposed to the same turnover of residents as other residential units since all placements were planned on a long-term basis. The relative success of residential schools, over other forms of residential care, in improving the young people's education and self-esteem may be related to this greater stability and continuity. The findings suggest that the potential of residential care in this area has not been utilised (Jackson 1989; Aldgate, 1990).

Foster Care

This was offered to only a minority of the teenagers placed away from home and in one agency was hardly ever considered. Nevertheless, one third of all placements were in foster care. Because of the acute shortage of suitable placements, notions of matching could not be fully applied. Similarly, only a few placements were with carers who were specially trained and supported. These factors may partly account for the fact that the foster placements were more likely than residential ones to finish ahead of the planned date and sooner than needed. The main difficulties, from the young people's point of view, were foster carers being too restrictive about evening activities and money or wanting too much family togetherness. Whilst breakdowns in arrangements led to disappointments, on the other hand the successful ones worked very well indeed and were serving as a base for adulthood, so the young person would not have to move to a 'preparation for independence' unit and then supported accommodation like their colleagues in residential care.

After-Care Services

Overall about one fifth of the sample lived on their own or in supported accommodation at some point during the year. Some moved from home supervision rather than care. Although the agencies in the study had developed programmes to assist in the transition from care to adulthood, social workers appeared to overestimate the amount of preparation given to the young people. Moreover those in our study who were trying to manage on their own still faced very similar problems to those identified nearly a decade ago before more concerted attention was given to older care leavers (Stein and Carey, 1986). Some had set out with high expectations, but were soon disillusioned by mounting debts, unsuitable housing, lack of support, loneliness and the uncertainties of the benefits system. Often they found it hard to deal with the various agencies which might help with money, work, education or housing and some gave up. This was the most vulnerable, unhappy and dissatisfied group of young people from amongst the whole sample. It should not be difficult to recognise this group early on, concentrating far more resources and attention to meet their complex needs, particularly the need for stability in life.

Several young people felt that the 'system' wanted to get rid of them before they were ready, especially in Scotland. Others were keen to move out, but found life on their own difficult emotionally, financially and socially. A few of these depended heavily and thankfully on help from their social workers, but more felt unsupported and abandoned. This inconsistent pattern seemed to be related to the pressures experienced by individual area teams and/or individual social workers. Support from former residential carers was often minimal, despite promises to the contrary. Some young people had been told they could return to the fieldwork office for help if needed, but this was unsatisfactory too. Either the young person did not feel able to take the initiative for fear of being seen to have failed or else help was not forthcoming because of staff changes or commitments. Even some young people who felt resentful about social workers, still felt abandoned if not visited. Parents and relatives often had low incomes and other family responsibilities themselves, so the most they could usually offer was emotional support, an overnight stay or an occasional meal.

Home-based Supervision

Little has been written about supervision of teenagers and perhaps in consequence social workers sometimes seemed uncertain how to tackle the dual tasks of modifying the young people's behaviour (usually offending) and improving their welfare. Often young people were not well motivated to use supervision as an opportunity to stay out of trouble or to improve their circumstances, so commitment had to be generated or inspired. Some social workers were not happy or comfortable having to supervise unmotivated and uncooperative youngsters, but in a number of cases barriers were overcome and trust established by a combination of friendly informality and direct action (eg advocacy). About a fifth of young people seemed to benefit a lot from home supervision, with many of the initial problems reduced or stopped. In another quarter or so cases, there was some amelioration. Little or no benefits were identified in about half the cases.

Youngsters with problems of offending and drug taking who had declared explicit intentions to stop or cut down seemed to achieve more than those who did not. This raises the question of whether others could have been challenged to set such goals. Because of the statutory responsibilities social workers carry they cannot be wholly neutral and challenging certain behaviours may be not only unavoidable but desirable. However, the process of how and when this is done seems crucial to the outcome. In the main, teenagers valued frankness about the consequences of anti-social behaviour and encouragement to change, provided this occurred within a relationship of personal acceptance. In many such cases, the boundary line between care and challenge was a flexible one leaving much more scope for negotiation, compared to what much of the professional literature on the subject tends to suggest. Some parents did not understand why social workers took time to build up trust before seeking to alter behaviour and thought the behaviour was being condoned. Much of this misunderstanding could have been avoided through better communication about aims and processes. In Chapter 6 we outlined what components of policy, practice and resources are required to make supervision more effective.

Group Work and Befriending

The study showed that meetings with peers and individualised attention from a 'friendly' adult could take many forms and be adapted to children both at home and away from home. Usually this kind of help was well liked by the teenagers, although both they and the social workers were more circumspect about how much effect it had on the initial problems. Activities were often a valuable incentive for young people to attend and were enjoyed, but a few parents saw this as indulgent. Many teenagers valued discussing issues of common concern in an informal setting. The impact of group activities was likely to be higher if combined with other forms of intervention, such as consistent individual and family work.

Participation in Decision-Making

The agencies in the study had clear policies stressing cooperation and joint planning with parents and young people. More parents than young people had been in favour of supervision or care. Subsequently, the position reversed and parents were more likely to feel negative or excluded. For example, many were dissatisfied that they had little influence on placement choice and were not kept informed of plans or developments. Parents often considered that decisions were too much influenced by what the teenager wanted. Parents who said that they did not have sufficient opportunities to get their views across or were uncertain about the opportunities offered them were very unlikely to express satisfaction with the services.

Fewer young people than parents felt they had an influence on the start and nature of the intervention, especially of course when this was imposed by a court or panel. Most felt they had been consulted about later decisions and that they were adequately prepared for moves. Young people's participation in decision-making was hampered by limited choices, ignorance about options and lack of skills in expressing themselves or negotiating with adults. Participation by young people in the choice of the type of placement and about the specific placement emerged as significant variables bearing on levels of satisfaction with the services. This was particularly important to those in care who felt that options were often limited by lack of resources. In all, participation without choice of specific placement seemed hollow to many young people and their families. Even when consulted, most young people still felt they had had little influence. When such feelings persisted, the probability of success was lowered.

The majority of the teenagers were reasonably happy with child care reviews. Either they felt well able to speak for themselves or else they were confident that social workers, key workers or parents would get their views across. There was some resentment at having too many adults present, especially people they knew hardly or not at all. Preparatory talks with social workers and key workers seemed to be helpful. Fewer were confident about speaking in court or at a panel. Generally there was not much support for having an independent representative to speak for them in legal or decision-making settings. When young people wanted assistance in putting their views across, they usually preferred familiar people – relatives, social workers, friends or teachers.

Most young people in care seemed to be aware of complaints procedures. Awareness was more common among those in residential than in foster care and also varied between agencies.

Changes and Overall Progress

Subjective Evaluations

More than two thirds of the young people had concluded that overall their lives were better at the end of the year than at the start, albeit not always in their view because of social work intervention. However this applied to only one third of those living independently. Much of the improvement may have been due to the natural tendency of crises to subside and be placed in perspective. Just under half the teenagers thought their stated expectations for the intervention at the start of the measures had been met (48%, compared with 41% for parents and only 29% for social workers, who had more ambitious hopes at the outset). Looking for positive outcomes in relation to stated expectations and needs a year earlier, proved complex, elusive and fraught with difficulties. This was mainly because objectives had not been jointly agreed and each party had a different perspective. Expectations also tend to shift, reflecting changes in the situation. Continued reviewing and redefinition was therefore required and this had seldom happened. As with expectations, social workers continued to see outcomes mainly in develop-mental terms, whilst the young people and parents looked at them largely in concrete and behavioural terms. The low level of shared planning, goal setting and reviewing ran from the identification and definition of the problem to the setting of expectations (Chapter 3) and finally to the evaluation of outcomes. Though numbers were small, there was some evidence to suggest that where there was congruence between the parties about needs and expectations, and the right resources were consistently deployed, then the likelihood of more positive outcomes was higher.

Changes in Behaviour, Self-Esteem, Health and Schooling

Parents and social workers noted positive changes in the behaviour of some young people during the year, but many still showed levels of disturbance which were well above average. Both improvement and the lack of it were found in a variety of situations and with respect to all of the presenting problems, so that there was no close connection between initial circumstances and behavioural outcome. More boys than girls had a higher sense of self-esteem and they were also more likely to improve in this respect.

The majority of teenagers were said to be in good health at follow-up but young people were more guarded about this aspect of their lives than their parents or social workers. Girls were more likely than boys to say that their health had varied or got worse during the year. A large proportion of young people had left school during the year, but few were now at work or on youth training schemes. Parents thought that one third of the teenagers who were still at school were not doing as well as they could, because of negative attitudes and attendance problems. Social workers considered that rather more young people had deteriorated over the year than had improved with regard to progress at school or work.

General Success and Progress

A global index was devised to assess overall change by combining a range of measures on several dimensions (eg satisfaction with the year; behaviour change; schooling or work). Good progress occurred in a wide range of circumstances and was not confined to easier cases nor closely linked to particular types of problem or intervention. However, certain factors were related to success on this measure:

- *pre-intervention* – high self-esteem; good school progress; absence of addictions;
- *intervention* – residential school and foster care placements; the particular agency; good communication with social worker.

Getting on well with the social worker did not necessarily lead to a reduction in problems, but there was some association between a good relationship and overall success. The living circumstances at the end of the year which included the highest proportions of 'not successful' cases were custody and independent living.

Packages of Services

More than one service might be provided at the same time (combination) and/or in succession (sequence). The number of cases in the study together with the diversity of circumstances and services made it difficult to generalise about which packages worked well, so any conclusions must be tentative.

Combinations

Supervision seemed to be most productive if individual and family counselling were combined with group work or befriending activities and a good open and sometimes challenging relationship was established between the social worker and the young person. Group work also often helpfully supported placements in care. When older teenagers left residential care, it was rare for contact with the field worker or former carers to be sufficient and in the few instances when a befriender gave complementary support this was valued. The success of residential schools seemed to be enhanced when the social worker carried out family work.

Sequences

These were either **planned** (eg residential unit awaiting foster care placement) or **unplanned** (eg young person moving without consulting social worker). This distinction does not necessarily equate with good or bad, since a planned service might outlive its usefulness, whilst an unexpected change of plan could be an effective response to altered circumstances or assessments. Examples of helpful sequences in particular cases were:

- respite care followed up by group work on return home;
- discharge from care following careful preparation by residential staff and followed by frequent counselling from field worker;
- recovery from a foster care breakdown in a residential unit;
- successful foster placement after several residential placements, with social worker acting as trusted continuity figure throughout.

Delays in obtaining resources could undermine plans, as when young people became restless waiting for a placement or accommodation. The higher positive ratings and comments conveyed by young people and parents about the services offered by one of the agencies, indicates that it is possible to increase the level of satisfactory outcomes for young people on supervision or in care.

Implications of the Findings for Policy Formulation, Social Work Practice and Social Work Training

The social work needs of adolescents and their families, as we have found, have some similarities to but also many differences from those of younger children. The term 'children' is often used by policy makers, practitioners and trainers alike to embrace too diverse and sometimes irreconcilable needs. Our findings call for a more distinctive and focused approach towards this group of service users.

Policy Implications

A Policy Strategy for Teenagers

Adolescents and older teenagers now form the majority of those supervised or accommodated by local authorities. Most young people featuring in our study were experiencing multiple stresses, such as unstable family relationships, lack of family support, school failure, few qualifications or training, poor job opportunities, involvement in anti-social activities and in drugs. As a result, social service measures of intervention have to address a range of issues, including: behaviour, relationships, feelings (the young people's and those of others), practical needs, schooling, training, housing and jobs.

A comprehensive policy matched with appropriate strategies and resources is therefore required to respond to the needs of this group of youngsters. The policy should start from prevention and diversion before being set in the wider context of 'through care' and the requirement to consider the welfare of children throughout their childhood. Our findings point to the need for greater integration between residential and field child care services, with much more recognition of the centrality of the key worker's role and of residential staff playing a bigger role with the family. There is also need for more localised and flexible residential facilities to include day school attendance and brief respite care facilities. Whilst some young people need only short respite periods in care, others benefit from longer periods, especially those with no social base and who should not leave care abruptly at 16 or 17. Some specialised units will also still be necessary for those who are emotionally or psychologically very damaged and/or have serious drug problems. More planned and consistent work with the family and the young person is required at all levels, with the aim, among other things, to help create a kind of permanent social base for the young person.

It is important to develop a policy which applies each of the principles of diversion, prevention, substitute care and independent living according to individual needs and circumstances based on careful assessment. Blanket policies which assume that care is always negative or favour a particular form of service be it foster care, residential care or supervision in the community will not meet the needs of some teenagers. Central aims should be to help the young person to:

- **resolve conflicts;**
- **achieve a satisfactory and satisfying living situation and education;**
- **develop adequate skills and a support network (or social base) to cope as an adult.**

Within the above broad definition there is a clear remit for work focusing on the family, school and support networks. This calls for integration within social work and social services departments, as well as co-ordination between them and other agencies, to incorporate some of the best features we found in our study. The following framework could form the basis for such integration and co-ordination:

a *Horizontal Integration*

Each agency should provide or have access to a spread of linked services that includes all of the options, that is residential care, foster carers specially trained to take adolescents, short-term respite/accommodation (for a cooling-off period), a range of discussion and activity groups, outreach/befriending schemes and individual and family counselling. More longer term groups and more comprehensive social and outreach activities are needed for teenagers. There is a particular need to develop group work/activities for girls living at home. The allocation of appropriate services must take account of the circumstances of the intervention as follows:

Preventive Work

A clearer policy is required in relation to preventive work with teenagers and their families. Earlier intervention would help to overcome crises and prevent conflicts escalating out of hand. Closer liaison with the police and schools would also result in the earlier identification of those involved in serious conflictual relationships and the offer could be made of pro-active mediation. The main resource requirement at this stage is practitioner time to respond to crises, be available to mediate, negotiate, arbitrate and counsel, along with the ability to offer services such as daytime special education, brief respite services to allow time for reflection, group and outreach activities. On the basis of our study, supervision and diversion measures have not been used comprehensively and consistently but variably and partially. One small scale initiative taken by one of the sample agencies in the form of planned preventive intervention, including the offer of short-term respite, has met with a fair amount of success and deserves replication.

Supervision/Care

A major contributing factor to positive outcomes has to do with process which in turn is closely associated with the continuity, availability, responsiveness, reliability and personality of field and residential staff. Many residential and group workers have good skills and a capacity to gain the trust of young people and their parents. Greater flexibility is indicated in the current roles assigned to field and residential staff to provide for clear links between key workers in residential establishments and parents. There is also a need to reduce the turnover of all staff, particularly of key workers and group workers.

Parents and young people should have the option to have their main relationship with either their key or field worker, depending on their preference. The difference in choice has to do with the regularity of contact initiated by these workers, their responsiveness to crises and to the kind of person they are. Policy formulation should provide for these preferences in a more explicit way.

Further consideration should also be given to the compensatory value of the forms of education offered in residential schools arranged whilst the young person is in residence or attending as a day pupil. This type of schooling should be more available from units within easy reach of the young person's locality.

With regard to *foster care*, commitment to recruiting significantly more foster carers for adolescents would ensure that foster placements were available when needed. More consistent adequate and continued training is also called for foster carers. These steps would enable better matching of the emotional needs and relationship styles of the teenagers with the expectations of the foster carers, which seems central for this age group.

b *Vertical or Chronological Integration*

Local authorities should plan for populations and individuals from their early teens through to young adulthood in ways which minimise discontinuities of living situations and relationships, so that young people at home or in care develop viable support networks as well as survival skills. All work with adolescents should be viewed both as a critical opportunity to remedy the current problem(s) and also to prepare these youngsters for a constructive transition towards life as independent adults. The creation or strengthening of specialist teams to work with the 16+ age group need not be done at the expense of younger teenagers. The nature of the work is multifactorial and may require the provision of support over long periods often at short notice and at unsocial hours. More consideration should also be given to using residential workers and foster carers in an 'outreach' capacity. As already pointed out, this would have implications for how their work is organised (and also their training).

Preparation, Support and Supervision for Greater Independence

Young people who are vulnerable should be able to stay in care longer, have more support when they leave and be able to return when necessary. It has to be recognised, and planned for, that for a minority of young people the agency will remain their main social base for some time. Preparation for independent living has to be more comprehensive, offering similar opportunities to those who are on voluntary or statutory forms of supervision. The most vulnerable young people in our study were those with no consistent family support, in serious conflict with their families, lacking in education, social skills, income and housing. These young people should be easy to identify in their early teens in order to begin to address their need for practical and emotional support in a comprehensive way.

More collaboration is needed between the agencies involved in assessing and providing for the needs of young people moving towards adulthood, including social work, education, health, social security and housing. Young people do not find it easy to negotiate and co-ordinate their requirements with all these agencies and frequently give up. A difficulty or barrier put up even by a single agency, can limit a young person's chances in other areas of their lives and particularly the opportunity to settle down. There is a strong case for a single agency or care manager co-ordinating all the services now provided by these separate ones. The model we have in mind is of social workers who are specially trained, developing needs-led, rather than service-led packages of practical and emotional support tailored to the requirements of each young person. Young people should know at the outset what to expect in terms of services and support and have only one door on which to knock.

c   Co-ordination

There is a need for agencies to develop co-ordinated policies which recognise the special factors affecting teenagers, as well as the commonalties and rights which should be accorded to everyone under 18, as stressed by the UN Convention on Children. This is particularly essential with regard to Education, Police, Housing, Social Security and the Health Services. Education authorities ought, for example, to systematise early warning systems, provide more special education linked to mainstream schools and flexible residential schooling. Secondary schools could also extend programmes which meet the needs of resistant youngsters. Similarly improved co-ordination with Housing agencies and Social Security could help, as outlined above, to protect young adults living or planning to do so independently. The co-ordination of services with the probation service, the police, courts and reporters (in Scotland) are other important areas. Access to general health services and information about sex are important but more discriminating use should be made of referrals to psychiatric and psychological services in respect of young people. The encouraging results achieved by joint strategies initiated by some sample agencies with education could be extended to other key services.

Young People's Involvement in Decision-Making

The purpose of intervention should be clearly stated and become the focus for early negotiations between the young person, the parents (where appropriate) and the social worker, leading to the drafting of contracts or of a care plan and of a greater say in the choice of placement. In order to overcome the perceived formality of Reviews and Hearings, fewer 'strangers' should attend meetings, reviews/courts/ panels. Continuity of membership should also be encouraged.

Teenagers should be able to attend pre-meeting discussions, possibly with the Chair, to make oral statements there, or prepare written comments beforehand, with the help of a person of their choice. They should also be allowed to choose who they trust and would like to support them in meetings and reviews about their future.

Young people who are at risk should be monitored through a review system by courts/hearings to ensure that agencies do not default on their responsibilities to them. Agencies ought also to make sure that complaints procedures are available and known to young people who should have access to an external 'ombudsman' or children's rights officer.

Implications for Practice

Our findings suggest that comprehensive services need to be accompanied by field and residential social workers who have the personal qualities which enable them to engage well with teenagers, be seen as effective in getting things done and maintain the confidence of parents. Key workers/fieldworkers and other care staff who could establish good relationships with young people seemed to provide compensatory experiences for many of them and sometimes their families as well. What was valued was the personal qualities of these workers displayed in the form of caring, interest and concern that were missing from the lives of many youngsters.

Other qualities expected of field and residential workers include availability, reliability, responsiveness, flexibility, continuity and honesty which provide the basic ingredients for a good working relationship. Dependability and trustworthiness were high on the young people's agenda and that of their parents. Respect for parents and clarity about what is being offered in terms of supervision or care and the rationale behind them is essential. At times there may have to be open acknowledgement with them that the worker will not have much impact without gaining the trust of the young person. This process should not signify identification with the teenager's point of view to the exclusion of that of the parent. Anti-social and other similar behaviours must be acknowledged but young people resent social workers trying to tell them what to do. On the other hand, teenagers are usually prepared to take account of warnings and words of caution put forward by social workers or even some challenge, if they have come to like and respect their social workers and have found them dependable. Work with teenagers involves issues about autonomy and a teenager's right and need for a certain amount of independent help (especially as they grow older), but parents and other significant network members should be engaged whenever possible.

The idea of planned work with young people must include clarity about the purpose of intervention, prioritising, shared planning and goal setting, as well as the acknowledgement of possible differences of opinion. Social workers should establish a common understanding of what is expected but it is also necessary for them to be aware of differences in orientation, especially between the practical concerns of parents and young people on the one hand and the social worker's stress on the young person's personal development and self-esteem on the other. Mediating between a parent and the young person, linking a young person to resources or acting as an advocate with schools or housing departments is likely to create the trust for sharing on more personal matters. The orientation of many young people and parents towards short term and practical goals calls also for regular feedback mechanisms, the review of plans and the resetting of goals, where necessary. On the basis of our data we would conclude that successful achievements are more likely when targets are specific and accessible and address the pre-occupations of the young person and where appropriate those of their parents. The use of a contract or care plans is of little value without such in-built feedback mechanisms.

In work with young people, a re-examination is also needed of the use of self in a more flexible way which includes more informal methods of interacting, to gain trust and facilitate communication. It could include a joint outing for shopping, sharing a meal, going swimming or taking part in some other activity or groups. The timing should follow the young person's readiness as much as the social worker's programme. Because of their position, residential staff may be more skilled in displaying flexibility of roles and this should be acknowledged in making care plans, where relevant.

Any functional analysis of social work that does not take account of process, relationships and values is unlikely to be experienced as satisfactory, at least by many young people and their families. Many of the instrumental competencies that appear to be increasingly used to provide community care packages cannot be used as benchmarks for the provision of social work services to families and children, as we have found. The different needs of the latter group, and possibly of some of those in the former, often require fundamentally different approaches, such as personal and family counselling without neglecting the orchestration of necessary resources.

In summary, social workers need to develop and improve mediation and conflict management skills; recognise parents' wishes eg for firmness, and the young person's wish for parents to allow for more autonomy and independence; be more explicit in establishing aims and expectations, even when these differ or conflict with those of the young person or parents; be aware of the need to listen, keep promises and keep confidences; engage in more planned family work; allow for time to establish trust with teenagers; be clear and straight; and finally develop skills in preparing packages of 'care' by co-ordinating the services provided by other agencies to young people. These developments would be dependent on adequate resourcing in terms of practitioner time and the range of services available.

Implications for Training

Our findings suggest a need for a much more informed approach to the social work needs of young people and their families by the social services. To respond to these needs, not only should child care hold a more central position on social work training (similar to that negotiated for probation students in England) and on in-service training, but child care training itself should go well beyond notions of child protection for young children. This should involve the knowledge, skills, value dimensions and practice experience necessary to carry out child care and family social work adapted to the ages and stages of children. Whilst it is right that course assessment procedures should be tailored to demonstrate the competencies developed in the field of child care, it would be inappropriate to rely exclusively on outcomes without regard to input and process.

Within the broader approach paid to social work training, particular attention needs to be paid to the skills and techniques required for working with teenagers and their families where intervention is necessary because of serious problems within the family, disturbed or disruptive behaviour, offences or difficulties with schooling. This form of training should be extended to all those working with teenagers, including social workers, foster carers, group leaders, outreach workers and the managers of these different practitioners. Training should include a very thorough grounding in both normal and deviant aspects of teenage development and behaviour; evolving family structures and dynamics; 'youth culture' and the different understanding many young people have of what is 'problematic' behaviour; the young people's concerns and often despair about future employment and housing prospects; community resources for teenagers; preparation for adulthood; rights and responsibilities. Those in training also need to be sensitised to consumer wishes. Both parents and teenagers want their viewpoints respected, a willingness to listen, reliability, openness and action. Students should learn how partnership, jointness and participation in the definion of the problem or situation, its assessment, the setting of goals, the sharing of the process, reviews and re-definitions can lead to the achievement of more positive outcomes.

Increased knowledge about adolescence, awareness of the whole range of resources and improved communication and assessment skills is necessary so that social workers can learn to negotiate and organise effective packages of supervision or care. The sharpening of assessment skills should also improve decisions such as when to make the main focus of intervention the whole family, without neglecting the separate needs of the young person, or solely the young person. The pursuit of such objectives should cover the acquisition of skills in crisis work as well as the role of case manager, task-centred worker, family group worker or counsellor as a means for attending to the 'deeds', 'wants' and 'needs' of teenagers and their families. Above all, training for this work requires an adaptation of existing social work methods to include skills concerned with the management of conflict through the use of negotiating, mediating and bargaining skills and the defusion of conflict.

Final Conclusions

Finally, we started this chapter by making reference to the widespread public concern about the criminal behaviour of some young people and the call for tougher measures. Without dismissing these concerns, our findings suggest that so far the response of the social services and of other relevant agencies to the needs of this group of young people has been largely unfocused, inconsistent, piecemeal and lacking in purpose. It is now time that teenagers and their families received the same concerted and coherent attention as social work in relation to child protection and permanency planning which, in spite of some blemishes, have made great strides. We found many individual examples of good practice which benefited a significant number of young people, but there remains a need to develop coherent policies for teenagers with a range of comprehensive services at all levels, including community alternatives. If the best services, innovations and collaborative programmes from each of our sample agencies were to be combined, integrated and made widely available, then the basis for a good service for adolescents and their families would be there.

We end with the chart opposite which provides an overview of elements in the most successful combinations identified in the study.

The Main Elements of Effective Packages of Services for Young People

- joint strategic planning and co-ordination between agencies, especially social work, education and housing;

- the availability of a wide range of services, particularly:

    individual and family counselling;
    varied forms of group work;
    befriending;
    specialist education;
    residential schools with flexi-care arrangements;
    residential units which encourage staff continuity;
    foster care schemes with specialist training and support.

- careful assessment of the young person's needs, relationship patterns, schooling and behaviour to match these with suitable services;

- joint setting and reviewing of expectations, aims and methods of work by social workers, young people, parents and other key parties;

- flexible use of field, residential and group work staff to respond to individual circumstances and needs;

- social workers' acquisition and exercise of mediation and conflict resolution skills in work with young people, parents, carers and schools;

- social workers and carers taking time to build trust with young people and parents, then challenging unhelpful attitudes and behaviour;

- preparation and support to young people (and parents) for participation in decisions which affect them;

- recognition that for some young people living away from home is a positive move which offers respite, shared care or, in extreme cases, long-term protection from risk;

- external monitoring of decisions for young people to return home or move to 'independence';

- ensuring that care or supervision ends only when systems are in place which provide continuity of support for young people.

References

Adler, R. M. (1985) *Taking Juvenile Justice Seriously*, Scottish Academic Press, Edinburgh.

Ahmad, B. (1990) *Black Perspectives in Social Work*, Venture Press, Birmingham.

Aldgate, J., Maluccio, A. and Reeves, C. (1989) *Adolescents in Foster Families*, BAAF, Batsford.

Aldgate, J. (1990) 'Foster children at school: success or failure?', *Adoption & Fostering*, 14, 4, 38–48.

Aldgate, J., Heath, A., Colton, A. and Simm, M. (1993) 'Social work and the education of children in foster care', *Adoption & Fostering*, 17, 3, 25–34.

Almeida, M. C., Hawkins, R. P., Meadowcroft, P., and Luster, W. C. (1989) 'Evaluation of foster-family based treatment in comparison with other programs: A preliminary analysis', in Hudson, J. and Galaway, B. (eds.) *The State as Parent*, Kluwer, Dordrecht.

Asquith, S. (1992) 'Coming of Age: 21 Years of the Children's Hearings System', in L. Paterson and D. McCrone (eds.) *Scottish Government Yearbook*, Unit for the Study of Government in Scotland, Edinburgh.

Asquith, S. and Hill, M. (eds.) (1994) *Justice for Children*, Martinus Nijhoff, Dordrecht.

Association of Metropolitan Authorities (AMA) (1993) *Children and Trouble – A Study of Juvenile Justice Issues for Local Government*, Child Care Series No.2.

Banks, M., Bates, I., Breakwell, G., Brynner, J., Emler, N., Jamieson, L. and Roberts, K. (1992) *Careers and Identities*, Open University Press, Milton Keynes.

Bannister, J., Dell, M., Donnison, D., Fitzpatrick, S. and Taylor, R. (1993) *Homeless Young People in Scotland, the role of the Social Work Services*, HMSO, London.

Barford, R. and Wattam, C. (1991) 'Children's participation in decision-making', *Practice*, 5, 2, 93–102.

Batty, D. and Robson, J. (eds.) (1992) *Statutory Reviews in Practice*, BAAF, London.

Bebbington, A. and Miles, J. (1989) 'The Background of Children who enter Local Authority Care', *British Journal of Social Work*, 19, 5, 349–368.

Bernard, H. S. (1981) 'Identity formation during late adolescence: A review of some empirical findings', *Adolescence*, 16, 62, 349–358.

Berndt, T. J. (1982) 'The features and effects of friendship in early adolescence', *Child Development*, 53, 1447–1460.

Berridge, D. (1985) *Children's Homes*, Basil Blackwell, Oxford.

Berridge, D. (1994) 'Foster & Residential Care Reassessed: A Research Respective', *Children & Society*, 8:2, 132–150.

Berridge, D. and Cleaver, H. (1987) *Foster Home Breakdown*, Basil Blackwell, Oxford.

Biehal, N., Clayden, J., Stein, M. and Wade, J. (1992) *Prepared for Living?*, (Leaving Care Research Project Leeds University), National Children's Bureau, London.

Bilson, A. and Thorpe, D. (1987) *Child Care Careers and Their Management*, Fife Regional Council for Social Work Department, Glenrothes.

Blaxter, M. (1981) *The Health of the Children*, Heinemann Educational Books, London.

Blom-Cooper, L. (1986) *A Child in Trust*, London Borough of Brent, London.

Blos, P. (1970) *The Young Adolescent, clinical studies*, New York, The Free Press.

Bogart, N. (1988) *A Comparative Study of Behavioural Adjustment between Therapeutic and Regular Foster Care in the Treatment of Child Abuse and Neglect*, Doctoral Dissertation, Memphis State University.

Bottoms, A. and McWilliams, W. (1979) 'A non-treatment paradigm for probation practice', *British Journal of Social Work*, 9, 2, 159–202.

Bottoms, A., Brown, P., McWilliams, B., McWilliams, W. and Nellis, M. (1990) *Intermediate Treatment and Juvenile Justice*, HMSO, London.

Bradshaw, J. (1972) 'A Taxonomy of Social Need' in McLachlan, G. (ed) *Problems and Progress in Medical Care*, Oxford University Press, Oxford.

Brooks-Gunn, J. and Paikoff, R.L. (1992) 'Changes in self-feeling during the transition towards adolescence' in McGurk,H. (ed) *Childhood Social Development: Contemporary Perspectives*, Lawrence Erlbaum Associates, Hove.

Brower, A. and Nurius, P. (1993) *Social Cognition and Individual Change: Current Theory and Counselling Guidelines*, Sage, London.

Buchanan, A. E. and Brock, D. W. (1989) *Deciding for Others: The Ethics of Surrogate Decision Making*, Cambridge University Press, Cambridge.

Buchanan, C., Maccoby, E. and Dornbusch, S. (1991) 'Caught Between Parents: Adolescents' Experience in Divorced Homes', *Child Development*, 62, 1008–1029.

Buchanan, A., Wheal, A. and Coker, R. (1993) *Answering Back*, (Dolphin Project), Department of Social Work Studies, University of Southampton.

Bullock, R., Little, M. and Millham, S. (1993a) *Residential Care for Children*, HMSO, London.

Bullock, R., Little, M. and Millham, S. (1993b) *Going Home*, Dartmouth, Aldershot.

Carlen, P. (1976) *Magistrate's Justice*, Martin Robertson, London.

Chamberlain, P. (1990) 'Comparative evaluation of a specialized foster care for seriously delinquent youths: A first step', *Community Alternatives*, 2, 2, 21–36.

Cheetham, J., Fuller, R., McIvor, G. and Petch, A. (1992) *Evaluating Social Work Effectiveness*, Open University Press, Buckingham.

Chisholm, L. (1990) 'A sharper lens or a new camera? Youth research, young people and social change in Britain' in Chisholm, L., Buchner, P., Kruger, H-H., and Brown, P. (eds) *Childhood, Youth and Social Change: A Comparative Perspective*, Falmer Press, London.

Chisholm, L. (1993) 'Youth transitions, gender and social change', *Sociology*, 27, 2, 259–279.

Church, J. (ed) (1990) *Social Trends 24*, Central Statistical Office, Newport.

Cliffe, D. with Berridge, D. (1991) *Closing Children's Homes: An End to Residential Childcare?*, National Children's Bureau, London.

Coffield, F., Borril, C. and Marshall, S. (1986) *Growing Up at the Margins*, Open University Press, Milton Keynes.

Coleman, J. C. and Hendry, L. (1990) *The Nature of Adolescence*, Routledge, Chapman and Hall, London.

Collins, W. A. and Laursen, B. (1992) 'Conflict and relationships during adolescence', in Schantz, C. U. and Hartup, W. W. (eds.) *Conflict in Child and Adolescent Development*, Cambridge University Press, Cambridge.

Colten, M. E. and Gore, S. (1984) *Adolescent Stress: Causes and Consequences*, Aldine de Gruyter, New York.

Colton, M. (1988) *Dimensions of Substitute Child Care*, Avebury, Aldershot.

Colton, M. and Hellinckx, W. (eds.) (1993) *Child Care in the EC*, Ashgate, Aldershot.

Coopersmith, S. (1990) *Self Esteem Inventories*, Consulting Psychologists Press Inc, Palo Alto.

Davie, R.,Butler, N. and Goldstein, H. (1972) *From Birth to Seven*, Longman,London.

Dennington, J. and Pitts, J. (1991) *Developing Services for Young People in Crisis*, Longman, London.

Department of Education (1992) *School Attainment Tables*, DES, London.

Department of Health and Social Security (1985a) *Social Work Decisions in Child Care*, DHSS, London.

Department of Health and Social Security (1985b) *Review of Child Care Law: Report to Ministers of an Interdepartmental Working Party*, HMSO, London.

Department of Health (1989) *An Introduction to The Children Act 1989*, HMSO, London.

Department of Health (1991a) *Children in the Public Care* (The Utting Report), HMSO, London.

Department of Health (1991b) *Patterns & Outcomes in Child Placement*, HMS0, London.

Department of Health (1992) *Choosing with Care* (The Warner Report), HMSO, London.

Dickerson, V. G. and Zimmerman, J. (1992) 'Families with adolescents: Escaping problem lifestyles', *Family Process*, 31, 341–353.

Dinnage, R. and Pringle, M. Kellmer (1967) *Foster Care: Facts and Fallacies*, Longman, London.

Downes, C. (1982) 'Assessing adolescents for time-limited foster care', *Adoption & Fostering*, 6, 4, 26–30.

Downes, C. (1992) *Separation Revisited*, Ashgate, Aldershot.

Dunn, J. (1984) *Brothers and Sisters*, Fontana, London.

Erikson, E. (1965) *Childhood and Society*, Hogarth Press, London.

Fanshel, D., Finch, S. J. and Grundy, J. F. (1990) *Foster Children in a Life Course Perspective*, Columbia University Press, New York.

Farmer, E. and Parker, R. (1991) *Trials and Tribulations*, HMSO, London.

Farrington, D. P. (1992) 'Juvenile Delinquency', in J. Coleman (ed.) *The School Years*, Routledge, London.

Fenyo, A., Knapp, M. and Baines, B. (1989) *Foster Care Breakdown: A Study of a Special Teenager Fostering Scheme*, PSSRU, University of Kent.

Ferri, E. (1976) *Growing up in a One Parent Family*, NFER/Nelson, Windsor.

Ferri, E. (1984) *Step Children*, NFER/Nelson, Windsor.

Field, S. (1992) 'Young Offender Community Support Scheme – Hampshire, England', *Community Alternatives*, 4, 2, 77–96.

Fisher, M., Marsh, P., Phillips, D. and Sainsbury, E. (1986) *In and Out of Care*, Batsford, London.

Fletcher, B. (1993) *Not Just a Name: The Views of Young People in Foster and Residential Care*, National Consumer Council/Who Cares? Trust, London.

Fogelman, K. (1975) *Britain's Sixteen Year Olds*, National Children's Bureau, London.

Fogelman, K. (ed) (1983) *Growing up in Great Britain*, Macmillan, Basingstoke.

Franklin, B. (ed.) (1986) *The Rights of Children*, Basil Blackwell, Oxford.

Freeman, I., Morrison, A., Lockhart, F., Swanson, M., and Duffy, C. (1994) *An Account of a Pilot Consultation Exercise with Young People*, Strathclyde Regional Council, Glasgow.

Freeman, M. (1993) 'Removing rights from adolescents', *Adoption & Fostering*, 17, 1, 14–21.

Fuller, R. (1988) *The MARS Project: A Study of Preventive Work*, University of Stirling.

Galbo, J. J. (1986) 'Adolescents' perceptions of significant adults', *Children & Youth Services Review*, 8, 37–51.

Gambe, P., Gomes, J., Kapur, V., Rangel, M. and Stubbs, P. (1992) *Improving Practice with Children and Families*, CCETSW, London.

Gardner, R. (1989) 'Consumer Views' in B. Kahan (ed) *Child Care Research, Policy and Practice*, Hodder & Stoughton, London.

Garnett, L. (1992) *Leaving Care and After*, National Children's Bureau, London.

Gavin, L. A. and Furman, W. (1989) 'Age differences in adolescents' perceptions of their peer groups', *Developmental Psychology*, 25, 5, 827–834.

Gibbons, J., with Thorpe, S. and Wilkinson, P. (1990) *Family Support and Prevention: Studies in Local Areas*, NISW/HMSO, London.

Giller, H. and Morris, A. (1979) 'Supervision Orders: the Routinization of Treatment', *Howard Journal*, 149–159.

Graham, J., Hazel, N., Richards, A. and Waddell, T. (1992) 'Foster family care for homeless young people – The RAFT program', *Community Alternatives*, 4, 2, 27–42.

Hardiker, P., Exton, K. and Barker, M. (1991) *Policies and Practices in Preventive Child Care*, Avebury, Aldershot.

Harding, L. F. (1991) *Perspectives in Child Care Policy*, Longman, London.

Harris, R. (1980) 'A Changing Service: The Case for Separating 'Care' and 'Control' in Probation Practice', *British Journal of Social Work*, 10, 2, 163–184.

Harris, R. (1991) 'The Life and Death of the Care Order (Criminal)', *British Journal of Social Work*, 21, 1, 1–17.

Harris, R. and Timms, N. (1993) *Secure Accommodation in Child Care*, Routledge, London.

Hartup,W.W. (1992) 'Friendships and their developmental significance' in McGurk,H. (ed) *Childhood Social Development: Contemporary Perspectives*, Lawrence Erlbaum Associates, Hove.

Hawkins, R. P. and Breiling, J. (1989) *Therapeutic Foster Care: Critical Issues*, Child Welfare League of America, Washington D. C.

Hawkins, R. P., Almeida, M. C., Fabry, B. and Reitz, A. L. (1992) 'A scale to measure restrictiveness of living environments for troubled children and youths', *Hospital and Community Psychiatry*, 43, 1, 54–59.

Hazel, N. (1981) *A Bridge to Independence*, Basil Blackwell, Oxford.

Hazel, N. (1990) 'The development of specialist foster care for adolescents: Policy and practice', in Galaway, B., Maglajlic, D., Husdon, J., Harmon, P. and McLagan, J. (eds.) *International Perspectives on Specialist Foster Family Care*, Human Services Associates, St Paul.

Heath, A., Colton, M. and Aldgate, J. (1994) 'Failure to Escape: A Longitudinal Study of Foster Children's Educational Attainment', *British Journal of Social Work*, 24, 3, 241–260.

Hill, M. (1987) *Sharing Child Care in Early Parenthood*, RKP, London.

Hill, M., Lambert, L. and Triseliotis, J. (1989) *Achieving Adoption with Love and Money*, National Children's Bureau, London.

Hill, M., Ford, J. and Meadows, F. (1990) 'The place of counselling in social work', *Practice*, 4, 3, 156–172.

Hill, M., Nutter, R., Giltinan, D., Hudson, J. and Galaway, B. (1993) 'A comparative survey of specialist fostering schemes in the UK and North America', *Adoption & Fostering*, 17, 2, 17–22.

Hill, P. (1993) 'Recent advances in selected aspects of adolescent development', *Journal of Child Psychology and Psychiatry*, 34, 1, 69–99.

Holman, R. (1988) *Putting Families First*, Macmillan, London.

House of Commons (1984) *Second Report from the Social Services Committee, Session 1983–84, Children in Care*, Volume 1, HMSO, London.

Hudson, J. and Galaway, B. (1989) *Specialist Foster Care: A Normalising Experience*, Haworth Press, New York.

Hurrelmann, K. and Engel, U. (eds.) (1989) *The Social World of Adolescents*, De Gruyter, Berlin.

Jackson, S. (1989) 'Education of Children in Care' in B.Kahan (ed) *Child Care: Research, Policy and Practice*, Hodder and Stoughton, London.

Jackson, S. and Bosma, H. A. (1992) 'Developmental research on adolescence: European perspectives for the 1990's and beyond', *British Journal of Developmental Psychology*, 10, 319–337.

Jones, H. and Gallagher, J. (1985) *Intermediate Treatment in Scotland*, Central Research Unit, Edinburgh.

Jones, G. and Wallace, C. (1992) *Youth, Family and Citizenship*, Open University Press, Buckingham.

Kadushin, A. and Martin, C. (1988) *Child Welfare Services*, Columbia University Press, New York.

Kahan, B. (1979) *Growing Up in Care*, Basil Blackwell, Oxford.

Kearney, B. and Mapstone, E. (1992) *Report of the Inquiry into Child Care Policies in Fife*, HMSO, Edinburgh.

Kelly, B. (1992) *Children Inside: A Study of Secure Provision*, Routledge, London.

Kendrick, A. and Fraser, S. (1992) 'A Literature Review' in Scottish Office, *The Review of Residential Child Care in Scotland: The Three Supporting Research Studies*, CRU Papers, Edinburgh.

Kendrick, A. and Mapstone, E. (1991) 'Who decides? Child care reviews in two Scottish social work departments', *Children & Society*, 5, 2, 1.

Kent Social Services (1986) *Kent Family Placement Service – 10 Years on 1975–1985*, Kent County Council, Canterbury.

Kerfoot, M. and Butler, A. (1988) *Problems of Childhood and Adolescence*, Macmillan, London.

Kiernan, K. and Wicks, M. (1990) *Family Change and Future Policy*, Family Policy Studies Centre, London.

Killeen, D. (1992) 'Leaving home' in J. Coleman and C.Warren-Adamson (eds) *Youth Policy in the 1990's*, Routledge, London.

King, J. (1991) 'The tip of the iceberg', *Community Care*, 21–11-91, pp. 20–22.

Knapp, M. and Smith, J. (1984) *The PSSRU National Survey of Children's Homes*, Report no. 2, University of Kent.

Kosonen, M. (1993) *Evaluation of Foster and Adoptive Care Services in Tayside*, Tayside Regional Council SW Department, Dundee.

Le Francois, G. (1990) *The Lifespan*, Wadsworth, Belmont, California.

Lerner, R. M. (1985) 'Adolescent maturational changes and psychosocial development: A dynamic interactional perspective', *Journal of Youth and Adolescence*, 14, 4, 355–372.

Levy, A. and Kahan, B. (1991) *The Pindown Experience and the Protection of Children*, Staffordshire County Council.

Lindley, R. (1991) 'Teenagers and other children', in Scarre, G. (ed.) *Children, Parents and Politics*, Cambridge University Press, Cambridge.

Lockyer, A. (1994) 'The Scottish Children's Hearings System: Internal Developments and the UN Convention', in S. Asquith and M. Hill (eds.) *Justice for Children*, Martinus Nijhoff, Dordrecht.

Lowe, K. (1990) *Teenagers in Foster Care*, NFCA, London.

McCord, J. (1990) 'Problem behaviours', in Feldman, S. S. and Elliott, G. R. (eds.) *At the Threshold: The Developing Adolescent*, Harvard University Press, Cambridge, Mass.

Maclean, K. (1989) 'Towards a fee-paid fostering service', *Adoption & Fostering*, 13, 3, 25–28.

Marsh, P. and Triseliotis, J. (eds.) (1993) *Prevention and Reunification in Child Care*, Batsford, London.

Martin, F., Fox, S. and Murray, K. (1981) *Children Out of Court*, Scottish Academic Press, Edinburgh.

Martin, F. and Murray, K. (1982) *The Scottish Juvenile Justice System*, Scottish Academic Press, Edinburgh.

Mead, M. (1961) *Coming of Age in Samoa*, Penguin, Harmondsworth.

Mayer, J. and Timms, N. (1970) *The Client Speaks*, Routledge and Kegan Paul, London.

Millham, S., Bullock, R., Hosie, K. and Haak, M. (1986) *Lost in Care*, Gower, Aldershot.

Monck, E. (1991) 'Patterns of confiding relationships among adolescent girls', *Journal of Child Psychology and Psychiatry*, 32, 2, 333–345.

Morris, P. and Beverly, F. (1975) *On Licence, a Study of Parole*, Wiley, London.

National Association for the Care and Resettlement of Offenders (NACRO) (1991) *Preventing Youth Crime*, NACRO Juvenile Crime Committee.

Newson, J. and Newson, E. (1968) *Patterns of Infant Care*, Penguin, Harmondsworth.

Newson, J. and Newson, E. (1970) *Four Years Old in an Urban Community*, Penguin, Harmondsworth.

Noller, P. and Callan, V. (1991) *The Adolescent in the Family*, Routledge, London.

O'Brien, D. (1990) 'Factors affecting outcomes and admission of children into care', *Practice*, 4, 3, 199–210.

Packman, J. (1968) *Child Care Needs and Numbers*, Allen & Unwin, London.

Packman, J., Randall, J. and Jacques, N. (1986) *Who Needs Care?*, Blackwell, Oxford.

Parker, R. (1966) *Decision in Child Care*, Allen & Unwin, London.

Parker, R. (1988) 'Residential Care for Children', in I.Sinclair *The Research Reviewed*, HMSO, London.

Parker, R., Ward, H., Jackson, S., Aldgate, J. and Wedge, P. (1991) *Assessing Outcomes in Child Care*, HMSO, London.

Parkinson, L. (1987) *Separation, Divorce and Families*, Macmillan, London.

Parsloe, P. (1976) 'Social Work and the Justice Model', *British Journal of Social Work*, 6, 71–90.

Pecora, P., Fraser, M. and Haapala, D. (1989) 'Intensive Home-based Family Treatment' in J.Hudson and B.Galaway (eds) *The State as Parent*, Kluwer, Dordrecht.

Peterson, C. and McCabe, A. (1983) *Developmental Psycholinguistics: Three Ways of Looking at a Child's Narrative*, Plenum Press, New York.

Petersen, A, C. (1988) 'Adolescent development', *Annual Review of Psychology*, 39, 583–607.

Pilling, D. (1990) *Escape from Disadvantage*, Falmer Press, London.

Pitts, J. (1988) *The Politics of Juvenile Crime*, Sage, London.

Pratt, J. (1985) 'Juvenile Justice, Social Work and Social Control. The Need for Positive Thinking', *British Journal of Social Work*, 15, 1–24.

Prosser, H. (1978) *Perspectives on Foster Care*, NFER Publishing Co., Windsor.

Quinton, D. and Rutter, M. (1988) *Parenting Breakdown*, Avebury, Aldershot.

Raynor, P. (1985) *Social Work, Justice and Control*, Blackwell, Oxford.

Rees, S. and Wallace, A. (1982) *Verdicts on Social Work*, Edward Arnold, London.

Rossi, P. H. (1992) 'Assessing family preservation programs', *Children and Youth Services Review*, 14, 77–97.

Rowe, J., Cain, H., Hundleby, M. and Keane, A. (1984) *Long Term Foster Care*, Batsford, London.

Rowe, J., Hundleby, M. and Garnett, L. (1989) *Child Care Now: A Survey of Placement Patterns*, BAAF, London.

Rutter, M., Tizard, J. and Whitmore, K. (eds) (1970) *Education, Health and Behaviour*, Longman, London.

Salmon, P. (1992) 'The peer group', in J. Coleman (ed.) *The School Years*, Routledge, London.

Scheirer, M. A. and Rezmovic, E. L. (1983) 'Measuring the degree of program implementation', *Evaluation Review*,7, 5, 599–633.

Scottish Office (1992) *Another Kind of Home. A Review of Residential Child Care*. (The Skinner Report), HMSO, Edinburgh.

Scottish Office (1993) *Scotland's Children: Proposals for Child Care Policy and Law*, HMSO, Edinburgh.

Senior, P. (1984) 'The Probation Order: Vehicle of social work or social control?', *Probation Journal*, June, 64–70.

Shaw, M. (1988) *Family Placement for Children in Care*, BAAF, London.

Shaw, M. and Hipgrave, T. (1983) *Specialist Fostering*, Batsford, London.

Shaw, M. and Hipgrave, T. (1989a) 'Specialist Fostering 1988 – A Research Study', *Adoption & Fostering*, 13, 3, 17–21.

Shaw, M. and Hipgrave, T. (1989b) 'Young people and their carers in specialist fostering', *Adoption & Fostering*, 13, 4, 11–17.

Singer, L. (1989) *Adult Probation and Juvenile Supervision*, Avebury, Aldershot.

Smith, P. K. and Cowie, H. (1991) *Understanding Children's Development*, Basil Blackwell, Oxford.

Smith, P. M. (1986) 'Evaluation of Kent placements', *Adoption & Fostering*, 10, 1, 29–33.

Spalton, S. (1976) 'Social Work Supervision' in Martin, F. and Murray, K. (eds) *Children's Hearings*, Scottish Academic Press, Edinburgh.

Spicker, P. (1990) 'Social Work and Self-determination', *British Journal of Social Work*, 20, 221–234.

Stalker, K. (1990) *Share the Care: An Evaluation of a Family-Based Respite Care Service*, Jessica Kingsley, London.

Stein, M. and Carey, K. (1986) *Leaving Care*, Basil Blackwell, Oxford.

Steinberg, L. (1990) 'Autonomy, conflict, and harmony in the family relationship', in Feldman, S. S. and Elliott, G. R. (eds.) *At the Threshold: The Developing Adolescent*, Harvard University Press, Cambridge, Mass.

Steinberg, L. (1993) *Adolescence*, McGraw Hill, New York.

Stewart, J. and Stewart, J. (1993) *Social Circumstances of Young Offenders under Supervision*, Department of Applied Social Science, University of Lancaster.

Sutton-Smith, B. and Rosenberg, B. G. (1970) *The Sibling*, Holt, Rinehart and Winston, New York.

Swanson, M. (1988) 'Preventing Reception into Care: Monitoring a Short-Stay Refuge for Older Children' in Freeman, I. and Montgomery, S. (eds) *Child Care: Monitoring Practice*, Jessica Kingsley, London.

Thoburn, J. (1990) *Success and Failure in Permanent Family Placement*, Avebury/Gower, Aldershot.

Thoburn, J. and Lewis, A. (1992) 'Partnership with parents of children in need of protection', in Gibbons, J. (ed.) *The Children Act 1989 and Family Support: Principles into Practice*, HMSO, London.

Thoburn, J. (1993) 'Prevention and reunification – an historical perspective', in Marsh, P. and Triseliotis, J. (eds.) *Prevention and Reunification in Child Care*, Batsford, London.

Tizard, B. and Phoenix, A. (1993) *Black, White, or Mixed Race?*, Routledge, London.

Trasler, G. (1960) *In Place of Parents*, Routledge & Kegan Paul, London.

Triseliotis, J. (1983) 'Identity and security in adoption and long-term fostering', *Adoption & Fostering*, 9, 1, 22–31.

Triseliotis, J. and Russell, J. (1984) *Hard to Place: The Outcome of Adoption and Residential Care*, Heinemann/Gower, London.

Triseliotis, J. (1989) 'Foster care outcomes', *Adoption & Fostering*, 13, 3, 5–17.

Triseliotis, J., Borland, M., Hill, M. and Lambert, L. (1993) 'The rights and responsibilities of adolescents in need or in trouble', *International Journal of Children's Rights*, 1, 315–330.

Truax, C. and Carkhuff, R. (1967) *Towards Effective Counselling and Psychotherapy, Training and Practice*, Aldine, New York.

Utting, D., Bright, J. and Henricson, C. (1993) *Crime and the Family*, Family Policy Studies Centre, London.

Vernon, J. and Fruin, D. (1986) *In Care: A Study of Social Work Decision Making*, National Children's Bureau, London.

Wagner, G. (1988) *Residential Care: A Positive Choice*, HMSO, London.

Walker, H. and Beaumont, B. (1985) *Working with Offenders*, Macmillan, Basingstoke.

Wallerstein, J. and Kelly, J. (1980) *Surviving the Breakup*, Basic Books, New York.

Wedge, P. and Prosser, H. (1973) *Born to Fail?*, Arrow Books, London.

Wedge, P. and Mantle, G. (1991) *Sibling Groups and Social Work*, Avebury/Gower, Aldershot.

Weiss, H. and Jacobs, F. (1989) *Evaluating Family Programs*, Aldine De Gruyter, New York.

Whitaker, D., Cook, J., Dunn, C. and Rockcliffe, S. (1985) *The Experience of Residential Care from the Perspectives of Children, Parents and Care Givers*, Final Report to the FSRC, University of York.

Willis, A. (1983) 'The balance between care and control in probation', *British Journal of Social Work*, 13, 339–346.

Wolfersdorff, C., Kersten, J. and Sprau-Kuhlen, V. (1989) 'Closed units in institutions for children' in Hudson, J. and Galaway, B. (eds.) *The State as Parent*, Kluwer, Dordrecht.

Woodruffe, C. and Glickman, M. (1993) 'Trends in Child Health' in Pugh, G. (ed) *30 Years of Change for Children*, National Children's Bureau, London.

Worthington, M. (1993) 'The Criminal Justice Act, 1991', *Youth & Policy*, 41, 20–23.

Yelloly, M. (1979) *Independent Evaluation of Twenty-five Placements in the Kent Family Project*, Kent CC, Maidstone.

Youniss, J. and Smollar, J. (1985) *Adolescent relations with mothers, fathers and friends*, University of Chicago Press, Chicago.

Yuan, Y-Y. T. and Revest, M. (eds.) (1990) *Family Preservation*, Sage, Beverly Hills.

Subject Index

Author Index

Adler, R. M. 33
Ahmad, B. 16
Aldgate, J. 2, 26, 35, 43, 118, 228, 231, 252, 275
Almeida, M. C. 3, 27
Asquith, S. 21, 202
Association of Metropolitan Authorities 20

Baines, B. 27
Banks, M. 17, 18
Bannister, J. 119, 195
Barford, R. 34
Barker, M. 19
Bates, I. 17, 18
Batty, D. 34
Beaumont, B. 23
Bebbington, A. 16, 24, 25
Bernard, H. S. 16
Berndt, T. J. 14
Berridge, D. 1, 2, 25, 26, 28, 30, 97, 98, 99, 174, 257, 262
Beverly, F. 85
Biehal, N. 32
Bilson, A. 20
Blaxter, M. 43
Blom-Cooper, L. 133
Blos, P. 196
Bogart, N. 27
Borland, M. 34
Borril, C. 14
Bosma, H. A. 16
Bottoms, A. 21, 22, 103
Bradshaw, J. 76
Breakwell, G. 17, 18
Breiling, J. 190
Bright, J. 20
Brock, D. W. 33
Brooks-Gunn, J. 16
Brower, A. 93
Brown, P. 21, 103
Brynner, J. 17, 18
Buchanan, A. 148, 211, 214
Buchanan, A. E. 33
Buchanan, C. 18
Bullock, R. 2, 23, 24, 25, 28, 29, 34

Butler, A. 16
Butler, N. 15

Cain, H. 26
Callan, V. 15
Carey, K. 118, 193, 275
Carkhuff, R. 135
Carlen, P. 71
Chamberlain, P. 27
Cheetham, J. 89
Chisholm, L. 35
Church, J. 229
Clayden, J. 32
Cleaver, H. 2, 26, 174, 262
Cliffe, D. 1, 26, 28, 30, 99
Coffield, F. 14
Coker, R. 148, 211, 214
Coleman, J. C. 15
Collins, W. A. 190
Colton, A. 228
Colton, M. 27, 95, 231
Colten, M. E. 14, 16
Cook, J. 252
Coopersmith, S. 15, 47
Cowie, H. 13

Davie, R. 15
Dell, M. 119, 195
Dennington, J. 33
Department of Education 230
Department of Health 3, 97, 118–119
Department of Health and Social Security 3, 19
Dickerson, V. G. 15
Dinnage, R. 26
Donnison, D. 119, 195
Dornbusch, S. 18
Downes, C. 27, 191, 192
Duffy, C. 212
Dunn, C. 252
Dunn, J. 14

Emler, N. 17, 18
Engel, U. 13
Erikson, E. 14
Exton, K. 19

Printed in the United Kingdom for HMSO
Dd300787 7/95 C10 G3397 10170